Sheridan Nurseries

Sheridan Nurseries

One Hundred Years of People, Plans, and Plants

Edward Butts and Karl Stensson

DUNDURN
TORONTO

Editor: Shannon Whibbs
Design: Jennifer Scott and Jesse Hooper
Printer: Trigraphik LBF

Library and Archives Canada Cataloguing in Publication

Butts, Edward
Sheridan Nurseries : one hundred years of people, plans, and plants / by Edward Butts and Karl Stensson.

Includes bibliographical references and index.
Issued also in electronic formats.
ISBN 978-1-4597-0564-7

1. Sheridan Nurseries--History. 2. Sheridan Nurseries--Employees--History. 3. Nurseries (Horticulture)--Ontario--Oakville--History--20th century. I. Butts, Edward, 1951- II. Title.

SB118.75.C3S74 2012 631.5'2097130904 C2012-904633-7

1 2 3 4 5 16 15 14 13 12

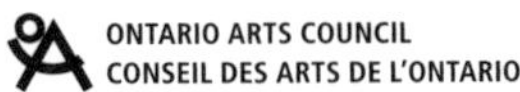

We acknowledge the support of the **Canada Council for the Arts** and the **Ontario Arts Council** for our publishing program. We also acknowledge the financial support of the **Government of Canada** through the **Canada Book Fund** and **Livres Canada Books**, and the **Government of Ontario** through the **Ontario Book Publishing Tax Credit** and the **Ontario Media Development Corporation**.

Printed and bound in Canada.

VISIT US AT
Dundurn.com
Definingcanada.ca
@dundurnpress
Facebook.com/dundurnpress

Dundurn
3 Church Street, Suite 500
Toronto, Ontario, Canada
M5E 1M2

Gazelle Book Services Limited
White Cross Mills
High Town, Lancaster, England
LA1 4XS

Dundurn
2250 Military Road
Tonawanda, NY
U.S.A. 14150

To Lorrie and Howard Dunington-Grubb for their vision; to my grandfather Herman Stensson for his tenacity; to my mom and dad, Lois and Fred Stensson, for instilling in me the passion for the business; and to the thousands of employees who contributed in building Sheridan into the industry leader it is today

— Karl Stensson

And I beseech you, forget not to inform yourself as diligently as may be, in things that belong to gardening.

— JOHN EVELYN (1620–1706)

CONTENTS

Sheridan Nurseries.

Lorrie and Howard Dunington-Grubb, the founders of Sheridan Nurseries.

INTRODUCTION

When we decided to write a book about Sheridan Nurseries' first hundred years, we were unsure of the shape the book should take. Larry Sherk, Sheridan's archivist and historian, and former chief horticulturist, suggested the themes of "People," "Plans," and "Plants." We certainly had plenty of material for each category.

The plans began in 1911, when Howard and Lorrie Dunington-Grubb arrived from England with the idea of bringing the concept of the English garden to Canada. Their most far-reaching plan took root in 1913 when they founded Sheridan Nurseries. It grew, branched, and blossomed over the decades. The company's growth has been well documented. The information had only to be selected and presented in an informative and (hopefully) interesting manner.

The same could be said of the plants. Starting with a few imported perennials, Sheridan Nurseries built one of the largest inventories of ornamental plants in Canada. The company introduced a spectacular array of new plants, many of which were developed by Sheridan nurserymen. That story, too, was thoroughly documented, especially in the Sheridan Nurseries catalogues. Again, there was a straightforward process of selecting the most important and most interesting information.

When we came to "The People," we faced a dilemma. From 1913 to the present, thousands of people have worked for Sheridan Nurseries. Many just came and went. A significant number made substantial contributions to the company's success and legacy. For some, this was done through long careers of dedicated service (such as nurseryman Constant DeGroot). Others had what might be considered an extraordinary relationship with Sheridan (in the case of the Japanese-Canadian internees). They all contributed in their own unique way. As we discovered when we began taping interviews as part of the research for this book, they all have stories to tell.

Unfortunately, we didn't have enough space for all of the stories. We could include only a selection of anecdotes that seemed to represent a cross-section of personal experiences. We made a great effort to mention as many of the members of the "Sheridan family" as possible. Regrettably, there wasn't room for all of the names. We hope that everyone will, nonetheless, enjoy this account of the company in whose history they played a part.

CHAPTER 1

Howard and Lorrie: Hearts and Flowers, Plants and Dreamers

There is no country of Canada's size, importance and wealth with so little to show in the way of botanical gardens.

— HOWARD DUNINGTON-GRUBB

When Howard Dunington-Grubb made that statement in 1959, he had already done more than any other person to rectify the very problem he was addressing. For when he had first arrived in Canada almost half a century earlier, there were few public or private gardens in the country. Canadians didn't plant flowers or shrubs around their homes. There was nothing like Niagara's Oakes Garden Theatre. Nor was there a company like Sheridan Nurseries that existed solely for the purpose of growing ornamental plants.

Howard Dunington-Grubb could fairly be called the Father of Landscape Architecture in Canada. He was an artist who worked with a pallet of living things: flowers, shrubs, and trees. His vivid imagination and creativity were expressed on landscapes, in urban gardens, and on a broad avenue in the middle of concrete utilitarianism. Howard sometimes found himself confronted with the pragmatic conservative philosophy that art has no practical use and therefore no fundamental value, as is shown in a conversation that allegedly took place in 1915:

> I well remember an interview on a very hot August afternoon during progress of the work on the gardens for the palatial Government House for the Province of Ontario. The Minister of Public Works had some excuse

> for being brusque. After inspecting stonemasons setting balustrade, cut-stone fountains, pavements, and steps for the terraces, he controlled himself sufficiently to merely ask if these things were necessary. The only possible answer was to admit quite frankly that they were all wholly unnecessary, that we were dealing unfortunately, not in necessities, but in luxuries, and that the only really necessary work involved was a plank walk to the front door so that people could get in and out without stepping in the mud. Garden design in a country devoid of gardens must necessarily be a gradual evolution.

Howard Burlingham Grubb was born in York, England, on April 30, 1881, to Edward and Emma Marie (née Horsnaill) Grubb, both from Letchworth. Edward was a Quaker, and had a distinguished reputation as an editor of Quaker journals. He earned his living as a tutor, and was secretary of the John Howard Society. That organization (still in operation today) was named for its founder, the great pioneer for the cause of prison reform. Edward and Emma named their son Howard in his honour. No doubt it was his parents' example that inspired in Howard the philanthropic leanings for which he would be known later in life.

Howard grew up amidst the great contrasts of Victorian England. The British Empire was at the height of its glory; a financial and industrial powerhouse. British factories made about 95 percent of the world's manufactured goods.

The British middle class was growing, but squalor existed side by side with prosperity in England's booming cities. The families of underpaid factory labourers, as well as hordes of unemployed, were crowded into unsightly, unsanitary slums that were the shame of London, Liverpool, Manchester, and other urban centres. Even the better-off middle-class suburbs were made up of row upon dreary row of low-cost housing, unbroken by green spaces.

Some of the more enlightened city administrators began to realize the need for parks and public gardens; the sort of spaces that had once been considered the exclusive domain of the aristocracy. Middle-class people with a yard and some disposable income wanted to turn their drab city lots into attractive "outdoor parlours" where they could entertain friends with tea and a game of whist on a Sunday afternoon.

This need for greenery and pleasant surroundings in urban areas brought about a demand for landscape architects. The English Garden became a status symbol. It marked the owner as both successful and cultured, even if it wasn't quite as magnificent as the Royal Botanic Gardens at Kew. Howard Grubb would bring the basic idea of the English Garden to Canada.

Howard grew up in a comfortable middle-class home. His parents expected him to become a teacher. But Howard didn't do well at school. According to his own account, he finished last in his class in every course he took. To make matters worse, he couldn't even make the school cricket or football teams. His family decided to ship him off to America.

This seems to have occurred around 1899. Continuing with Howard's narrative: after "many years" he "stumbled by accident, without qualifications, into society's worst-paid profession." By that, he meant landscape architecture.

Was it really by accident? Was Howard really "without qualifications"? Maybe so. But it seems more likely that Howard had sought and found his calling. In spite of the supposedly dire financial prospects for a young man drawn to "society's worst-paid profession," his family evidently accepted and supported his choice.

In 1904, Howard enrolled in Cornell University at Ithaca, New York. Four years later he graduated with a Bachelor of Science in Agriculture degree. Not one to wait for opportunity to come knocking, Howard pursued it before he had even finished school. In 1907 he wrote a letter to Thomas Mawson, one of England's most respected landscape architects. He wanted a job.

Mawson replied, politely advising Howard to stay in the United States. He said prospects there would be better. Three months later, the newly graduated Howard Grubb showed up in his office.

"My name is Grubb," the young man said.

"Well, what can I do for you?" asked the bemused Mawson.

"I have come to work for you," Howard said.

"I am sorry to disappoint you," Mawson replied, "but it is quite impossible. As you will see for yourself, every seat in the office is occupied."

Not willing to be turned away, Howard said, "Well, sir, I have travelled all the way from America for the purpose of working for you; so you must find me a seat somewhere."

Probably a little taken aback by the youth's brashness, Mawson said, "But my dear fellow, I simply cannot do it."

Howard persisted. "Listen to me, sir. I worked my way back from America on a cattle boat, so that I might have the honour of working for you, and so you simply must take me on."

When Mawson wrote about the encounter years later, he said, "What could I do in a case like this? It would be wrong not to give such an audacious youth its chance. Within two years Grubb was in charge of my London office."

Sheridan Nurseries.

Thomas Mawson personally signed this likeness of himself: "To my old friends Mr. & Mrs. Dunington Grubb [sic]."

Between 1908 and 1910, Howard was in charge of one of Mawson's most prestigious projects, the Palace of Peace that was being constructed at The Hague, in the Netherlands. The building was to become the home of the International Court of Justice. Howard had his work cut out for him, because even though Mawson had won the contract, he had to work within a smaller budget than he had anticipated.

LORRIE DUNINGTON

Sometime in 1910, Mawson took Howard to a lecture on garden design at the Architectural Association. The lecturer was Lorrie Alfreda Dunington. She had the distinction of being more than a respected garden designer. Lorrie was the first female landscape architect in England.

Born in England in 1877 (making her about four years older than Howard), Lorrie had grown up in India, South Africa, and Australia. At the age of seventeen, she became one of the first female students admitted to the Horticultural College in Swanley, Kent, when she enrolled to study garden design. Upon graduation two years later, she became the head gardener on an estate in Ireland.

Lorrie met the noted gardener H. Selfe-Leonard, who was especially well known for his rock gardens, and formed a partnership with him. They designed gardens all over Britain, and it was quite likely from Leonard that Lorrie acquired the love of herbaceous borders that became her trademark. Leonard had been influenced by the great English garden designer Gertrude Jekyll, and passed her ideas on to Lorrie. It's possible that through Leonard, Lorrie met Jekyll personally.

Lorrie wanted to go beyond garden design into landscape architecture. At the time there were no conventional courses on landscape architecture in England, so she had to improvise and obtain knowledge piecemeal. She took private lessons from an architect, and she attended a course at a technical college. Lorrie finally opened her own office in London. She practised for several years throughout the British Isles, and won a competition at the Letchworth Garden City. For Lorrie to have been invited to address the Architectural Association, where she was introduced by Mawson and then thanked by the eminent Sir Edwin Lutyens, indicates that her colleagues held her in high regard.

After the lecture, Mawson personally introduced Howard to Lorrie. The attraction must have been swift and mutual, because three months later they became engaged. They each wrote a letter to Mawson, telling him of the engagement and promising to hold him responsible if things didn't work out. In the spring of 1911, Howard and Lorrie were married.

At that time it was the unquestioned custom for the wife to take the husband's name. Lorrie would have been expected to formally become Mrs. Howard Grubb. Instead, the newlyweds combined their names and became Mr. and Mrs. Dunington-Grubb. In this regard, Howard and Lorrie were about two generations ahead of the feminist movement. However, it might have been that even though Howard's friends affectionately called him "Grubby," Lorrie, who most certainly had a mind of her own, didn't like the sound of "Mrs. Grubb." There might also have been a pragmatic reason for the hyphenated name. Lorrie Dunington was a recognized and respected name in the profession. There would have been no sense in losing that connection.

Lorrie had an established business in London, and Howard was well employed with Mawson's company. Nonetheless, Lorrie convinced Howard that they should pull up stakes and cross the Atlantic to start their new life together. It indeed appears that Lorrie made many of the crucial decisions for both of them. Howard was something of a dreamer and a perfectionist. Lorrie was more dynamic, and was a driving force when it came to business.

OFF TO THE COLONIES

Their original plan was to go to New York City. The United States was booming with opportunity. Howard and Lorrie even had a briefcase full of letters of introduction to prominent New Yorkers.

Then they made the fateful decision to try Canada instead. To Britons like the Dunington-Grubbs, Canada was a cultural backwater, where private gardens and landscape architecture were virtually unknown. That could have been the very thing that drew them to it. There would be practically no competition.

Lorrie arranged for them to cross Canada by rail in the summer of 1911. All expenses were paid by the Canadian Pacific Railway. Lorrie was a good writer, and had contracted do a series of articles about their journey for the London *Daily Mail*. The businessmen who ran the CPR hoped that Lorrie's articles about the wonderful prospects in Canada would help lure immigrants who would eventually travel on their trains.

The Dunington-Grubbs' honeymoon was a combination of business and romantic adventure. They crossed what was then called the Great Lone Land at a time when it still had a frontier atmosphere. They visited towns that were the beginnings of great cities. The couple might have decided to put down roots just about anywhere between Winnipeg and Vancouver, but they found "no encouragement" in the West. They finally chose Toronto.

With a population of about three hundred thousand, Toronto was Canada's second-largest city. In 1911 it was the staid bastion of Protestant values that earned it the nickname

This 1912 Christmas card designed for Dunington-Grubb & Harries by A.S. Carter was later used for the 1925 Sheridan Nurseries catalogue cover.

Sheridan Nurseries.

Toronto the Good. You couldn't so much as buy a sinful box of chocolates on a Sunday. Outside of working-class neighbourhoods that housed Italian, Irish, and Eastern European ethnic minorities, the city was essentially British. Union Jacks in their thousands decorated Yonge Street on patriotic holidays.

Toronto was a city of historic Loyalist roots and strong Anglo-Saxon heritage. A local aristocracy descended from the old land-owning Family Compact, and an upper middle class, whose wealth came from industry and commerce, still saw Mother England as the model for all things a civilized society should be. Toronto seemed the perfect place for Howard and Lorrie. No doubt Thomas Mawson had some influence on their decision. He had visited Canada at the invitation of Governor General Earl Grey, and had made numerous important social connections in Toronto. The Dunington-Grubbs moved into living accommodations at 265 Sherbourne Street, and then went straight to work.

Listing themselves as "Landscape Gardeners," Howard and Lorrie opened an office at number 10, 6 Temperance Street. They would soon change their self-description to "Landscape Architects." In the years to come they would move around Toronto to a variety of domestic and business addresses. But in those crucial early months they had to establish themselves so they could build a clientele. For a short period during 1912–13, the Dunington-Grubbs were associated with another landscape architect, William E. Harries.

There was a definite need in Toronto for experts in garden design and landscape architecture at both the private and municipal levels. Howard and Lorrie advertised themselves as: "Consultants on all matters relating to Park and Garden design, Real Estate and Suburban Development, Civic Art and Town Planning." There is also documented evidence that they were representing Thomas Mawson's interests in Canada. The following item appeared in the August 1912, issue of *The Canadian Municipal Journal*:

> Mr. H. Dunnington-Grubb [*sic*], Landscape Architect, Toronto, who is associated with Mr. Thomas Mawson, the English Landscape Architect, will submit plans for the grounds of the University at Calgary, Alberta. Mr. Mawson looked over the ground upon a recent visit some months ago.

It was certainly beneficial to the team of Dunington-Grubb to be associated with so illustrious a name as Mawson. But in all likelihood they'd have prospered even without his endorsement, because no sooner did they hang out their shingle than they were getting work. Wilfrid Dinnick, the developer of the new Lawrence Park Estates, retained them as advisors in 1911 and 1912. Lawrence Park was a suburb of Toronto designed in the style of the English Garden City movement, which featured the integration of architecture and garden. Howard and Lorrie did the landscape designs and the planting schemes for the boulevards and parks. People moving into new homes would have Howard do their landscaping.

THE FOUNDING OF SHERIDAN NURSERIES

At that time there was no nursery in Canada specializing in ornamental plants. Lorrie decided to start one. She rented

Sheridan Nurseries.

ten acres of land in Lawrence Park, and ordered some shrubs from Europe. The imported plants would provide material for the enhancement of design work. Because landscape architects were not very highly paid, the sale of ornamental trees and shrubs would supplement the Dunington-Grubbs' income.

The Lawrence Park project ran into financial and developmental problems in 1912, and had to be suspended. It would not actually be completed until the 1930s. Lorrie moved the nursery to the Lambton Flats and called it Humber Nurseries. Unfortunately, this venture was short-lived. Why Humber Nurseries failed isn't known, but in 1913 Howard and Lorrie were looking for land outside Toronto.

Sheridan was a hamlet to the west of Toronto, just outside the town of Oakville. It was located mainly on the southwest corner of Town Line and Middle Road. To visit the site today, you'd have to stand in the middle of the intersection of the Queen Elizabeth Way (QEW) and Winston Churchill Boulevard. But in 1913, all around it were farms, rolling hills, and dirt roads. It was there in the autumn that Howard and Lorrie found what they were looking for; a "small patch of sandy loam." A farmer named Greeniaus had one hundred acres of land available. As it turned out, only about 20 percent of the soil was suitable for the kind of plants Howard and Lorrie wanted to grow. The rest of it was mostly clay.

1913 Dunington-Grubb Christmas card, which was also reused for the 1934 Sheridan Nurseries retail catalogue cover.

Sheridan Nurseries.

A.S. Carter's brochure cover for the short-lived Humber Nurseries.

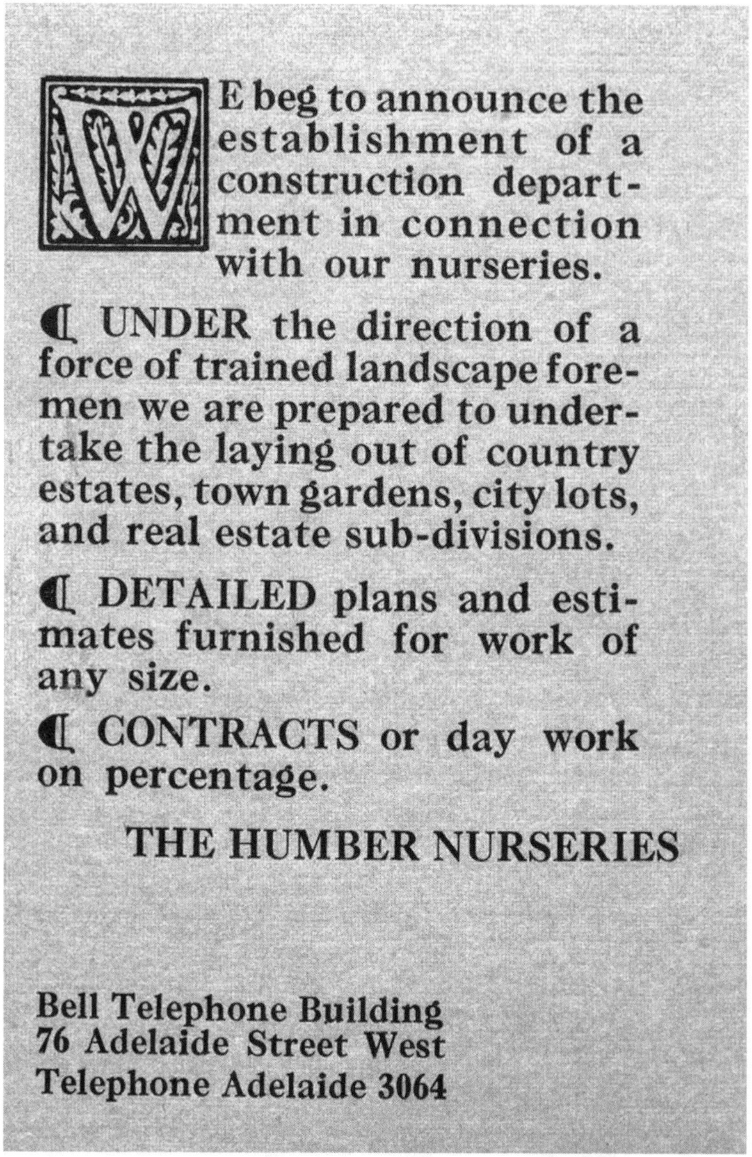

E beg to announce the establishment of a construction department in connection with our nurseries.

¶ UNDER the direction of a force of trained landscape foremen we are prepared to undertake the laying out of country estates, town gardens, city lots, and real estate sub-divisions.

¶ DETAILED plans and estimates furnished for work of any size.

¶ CONTRACTS or day work on percentage.

THE HUMBER NURSERIES

Bell Telephone Building
76 Adelaide Street West
Telephone Adelaide 3064

University of Toronto Fisher Rare Book Library.

Inside cover of brochure announcing the establishment of Humber Nurseries.

Howard and Lorrie arranged a bank mortgage to purchase the land. People thought they were crazy. This wasn't just a matter of renting a patch of ground to raise a few shrubs; it was a major investment, for a *nursery*, of all things! Hadn't they learned a lesson from the failure of Humber Nurseries? Couldn't they see the danger of investing money in such a "mad enterprise" as a nursery? Years later, Howard wrote of that landmark occasion:

> "Never use your own money," said the banker, "just sell shares." Having neither money for promotion nor financial connections we burned our boats by investing our last few dollars on a preliminary payment for 100 acres of real estate, at much too high a price, to learn the methods of (indecipherable) finance at first hand.

The papers were signed, and Sheridan Nurseries was born. There was no guarantee it would survive infancy. Fortunately, the right person would come along to make sure the fledgling company took root and thrived.

Howard and Lorrie had no intention of moving out to Sheridan. Their landscape-architecture business was based in Toronto, and they were getting good contracts. In 1913 they were commissioned to produce plans for the subdivision of Colvin Park in Buffalo, New York; Oriole Park in Toronto; and the Workman's Garden Village for the Riordan Pulp and Paper Company in Hawkesbury, Ontario. Their fine work led to a growing number of diverse projects, from a suburban social centre called the Old Mill Tea Room, to "the extensive and beautiful rock gardens" of the Humber Valley Surveys.

In 1915, Howard and Lorrie became involved in the now legendary Chorley Park project. Chorley Park was the magnificent, fifty-seven room chateau that was being built as the official residence of the lieutenant governor of Ontario.

Sheridan Nurseries.

The cairn that marks the site of the vanished village of Sheridan, erected in the southwest quadrant of the intersection of the Queen Elizabeth Way and Winston Churchill Boulevard. Dedication date: May 24, 1986.

Located on a fifteen-acre site in north Rosedale, with a view of the Don Valley, Chorley Park was considered the most beautiful government house in Canada. It even surpassed Rideau Hall, the governor general's residence in Ottawa. Chorley Park cost over a million dollars to build, a staggering sum at that time.

Originally, the gardens and landscaping at Chorley Park were to be done by C.W. Leavitt, a prominent American landscape architect. He drew up an excellent plan that combined a formal approach with the natural setting. However, Toronto's own growing community of landscape architects angrily complained about a foreigner being brought in to do a job they felt should have gone to someone local. It became a hot political issue. Finally, Leavitt was dropped, and Howard and Lorrie took over. Being British made them acceptable.

Howard and Lorrie drew up magnificent plans for Chorley Park. To their disappointment, most of them were rejected. Chorley Park was already going over budget, and the cost of Canada's involvement in the war in Europe was mounting. They completed the project with few changes to Leavitt's design. Nonetheless, the gardens they created on the estate were praised as "the finest in the Dominion."

Chorley Park's history as a government house was short and controversial. Although its guests included such dignitaries as the Prince of Wales (later Edward VIII) and Winston Churchill, critics complained from the start that it was too pretentious and too expensive to keep up. The Great Depression made Chorley Park even more of a burden on the provincial government. In 1937, Premier Mitchell Hepburn closed it down. Thereafter, Chorley Park was used as a military hospital, RCMP headquarters, and a home for refugees from the Hungarian Revolution of 1956. Howard and Lorrie's lush gardens were dug up to make space for utilitarian outbuildings. Finally, in 1959, the whole thing was demolished. All that remains is the bridge to the forecourt.

However, in 1913 the Chorley Park saga lay in the future. It would be just one of the many projects that would help Howard and Lorrie build Sheridan Nurseries. It was also important that the Dunington-Grubbs maintain themselves in Toronto society. Sheridan was out in the country. They needed a qualified person to run Sheridan Nurseries while they took care of business in Toronto. Lorrie placed an advertisement in the November 1, 1913, issue of *The Gardeners' Chronicle* in London, England:

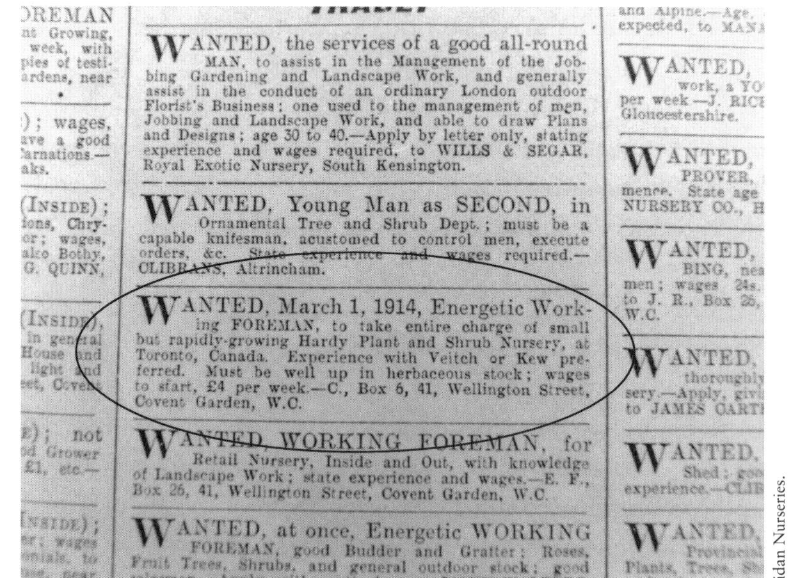

WANTED, the services of a good all-round MAN, to assist in the Management of the Jobbing Gardening and Landscape Work, and generally assist in the conduct of an ordinary London outdoor Florist's Business; one used to the management of men, Jobbing and Landscape Work, and able to draw Plans and Designs; age 30 to 40.—Apply by letter only, stating experience and wages required, to WILLS & SEGAR, Royal Exotic Nursery, South Kensington.

WANTED, Young Man as SECOND, in Ornamental Tree and Shrub Dept.; must be a capable knifesman, acustomed to control men, execute orders, &c. State experience and wages required.—CLIBRANS, Altrincham.

WANTED, March 1, 1914, Energetic Working FOREMAN, to take entire charge of small but rapidly-growing Hardy Plant and Shrub Nursery, at Toronto, Canada. Experience with Veitch or Kew preferred. Must be well up in herbaceous stock; wages to start, £4 per week.—C., Box 6, 41, Wellington Street, Covent Garden, W.C.

WANTED, WORKING FOREMAN, for Retail Nursery, Inside and Out, with knowledge of Landscape Work; state experience and wages.—E. F., Box 26, 41, Wellington Street, Covent Garden, W.C.

WANTED, at once, Energetic WORKING FOREMAN, good Budder and Grafter; Roses, Fruit Trees, Shrubs, and general outdoor stock; good salesman.—Apply, with particulars, to JAMES WALTERS, Rose Grower, Exeter.

Sheridan Nurseries.

The want ad Lorrie placed in the Gardener's Chronicle *that caught the attention of Herman Stensson.*

> Wanted, March 1, 1914, Energetic Working FOREMAN, to take entire charge of a small but rapidly growing Hardy Plant and Shrub Nursery at Toronto, Canada. Experience with Veitch or Kew preferred. Must be well up in herbaceous stock; Wages to start, £4 per week.

The ad caught the attention of Herman Stensson, a Scandinavian horticulturist working in England. He decided to respond. As we shall see further on, the story of Sheridan Nurseries is inextricably woven with that of the Stensson family.

HIGH SOCIETY AND SOCIAL CONSCIENCE

Well before their business ventures brought them financial success, Howard and Lorrie were rubbing shoulders with the cream of Toronto's high society. They were, after all, designing the landscaping and gardens for some of the finest homes in the city. This was not necessarily social-climbing or elitism. For one thing, it was good for business for Howard and Lorrie to socialize with the people whose gardens they wanted to design, and who sat on committees that oversaw civic projects. But the Dunington-Grubbs were more than socially active; they were also socially conscious. Lorrie's name first appeared in the society section of a Toronto newspaper on November 6, 1911, when the *Globe* reported that at a meeting of the University Women's Club, she had spoken on "Civic Improvement and the Housing Problem":

> Mrs. Dunnington Grubb [*sic*] criticized Toronto rather freely with regard to the congestion on Yonge Street, which she thought infinitely worse than the Strand, London, and with regard to our slum district. She told of the large boarding houses in London for girls which were run on a paying basis, yet cost the girls not more than they could afford to pay. The address evoked some discussion.

That wouldn't be the only time that Lorrie spoke publicly on the problem of decent housing for Canada's urban poor. She and Howard had liberal views on many social issues. As a member of the Local Council of Women, Lorrie took up such causes as a boycott to protest the high price of potatoes, a staple in the diet of low-income families; and a demand for female magistrates in women's and children's courts, and female inspectors for institutions in which women and children were incarcerated.

Howard attended meetings of the League for Social Reconstruction. That was the reformist intellectual wing of the Cooperative Commonwealth Federation (CCF), the forerunner of the New Democratic Party (NDP). He quite likely knew such leading socialists as J.S. Woodsworth, the founder of the CCF, and Agnes Macphail, Canada's first female Member of Parliament.

The Dunington-Grubbs frequently lectured on horticulture, landscaping, and the history of gardening. These events were always well-attended and were covered in the newspaper society pages. Howard and Lorrie hosted and attended garden parties and soirees that were high on any socialite's list of places to be seen. The names of many of the guests who turned up at these genteel affairs could be found in the *Canadian Who's Who* of the time. There were, for example, members of the Eaton, Massey, and Gooderham families. A guest might share tea and conversation with Sir Henry Pellatt, the millionaire who built Casa Loma; Hector Charlesworth, a famous Toronto journalist and critic; or Jeanne Gordon, the celebrated Canadian opera star. Lorrie felt herself honoured to be presented to such dignitaries as the Dowager Countess Grey, Lady Byng of Vimy, and Princess Alice the Duchess of Gloucester (Queen Elizabeth II's aunt).

Canadians today could hardly comprehend the importance of these events to people of that time. You got your name in the newspapers if you had the honour of pouring the tea. Ordinary people eagerly read the accounts just to keep up with what high society was doing.

It is evident from the many newspaper articles and the reminiscences of their acquaintances that people enjoyed the Dunington-Grubbs' company. Humphrey Carver, an urban planner and author, described Howard as, "a witty Englishman, as tall as a Lombardy poplar, with a quick teasing style and an infectious laugh."

According to Carver, Howard was a man who always sat up straight, but had a quizzical expression. Carver thought that he "looked rather like a caterpillar." Howard had a snorting laugh, Carver said, and would tease and argue with Lorrie, while always "sticking to his position."

Howard was a vegetarian whose diet of raw fruits and vegetables was "famous among his friends and acquaintances, for he often enjoyed a dessert of a whole pineapple or several apples or pears, and has been known to eat a basket of cherries or many bunches of grapes during an evening." Carver's comment on Howard's vegetarianism was, "He loved the green landscape, and he et it."

Cleeve Horne, the Canadian painter and sculptor who was renowned for his portraits, including one he did of Howard Dunington-Grubb, spoke of Howard as, "a marvelous guy … a big man in more than size alone. For one so prominent in his profession, he was unusually humble, with no affectations whatsoever. He was extremely warm and had a magnificent sense of humour. A most delightful character."

Carver found Lorrie to be more reserved than Howard. He said of Lorrie:

> [She] was a lovely person … I connect Mrs. Grubb with the herbaceous border, the flowers, the beauty of the individual flower and the stalks and shapes of the leaves. In the 19th century, the explorers and the botanists of England were in the distant outposts of the Empire and they brought back all sorts of exotic plants and seeds which the ladies of the period arranged most tastefully — crimsons, blues, purples — arranged them in herbaceous borders and in millinery. These same flowers were on the Grubbs' William Morris wallpapers, creeping and crawling up the walls of their drawing rooms and on the chintzes in those same rooms. This is the way I think of Lorrie Grubb, that she was a lady of flowers, and I simply assume that she was a person who gave this knowledge to her husband

Howard. I'm not talking about a frivolous enjoyment of flowers; Mrs. Grubb was a literary person, an aristocrat and a scholar.

A PASSION FOR THE ARTS

> *We all realize that art is one thing that does rise above nationalities and personal animosities.... Even during the war, despite any feelings of bitterness that might be entertained, we could not exclude from our lives beautiful German music.*
>
> — LORRIE ALFREDA DUNINGTON-GRUBB, speaking at the annual luncheon of the Women's Art Association, Toronto, February 3, 1928. From the Toronto *Globe*.

Besides landscape architecture and gardening, Howard and Lorrie shared a passion for the arts. Music, theatre, literature, and the visual arts collectively influenced who they were and what they did. They were, after all, artists in their own right.

Howard was a member of the Arts & Letters Club of Toronto, which was founded in 1908 by a group of writers, musicians, architects, academics, and supporters of the arts. The club had quarters on King Street and then Adelaide Street before finally moving to St. George's Hall at 14 Elm Street in 1920. It is still there today.

Until 1985, the Arts & Letters Club was a male bastion, much like the gentlemen's clubs of England. When Howard joined in 1913, strong-willed Lorrie might have privately bristled at the idea of women being excluded. But she knew Howard's membership could be important to them, both socially and professionally.

The Arts & Letters Club was a mecca for Canadian writers and artists of every discipline. They met there to eat and drink, to exchange ideas, and to have a good time. The membership list of more than a century reads like a *Who's Who* of Canadian culture: editor H. Napier Moore, journalist Hector Charlesworth, artist C.W. Jefferys, all of the members of the Group of Seven, and such luminaries as Vincent Massey, Marshall McLuhan, Mavor Moore, and Edmund Wyly Grier.

Howard was an active member. He served on committees and performed in low-brow comedy skits on stage. A report dated October 30, 1920, states that in a mock trial, Howard and another man were policemen and "had a lot of funny business."

Howard's image was captured in caricature by Arthur Lismer of the Group of Seven, and is part of the Arts & Letters Club's collection. Much more formal in mood is a photograph taken in 1938, which now hangs in one of the club's galleries. The Arts & Letters Club owns what is probably the only footage of Howard on film. It is a silent, black-and-white study, thirty seconds long, called *Behold the Lily*. The film shows a formally dressed Howard sitting at a desk, packing his pipe with tobacco.

Lorrie and Howard were both active in amateur theatrical productions. These ranged from morality plays and patriotic historical dramas, to Shakespeare. On one occasion, as a member of the Canadian Drama League, Howard was part of the cast for a production of *Love's Labour Lost* produced by the Lyceum Women's Art Association. We don't know what the professional critics thought of it, but, according to the society columns, the play was a success.

Lorrie was vice-president and an executive committee member of the prestigious Rose Societv of Ontario. She became involved with the Women's Art Association about 1915, and through it met such important artists as Frances Loring and Florence Wyle. In 1925 she was elected president of the association and held that position until 1930. This organization was founded in 1886 to further the role of women

Sheridan Nurseries.

Howard Dunington-Grubb (centre) in later years, often took part in skits at the Arts & Letters Club.

in the arts, and is still active today. The WAA's Toronto home is a nineteenth-century house at 23 Prince Arthur Avenue, where a garden has been named in Lorrie's honour.

In 1922, Howard and Lorrie became members of the Committee for War Memorials, which was set up to "advise [the people of Canada] in regard to the betterment of War Memorials and other art objects ..." They were considered valuable colleagues who actively promoted other artists in collaborative efforts. It is noteworthy that Lorrie, the businesswoman, felt that "Committees formed by Municipalities ought to pay for any information given by the Advisory Council, on the strength that free advise [*sic*], no matter how good, was not worth paying attention to."

As a boy, Howard had not excelled at sports. Nonetheless, as an adult he did have an interest in athletics. He was a member of the Toronto Golf Club, and once placed second in an amateur tournament at the Mississauga Golf Club.

Howard also belonged to the Toronto Skating Club. In addition to skating parties where members and their families gathered for recreation and tea, such clubs also put on spectacular theatrical shows. On March 21, 1920, Howard participated in a production of *Arabian Nights* which featured the Canadian figure skating champion Jeanne Chevalier. The Toronto *Globe* reported:

> The grand march, with which the pageant opened, drew a jewelled garland of gay figures from the Persian court to a dais upon which an ermine-draped chair awaited the Grand Vizier, and places of lesser grandeur the Princesses and courtiers. The stage decorations and floral display were arranged by Mrs. Arthur Kirkpatrick. Mr. H.B. Dunington Grubb [*sic*] and a group of other gentlemen were the Royal Guardsmen ...

GARDENS OF WORDS

Howard and Lorrie were prolific writers. They wrote authoritative articles on gardening and landscaping for publications such as *The Canadian Home Journal* and *Canadian Homes and Gardens*. Lorrie often headed her articles with literary quotations from poets such as Sir Walter Scott, Alfred Lord Tennyson, or Ralph Waldo Emerson. Her writing style was

Sheridan Nurseries.

Howard and Lorrie Dunington-Grubb in the late 1930s.

formal and instructive, but appealing and easy to follow. An editorial note in *Women's Century* in 1921 says, "The followers of Mrs. Dunington-Grubb's articles ... will appreciate her interested endeavors to get just the right sort of information for our garden loving readers."

Like many people of her time, Lorrie also wrote for her own pleasure, and to keep detailed records of exceptional events in her life. In the Dunington-Grubb Collection in the Archival Library at the University of Guelph, there are several essays, in typewritten form and in Lorrie's own handwriting, about a trip she took to the Canary Islands. One essay, titled "Canaria Days" beautifully records her observations during a single day in an exotic place.

> The mountains are a glorious salmon pink. No need for a watch to tell the time. The "smiling morn" proclaims that it is just 5 a.m. and while I look, already the colour begins to pale; in a few minutes it will be fleeting gold. Yet with this brief announcing the Spanish day begins. All breathing things in slow succession come to life. Cocks crow, donkeys bray with strangely raucous notes and sheep bells tinkle in the distance.

Howard's professional writing was also informative, and done in an appealing and readable style. However, Howard's writing persona was a little more casual than Lorrie's. He was more likely to sprinkle his articles with subtle examples of his dry sense of humour. The following is from "The Grassless Garden":

> "It's like this," I tell the neighbours, "I got rid of my grass because: (A) I don't like pushing lawn mowers, holding sprinklers, or any other form of heavy labour; (B) The grass didn't grow well in such a shady garden; (C) I wanted a garden that would look green right through the winter; (D) there was a lot of planting material that I wanted to try out; (E) A landscape architect is expected to do something different anyway.
>
> "New? Why, there's nothing new about the grassless garden. Good heavens!!! The thing that's new is grass. If you don't believe it, try mowing a lawn with a scythe, sickle or shears. That's what they had to do before lawn mowing machinery was invented. Only the rich could afford a lawn then."

In the 1930s Howard undertook an ambitious project. He wrote a 219-page book titled *The Garden Today*, "to assist the layman in the development of a property as a house and garden." Howard believed that, "The time has arrived when [the principals of layout and design] should be clearly stated in simple language, and submitted to the public in book form."

To Howard's great disappointment, he couldn't find a publisher. Editors found his prose style turgid. Even so, given Howard's reputation in his field, the book might have found a market. But the Great Depression was on, and nobody wanted to risk publishing a book of limited appeal. Howard collected thirteen rejection slips before he gave up on it.

The manuscript for *The Garden Today* is in the Sheridan Nurseries archives. Although the main text is technical in nature, the first chapter, which is a concise history of gardening, contains colourful information and snippets of Howard's wit. The passage below begins with a section describing the garden in ancient Egypt:

> His [the Egyptian's] home was an area of land enclosed by high walls, a fortress, to shut out the savage desert no less than savage man. On one point he was perfectly clear, the area inside the walls must have not the slightest resemblance to anything he had ever seen in nature, for he had seen nothing but the desert. His garden should be as different from its surroundings as the hand of art could make it. Water in the form of tanks, canals and fountains was taken to every part of the home. The arrangement was simple, orderly and straightforward. It was an outdoor architectural design meeting the actual needs of the family in as direct and logical a manner as does the floor plan of a first prize design for a model house today ... Is it any wonder that the word *paradise* appearing in every language, and meaning originally an enclosed space laid out with buildings for the use of the family, in other words, a *garden*, should have come to signify *heaven*? It was the most attractive refuge people were able to think of, the most restful, soul-satisfying conception which art could visualize.

PAGEANTRY AND TRAGEDY

Lorrie was often involved with community groups and committees. In 1928, for example, she lectured at various times on gardening, art, and literature. She helped organize a masquerade ball for students of the Ontario College of Art, hosted a convention for the National Council for Women, presided over a YMCA World Unity conference, and was re-elected president of the Women's Art Association.

Lorrie was a prominent member of the Lyceum and Heliconian clubs of Toronto, both of which were devoted to the involvement of women in the arts. She was an enthusiastic participant in the Heart of the World Pageants. Founded in 1927, the pageant was a theatrical and musical extravaganza that celebrated Toronto as "the living panorama of nations at peace in the love of mankind." Performers representing numerous nationalities and ethnic groups went on stage to sing, dance, and act in the cause of racial and international harmony. As the reviewer of one performance put it, "The general idea was that all nations have to work together ... to find their right places in the grand concourse of the world."

Lorrie was in the first production in 1927, and was still with the pageant in 1938. Howard got into the act, too. In a review of one Hearts of the World production, a Toronto *Daily Star* journalist wrote: "I could not have asked for ... a more menacing and dreadful Mars than Dunington-Grubb; [or] a more graceful, poetic and charming figure as Tolerance, Mother, and finally Peace, than Mrs. Dunington-Grubb."

Sadly, sometime in the late 1920s, Lorrie began to show the symptoms of tuberculosis. At that time, there were no effective medications to fight TB. Lorrie's prospects were not good.

For a few years Lorrie received nursing care at home, and still worked with Howard professionally. She also tried to keep up with her many social commitments. She was involved in a musical study club, appeared at Lyceum Club functions, and attended garden parties. However, the debilitating effects of the disease gradually proved to be too much even for Lorrie's indomitable spirit.

On March 1, 1944, at an exhibit of rare old laces sponsored by the Lyceum and Women's Art Association, Lorrie wore a Limerick veil that had been in her family for over a hundred years. Three months later, her name appeared in the *Daily Star* as a guest at a Lyceum Club garden party. That was the last time Lorrie made the social pages.

Soon after, Lorrie was admitted to the Mountain Sanatorium (now Chedoke Hospital) in Hamilton. She died there at the age of sixty-seven on January 17, 1945. The obituary in the *Daily Star* requested that mourners visiting the funeral home or attending interment in Mount Pleasant Cemetery "Kindly omit flowers." Whatever Howard's reason for that decision, he kept it private. After all, no one had known the Lady of Flowers more intimately than he.

In August of 1941, with the Second World War raging and Canada firmly committed to the Allied cause, Howard joined the Camouflage Corps. That was a group of twenty-five architects, artists, sculptors, photographers, and engineers who got together with an expert once a week to see how they could use their skills and talents in the art of camouflage. The destruction that heavy bombing had wreaked upon European cities clearly demonstrated the importance of using camouflage to protect civilian centres and industrial installations from air attack. It was one way in which a pacifist like Howard could conscientiously contribute to the war effort.

In March of 1942, Howard's attention was turned to the more domestic problem of highway traffic accidents. Speaking at the University of Toronto to members of the Men of Trees Society, he suggested that trees would be a safety factor on Ontario roads.

> Tree plantings along Ontario highways would provide untold benefits to the motorist. A centre boulevard of thickly planted trees would eliminate disasters caused by glaring headlights and head-on collisions. Wide plantings on either side of the highways would control high winds and hold drifting snow, a hazard to winter driving and which necessitates costly removal.

A few months later, Howard was made an advisor to the Toronto City Planning Board. At the time of her death, Lorrie was president of the Canadian Society of Landscape Architects, an organization that she and Howard had helped to found. He took over her duties for the remainder of her term, and then was elected president for the following year.

LIFE AFTER LORRIE

Howard was a widower at the age of sixty-three. Lorrie's passing deeply grieved him, but he was in robust health. He was financially well off. However, the idea of retiring didn't occur to him. He was president of the increasingly successful

Sheridan Nurseries, and there was no shortage of landscape architecture projects.

In 1956, there was growing concern that Canada was falling behind the United States in the development of parklands along the new St. Lawrence Seaway. The Americans had mobilized their own very best landscape architects, while in Canada much of the work had gone to "outsiders." As the president of the École des Beaux Arts in Montreal put it, "We are still plain gardeners to too many." The *Globe and Mail* wrapped up Canadian anxiety in a few words: "If Queen Elizabeth opens the seaway, Ontarians and other Canadians would be chagrined if the Canadian side takes an inferior position to that of the United States ..."

Howard was one of several Toronto landscape architects who were consulted on how Canada could keep up with the Americans. The situation exemplified Howard's long-held beliefs that Canadians lacked awareness of the importance of landscape architecture, and the country needed improved facilities for teaching it. For twenty years, Howard was a special lecturer on landscape design at the University of Toronto's architectural facility, and he constantly lobbied for more facilities and faculty

In 1958, Howard bought land along the Credit River in Meadowvale (now part of Mississauga) for the establishment of the Meadowvale Botanical Gardens. This was his personal dream project. He wanted to create: "a botanical demonstration garden for the citizens of Toronto and environs." His intention was that the garden would display ornamental plants and "disseminate ... gardening education and information ... to the general public." On June 25, 1959, the Toronto *Daily Star* reported:

Once upon a time, a man with a million dollars sat down to figure out what to do with his fortune. His answer was an ambitious plan for a 100-acre botanical garden in the Toronto area. Preliminary sketches for the Meadowvale Botanical Garden were unveiled for the first time yesterday. The garden, stretching along the Credit River, is less than a mile from Highway 401. Guiding and financing the initial stages of the project is H.B. Dunington-Grubb, well-known Toronto

Sheridan Nurseries.

Howard Dunington-Grubb's dream of a Meadowvale Botanical Garden was never fully realized due to funding problems. Instead, funds from the Dunington-Grubb Foundation have been used to support worthy projects and organizations.

> landscape artist. Mr. Grubb, aged over 70, yesterday admitted that he first had the idea for the garden because he had no one to inherit his money. Although unconfirmed, it is believed that his fortune runs into seven figures ... He said an important function of the Meadowvale Botanical Garden would be to help the average homeowner landscape and choose plants for his garden.

Howard envisioned a botanical park that included a rock garden, a rose garden, and a hedge garden. There would also be special areas for climbing hybrid tea and floribunda rose varieties. Work was begun on the site with some tree plantings, the raising of a wall along the road front, and the construction of a house for the keeper.

Howard put up one million dollars of his own money to get the Meadowvale project under way. It soon became apparent that maintaining the gardens would cost about $100,000 a year. Howard decided to put the project on hold until additional financial support could be found. Unfortunately, that didn't happen.

Howard had overlooked the fact that much of the site he had purchased was Credit River floodplain, and was underwater during wet seasons. After his death, the Meadowvale Botanical Gardens was converted to the Dunington-Grubb Foundation. The trustees explored several ideas for the development of Howard's legacy, including a major conservatory. But they were stymied by prohibitive costs. The Foundation finally sold the Meadowvale property to the Credit River Conservation Authority, and decided to fund many philanthropic garden- and landscape-related projects in Howard's honour.

That still left the matter of ensuring that Howard's financial legacy would be used in accordance with his wishes. In the early 1970s, the Toronto Civic Garden Centre planned a much-needed expansion of its facilities. The Foundation provided seed money for the expansion, and then donated $650,000 to the Centre, on the condition that the City of Toronto matched the amount. The deal was done, and a floral hall/auditorium was named the Howard Dunington-Grubb Hall. The Dunington-Grubb Foundation went on to fund many other worthy projects.

ACCOLADES, BUT PLEASE, NO FLOWERS

In the last twenty years of his life, Howard was recognized as one of the most prominent Canadians in his profession. He represented the Canadian Society of Landscape Architects (CSLA) on the Canadian Arts Council from 1947 to 1954. In 1949 he was named chairman of the committee to write a brief to the Vincent Massey Royal Commission on the Arts, Letters, and Sciences. From 1950 to 1951, Howard was the first chairman of the CSLA Education Committee, and in 1953 he was secretary for the organization. He was elected a Fellow of the CSLA in 1964. In 1961, Howard was one of six landscape artists invited to design gardens for the Garden Club of Toronto's annual Flower Show, being held that year at Casa Loma. Sheridan Nurseries was one of the four landscape and nursery companies contributing to the project.

Howard was also honoured with several prestigious awards. In 1954, the Ontario Association of Architects presented him with its Allied Arts Medal. That same year he received the Royal Architectural Institute of Canada Medal in Montreal. As president of Sheridan Nurseries, which had become the largest grower and retailer of plants in Canada, Howard was made an honorary member of both the Canadian and Ontario Nursery Trades Associations.

Sheridan Nurseries.

Ontario Landscape Contractors Association Award given to Howard Dunington-Grubb in 1965.

Sheridan Nurseries.

Howard Dunington-Grubb in later years.

In 1963 Howard became the first Canadian to be given an honorary membership in the International Shade Tree Association. In January of 1965, he became the first person to be made an honorary member of the Ontario Landscape Contractors Association.

An unofficial honour in which Howard took special pride came in May 1954. The Architectural Conservancy of Ontario selected his house at 3 Dale Avenue in Rosedale as one of five Toronto residences to be shown to the public on a special tour. The houses were chosen as examples of artistic excellence. Howard's home was the subject of a photo-feature in the May 11 edition of the *Globe and Mail*. A decade later, in an article that appeared in the *Daily Star* on January 6, 1964, journalist Lotta Dempsey wrote: "My favourite house in Toronto? That's easy. The completely charming residence which landscape architect Howard Dunninton Grubb [*sic*] designed himself and built in a coach house poised on a ravine's edge on Dale Avenue. It is not a large house, but every inch and corner is handsomely done with complete charm and warmth."

One day an invitation dated February 18, 1965, arrived in Howard's mailbox. In the envelope were two tickets and a handwritten card inviting him to the Canadian premiere of a film called *This Garden — England* at the O'Keefe Centre on March 9. The lieutenant governor of Ontario would be in attendance. The invitation had been sent by the secretary of the Garden Club of Toronto. She received a reply from Howard's office, dated February 22: "We regret to inform you that Mr. H.B. Dunington-Grubb is ill and will be unable to accept your kind invitation to the Preview Party of the Garden Club of Toronto on March 9th."

Howard Dunington-Grubb died in his home at the age of eight-four on February 25, 1965. He was buried next to Lorrie in Mount Pleasant Cemetery. Howard's obituary closed with the words, "Flowers gratefully declined."

CHAPTER 2

The Stensson Family: Pioneers of Horticulture

THE PATRIARCH

A Sheridan Nurseries' directors' report written in March 1964, states that the history of the company would read like a "long series of extraordinarily lucky breaks and bold decisions." One of those lucky breaks came the day in the fall of 1913 that Sven Herman Stensson saw Lorrie Dunington-Grubb's ad in *The Gardeners' Chronicle* in England. There doesn't appear to be any documented explanation as to why Herman (the name he preferred) chose to respond to an advertisement for a job in far-off Canada. Perhaps he simply felt, like so many other Europeans in the early twentieth century, that the New World offered greater promise than the old. Whatever Herman's reasons, Lorrie and Howard couldn't have found a more qualified manager to run their nursery.

Herman, one of seven children, was born in Oretorp, Sweden, on April 17, 1877, to Nils and Christiane (née Rasmussen). While Herman was still very young, his family moved to Denmark where Nils had been offered a job as gardener at Knuthenborg Park. This huge estate, owned by the aristocratic Knuth family, was being transformed into a park which displayed rare plants from all over the world. The landscape design was the last major project of the great English landscape architect Edward Milner. Nils became the chief landscape gardener of the Count of Knuthenborg. The count gave the Stenssons the use of a hunting pavilion, one of several fine Victorian-era homes on the property. That was where Herman grew up.

Herman learned gardening and landscaping while working with his father at Knuthenborg. He also attended the School of

Sheridan Nurseries.

The Hunting pavilion in Knuthenborg Park, a royal Danish estate, where Herman Stensson grew up. Note Herman sitting in the window.

Horticulture in Copenhagen. He loved horticulture, and was a hard worker and an eager student. In addition to his skills as a landscaper, Herman also had a great natural talent as an artist. He made beautiful drawings of the Knuthenborg Palace and gardens. Much of the design Nils and Herman created at Knuthenborg remains today. As a reward for Herman's excellent work, the count gave him a gold-and-amethyst brooch. It was to be a gift for the woman, as yet unknown, whom Herman would marry. The brooch is still a Stensson family heirloom.

At some point Herman left home to strike out on his own. According to his son Howard, Herman served about a year in the Danish Army. Letters of reference from a nursery in Erfurt, Germany, indicate that he worked there in 1898 and 1899. It's possible that he worked at landscape gardening in France and the Netherlands, as well. Then Herman went to England, where horticulture was becoming fashionable.

The increasing popularity of garden culture in England attracted many ambitious and talented young men like Herman. There was plenty of work available in public projects and on private estates. Moreover, nurseries were developed specifically to grow ornamental plants. No known document states exactly when Herman arrived in England, but a letter of recommendation written by an English employer suggests that it must have been in 1899. In fact, Herman collected an impressive body of excellent references. They provide a guide to his years in England.

From April to September 1899, Herman worked for the Happy Lane Nursery at Waltham Abbey. Then he went to H.E. Milner & Son in Surrey, where he was underforeman for three years. In 1904 and 1905 Herman worked for a nursery in Cambridge, and grew orchids for Sander & Sons of

Sheridan Nurseries.

The Count of Knuthenborg gave this brooch to Herman Stensson as a gift for his future wife. It is still a Stensson family heirloom.

Sheridan Nurseries.

Herman Stensson at the time he was living in England.

London, who advertised themselves as "Warrant Holders to His Majesty King Edward VII" and "Purveyors of Orchids to Her Late Majesty Queen Victoria."

Then Herman found employment with the firm of William Wells & Sons in Hitchen, Hertfordshire. He stayed for over seven years. At some point Herman had the opportunity to work in London's famous Kew Gardens and assisted in laying out England's first "Garden City" at Letchworth. He must also have gone back to work in Germany for awhile, because years later his children would recall seeing a folder full of German postcards he had sent to their mother while he was courting her.

There is a consistency in the letters of reference Herman collected from his Danish, German and English employers: that he was "honest, sober, industrious and attentive to his duties." They praised his knowledge of horticulture, his skill as a draughtsman, and his managerial abilities. In 1905 Herman must have written back to his old employer at Knuthenborg. A letter on Knuthenborg stationery, dated July 10, 1905, is among his papers.

> Mr. H. Stensson,
>
> In reply to yours of the 8th inst. I have much pleasure in stating that I feel confident through my knowledge of you through a good many years and from conversations I have had with you on the subject of your profession, in recommending you to any position within the latter. Of your trustworthiness and steady character I cannot speak too well.
>
> ______ Knuth

The first name in the signature is illegible. An archivist at the Danish State Archives in Copenhagen has suggested that the author of the letter might have been Eggert Christopher Knuth, who was the Count of Knuthenborg at that time.

HERMAN AND ANNIE

One person in England was impressed with Herman for reasons other than his gardening and landscaping expertise. Annie Benning, a charming and attractive woman, was born on November 23, 1874, making her two-and-a-half years

Sheridan Nurseries.

The original Sheridan Nurseries barn. The car and truck indicate mid-1920s.

older than Herman. He met her while he was boarding at her parents' home. On January 9, 1906, Herman and Annie were married in Hitchen. Their son Jesse Vilhelm was born on July 23, 1907 (he would be known to family and friends as Bill, but more often, J.V.). He was followed by Karl Frederick (Fred), September 17, 1908; Christian Kenneth (Chris), October 10, 1909; and Howard Herman (Howard), December 2, 1912.

On March 13, 1912, Herman became a naturalized British subject. A little over a year and a half later, he saw the advertisement that would draw him and his family to Canada. On November 7, 1913, Herman wrote to Lorrie and Howard Dunington-Grubb, expressing his interest in the position. He received a reply, signed by Howard, dated December 22.

> Negotiations are now in progress for the purchase of one hundred acres of land about 22 miles from Toronto and close to the lake. This site is an admirable one in every respect as the soil varies from heavy clay to light black loam and sand. The site slopes gently to the South and is well protected from the North. Through the Southern section passes the most travelled railway in Canada giving considerable possibilities for advertising ... There is a small farm house on this property which you can have rent free and good barns ... Available labour will limit the amount of stock we shall be able to plant in any one season to 3 or 4 acres so that we shall have to try and grow some paying crop on the rest of the farm. Have you any knowledge of farming?"

The letter went on to offer Herman $60 toward travelling expenses on the condition that he agreed to keep the position for at least two years. It promised him raises in salary and "a substantial interest in the concern" if he should prove to be the right man and the nursery became profitable. The Dunington-Grubbs would employ three men to help Herman with seasonal work.

The letter was followed by another, dated December 23.

> Since writing you yesterday we have completed arrangements for the purchase of the farm of which I spoke. There will be horses and all necessary equipment. As the land is specially adapted for the raising of small fruits like gooseberries, currants and strawberries, we think it might be well to go in for these in a small way until we are likely to need the land for other purposes ...
>
> Please understand that your wages will be $20.00 per week with house rent free on the property. Do not tell the immigration officials that you are coming out on any definite engagement as I am given to understand that it may cause trouble.

The last sentence poses something of a mystery. Why would Howard instruct Herman *not* to tell immigration officials that he had a "definite engagement"? Wouldn't officials prefer that newly arrived immigrants already have employment arranged? Howard's concern might have had to do with the nature of the position Herman was filling. He was not

a common labourer, but an artisan who would be working at management level. Immigration officials might have wondered why Howard had gone outside Canada for such an individual instead of hiring locally. Or it could have been that the Dunington-Grubbs just didn't have much patience with government bureaucrats.

As Herman and Annie prepared for the big trip across the sea, they received another letter; this one dated January 28, 1914. Some of the information in it must have made them wonder just what they were getting into.

> Replying to your three letters of recent date I note that you expect to be in Toronto March 21st. Address your baggage to Clarkson station, Ontario, Grand Trunk Railway. We have a man and his wife living in the house now and looking after the farm. I do not know whether the stove now there belongs to them or to us but think it would be well for you to bring your stove in any case. The roads are not very good out in the country here but you might bring your bicycle in any case as the Government intends to build a new road from Hamilton to Toronto this year.

THE JOURNEY

The Stensson family departed from Liverpool on the steamer RMS *Alaunia* in early March 1914. On the passenger list, Herman's occupation was entered as "farmer." Canadian immigration officials would have no objections to that. Canada welcomed farmers. Nobody was likely to ask Herman what he intended to grow. The *Alaunia* was a new ship, especially made for the Cunard Line for ferrying immigrants. She was no luxurious *Titanic*. All passengers on the *Alaunia* were second or third class.

The *Alaunia* was launched on June 9, 1913, and made her maiden voyage on December 27, 1913. When the First World War began, she was requisitioned as a troop ship. RMS *Alaunia* was the first Cunard ship to transport Canadian troops. She was sent into the Gallipoli campaign by the summer of 1915. Then she carried troops to Bombay later the same year. She returned to the North Atlantic and carried troops from Canada and the U.S. in 1916. The *Alaunia* struck a mine and sank on October 19, 1916. The Stenssons were fortunate to have sailed before the carnage on the seas began.

Library and Archives Canada, PA149833.

SS Alaunia *of the Cunard Line, the ship that brought the Stensson family to Canada in 1914. The* Alaunia *was sunk by a mine in the First World War.*

What must Herman and Annie have been feeling as their ship headed out to the open sea toward a strange new country? Herman was thirty-six years old, and Annie thirty-nine; much older than most emigrating married couples. They had four small children in tow: J.V., six; Fred, five; Chris, four; and Howard, just fifteen months. Howard actually took his first baby steps on the deck of the ship. (He would joke in later years that because of that, he walked with a wobble.) The *Alaunia* was certainly an improvement over the cattle boats that had carried Europeans to the Americas just a generation earlier. But the days were still long and boring, and people still got seasick.

The ship docked in Halifax on March 13, and the Stensson family first set foot on Canadian soil. Once they had gone through customs and immigration, they went to the train station. There they boarded the Intercolonial Express for the trip to Toronto, 1,857 kilometres (1,150 miles) away. Twenty-seven hours and a dozen stops later, they changed trains at Montreal and boarded the Grand Trunk Express for the nine-hour run to Toronto. That meant about thirty-six hours in a railway coach, plus the time spent in the Montreal station between trains — with children who got hungry, thirsty, sleepy, bored, and had to go to the bathroom.

As the train rolled through eastern Canada, Herman and Annie no doubt experienced something that had been felt by so many newcomers who had travelled that route before them: a sense of wonder at the enormity of the country. Through the windows of their coach they would have seen mile after mile of forest and farmland, broken only by distantly spaced urban centres. Nothing at all like England! Herman might very well have wondered if his prospective employers' idea of establishing a nursery in this wild country made sense, and if he had made a wise decision himself in uprooting his family on such a gamble.

THE VILLAGE OF SHERIDAN

The Stenssons most likely met the Dunington-Grubbs in Toronto. They would have taken the train to Clarkson, and then a carriage to the nursery. We can only imagine what Herman and Annie must have been thinking.

In the early twentieth century, not many newcomers from Britain were fully prepared for life in rural Canada. Even if they had been told in letters of what to expect, they couldn't actually grasp the reality of it until they arrived and began to experience it for themselves. Even a region like southern Ontario, which had been under agricultural development for a century, hardly resembled the quaint English countryside.

Railways linked communities, but country roads were terrible. They were obstacle courses of ruts, mud, rocks, and washouts. In winter, the best way to get around was still by horse-drawn sleigh.

At the time the Stenssons first saw it, Sheridan was a hamlet of about fifty people. It had originally been called Hammondsville, after a United Empire Loyalist named William Hammond. In the mid-1850s, when the village boasted of a population of two hundred, the people wanted their own post office. Apparently the provincial government felt the name Hammondsville sounded too much like that of another community. This could have been Hammondsville, Ohio, or Hammondville (now Hammond) in Perth County, Ontario.

Stephen Oughtred, the local blacksmith, suggested re-naming the community after the Irish-born British playwright Richard Brinsley Sheridan. Now bearing that illustrious name, the hamlet got its post office in 1857. It was located on a thoroughfare called the Middle Road, which would one day be the QEW. The Sheridan Post Office remained in operation until 1956.

Besides the post office, Sheridan had a general store, a blacksmith's shop, a tannery, a chair factory, and a shoemaker's shop. There was a United Church, but no tavern. An old Zion church was used as a community centre and Women's Institute Hall. An old school had been converted into a temperance hall. (This building can still be seen in the Ontario Agricultural Museum near Milton. The only other known surviving building from the Sheridan area is a barn from Sheridan Nurseries that was donated to the Peel Board of Education in Mississauga and is now on an educational farm on Highway 10 south of the 401.)

Sheridan Nurseries

The Sheridan general store was also the local gas station. This location is now the intersection of the QEW and Winston Churchill Boulevard. Note the gas pump just past the hood of the car.

THE "COTTAGE" AND THE HUNDRED ACRES

When the Stenssons finally arrived at their new home, Annie's heart must have sunk. The "house" could at best be described as a small cottage. It had no electricity, telephone, or indoor plumbing. Drinking water came from a well. The toilet was an outhouse.

Sheridan Nurseries.

The original cottage the Stensson family moved into upon their arrival in Canada in 1914. The house had no electricity or indoor plumbing at the time.

A quick inspection of the hundred acres was all Herman required to realize most of the land wasn't suited for the types of plants he was going to cultivate. Only a fifth of it was good, sandy loam. The rest was clay.

But Herman was an industrious and courageous man. He was determined to make a life in Canada for his family. To do that, he committed himself to making the Dunington-Grubbs' dream of a genuine ornamental plant nursery a reality, even if he had only a small stock of imported perennials with which to start.

Herman spent his first spring and summer improving the ground, and overseeing a few hired men who planted and tended perennials, shrubs, and trees. At the same time his family learned, day by day, the ins and outs of rural Canadian life.

Local people would have come by to welcome the new neighbours and invite them to social gatherings where the attractions were tea and games of horseshoes. Annie made trips to Sheridan to do one-stop shopping at the general store and pick up mail. The Stensson boys would have been thrilled the first time they looked out their bedroom window early one morning and saw deer. The Stenssons would also have found that the local wildlife also included "pests" like rabbits, skunks, coyotes, foxes, and porcupines. Herman eventually applied for a firearms permit so he could buy a shotgun.

One thing is consistent in the chronicles of immigrants in nineteenth and early twentieth century Canada: the shock of the first winter! One account after another provides first-hand anecdotes from horrified narrators about sub-zero temperatures, waist-deep snow, and blizzards that paralyzed

the cities and countryside alike. Herman would have remembered cold winters in Denmark, but for Annie and the boys, the long season of ice and snow was a first-time experience. Talking about those times years later, Howard Stensson said the "ramshackle" house in which they lived was cold, but he didn't give any details. However, reminiscences of other people who lived in frame houses with no electricity provide a good idea of what daily life was like in the Stensson home during the winter.

Annie, who was a good cook, probably prepared the meals on a wood-burning stove which made the kitchen the warmest room in the house. There might also have been a fireplace, a wood-burning pot-bellied stove, or maybe even a coal-oil stove in another part of the house. These would have kept the rooms in which they were located comfortable in the daytime and the early evening, but chilly drafts would still find their way in, and there would frequently be frost on the insides of the windows.

After sundown the family would have supper by the light of coal-oil lamps. Mixed with the aroma of cooking would be the dank smell of wet woollen mittens, scarves, and socks drying near the stove. No electricity meant that the family couldn't listen to the radio programs that were becoming popular. The Stensson family would probably retire early to chilly bedrooms.

Long flannel underwear, a woollen nightshirt, and heavy quilts kept a sleeping body warm, even as a north wind howled outside. It also helped if more than one warm body shared a bed. There would have been a pot under the bed, because nobody liked the idea of a trip to the freezing outhouse in the middle of the night.

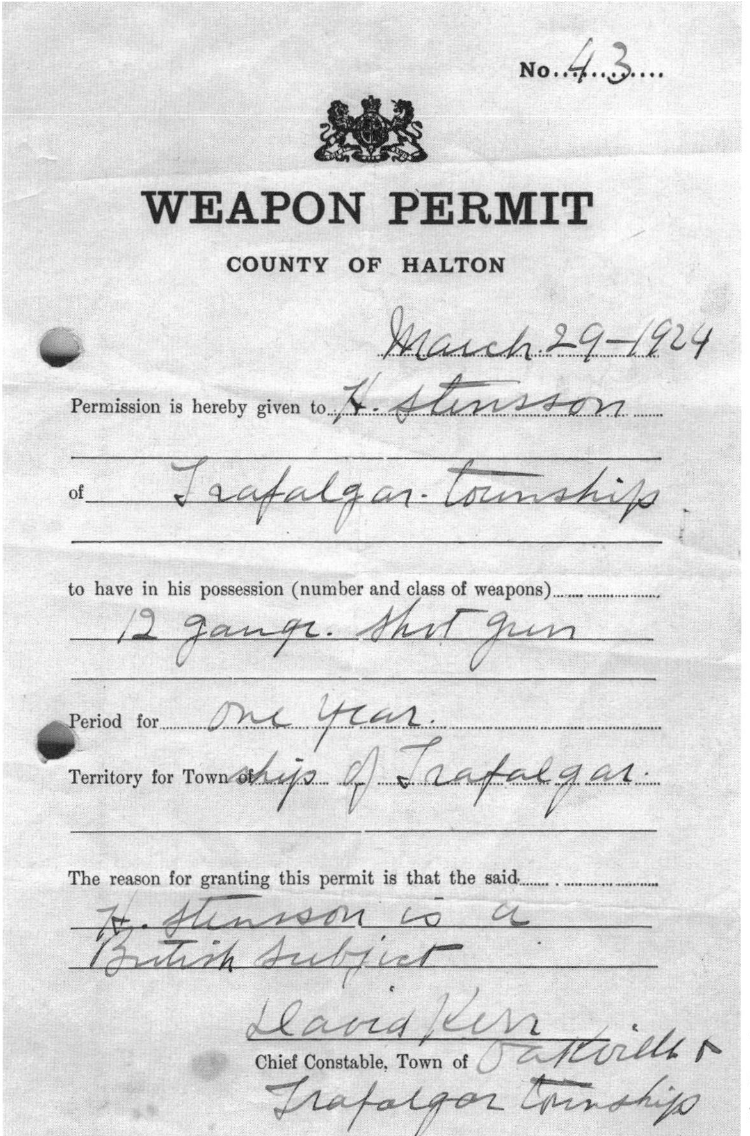
No. 43

WEAPON PERMIT

COUNTY OF HALTON

March 29–1924

Permission is hereby given to H. Stensson

of Trafalgar-township

to have in his possession (number and class of weapons) 12 gauge. Shot gun

Period for One Year.

Territory for Township of Trafalgar.

The reason for granting this permit is that the said H. Stensson is a British Subject

David Kerr

Chief Constable, Town of Oakville & Trafalgar township

Sheridan Nurseries.

Herman Stensson's permit for a twelve-gauge shotgun, dated March 29, 1924.

Of course, the Stensson boys would have learned from other children that winter could be fun. They skated on frozen ponds and enjoyed sleigh rides and snowball fights. Neighbouring families overcame the isolation of winter by getting together on Saturday evenings for games of cards and checkers.

But in spite of the diversions, winter was tough. Herman, who was a very patient man, took everything in stride. But after that first winter, Annie wanted to go back to England.

However, in the summer of 1914 the First World War had started. Everyone had been certain it would be over by Christmas, but the struggle was bogged down in the mud and blood of the trenches in France and Belgium. It was clear to almost everyone except the generals that the carnage would not end any time soon. Ships sailing between the Americas and Britain had to run a gauntlet of minefields and German submarines. In May 1915, the stunning news came of the sinking of the *Lusitania*. The big passenger liner, en route from New York to Liverpool, was torpedoed off the coast of Ireland with the loss of 1,119 lives. War had made sea travel extremely hazardous.

There's no way of knowing how much the war influenced Annie's change of heart. Perhaps Herman assured her that after that first tough winter, things would get better. He may have reminded her that he had an agreement with the Dunington-Grubbs, and that it would be to their great disadvantage if he were to break it. Howard and Lorrie might even have had a hand in convincing her to think things over. Whatever the reason, Annie decided to give Canada another chance.

PUTTING DOWN ROOTS

Herman had made a good start in his first season. Doubtless, it had been an enormous learning experience as he came to grips with the realities of cultivating *anything* in that part of Canada. As a newcomer, he likely got useful advice from his neighbours, even though the farmers must have wondered at the folly of cultivating plants that weren't food crops. But Herman was an optimist. He had a big sign advertising Sheridan Nurseries placed in a spot beside the railway tracks where people would be sure to see it.

The nursery didn't have a stream for irrigation. Herman fetched tanks of water from Lake Ontario in horse-drawn wagons. He eventually got permission to pipe water in from a neighbour's pond. The best fertilizer available was "barnyard shavings," the polite local term for horse manure.

Howard Dunington-Grubb had told Herman that he would probably have to raise some crops such as strawberries. In those days the Clarkson area was famous for its strawberries. In season, the loading platform at the Clarkson train station would be piled high with crates of berries awaiting shipment to Toronto and Montreal. It's likely that Herman grew strawberries in those early days to bring in some operating money. Herman also raised vegetables to feed his family and help offset wartime shortages.

As the war years dragged on, the papers carried grim news about Canadian losses in bloody battles like Ypres, Vimy Ridge, and Passchendaele. But on January 10, 1917, Herman, Annie, and the boys had cause to celebrate. A baby girl, Betty Christine, was the first member of the Stensson family to be born in Canada. Like a true Canadian pioneer, Betty arrived during a howling snowstorm.

As the "baby of the family" and the only girl, Betty had a childhood somewhat different from her brothers. Howard, the nearest in age, was a whole four years older. But Betty learned to hold her own and be independent. Because money was tight, Betty sometimes had to wear clothes that her mother had made from sugar sacks. That must have resulted in some

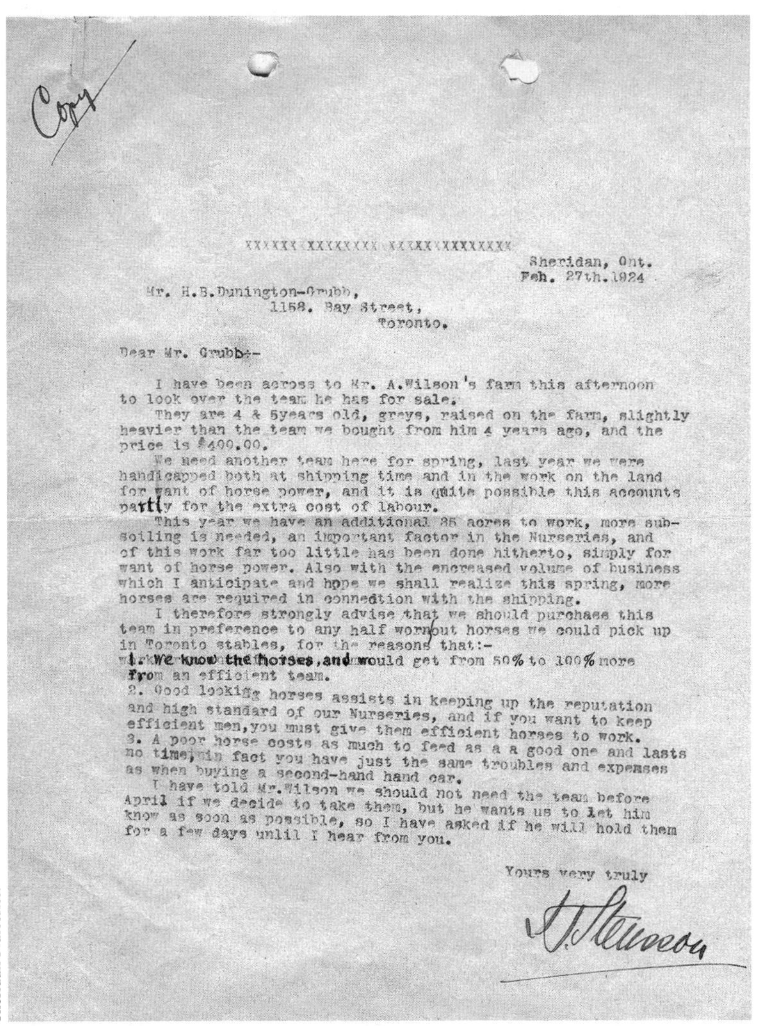

Copy

Sheridan, Ont.
Feb. 27th.1924

Mr. H.B.Dunington-Grubb,
1158. Bay Street,
Toronto.

Dear Mr. Grubb:-

I have been across to Mr. A.Wilson's farm this afternoon to look over the team he has for sale.

They are 4 & 5years old, greys, raised on the farm, slightly heavier than the team we bought from him 4 years ago, and the price is $400.00.

We need another team here for spring, last year we were handicapped both at shipping time and in the work on the land for want of horse power, and it is quite possible this accounts partly for the extra cost of labour.

This year we have an additional 35 acres to work, more sub-soiling is needed, an important factor in the Nurseries, and of this work far too little has been done hitherto, simply for want of horse power. Also with the encreased volume of business which I anticipate and hope we shall realize this spring, more horses are required in connedtion with the shipping.

I therefore strongly advise that we should purchase this team in preference to any half wornout horses we could pick up in Toronto stables, for the reasons that:-

1. We know the horses, and would get from 50% to 100% more from an efficient team.

2. Good lookigg horses assists in keeping up the reputation and high standard of our Nurseries, and if you want to keep efficient men, you must give them efficient horses to work.

3. A poor horse costs as much to feed as a a good one and lasts no time, in fact you have just the same troubles and expenses as when buying a second-hand hand car.

I have told Mr.Wilson we should not need the team before April if we decide to take them, but he wants us to let him know as soon as possible, so I have asked if he will hold them for a few days unlil I hear from you.

Yours very truly

H. Stensson

Herman Stensson's letter, dated February 27, 1924, informing Howard Dunington-Grubb of the need for a new team of horses.

Sheridan Nurseries.

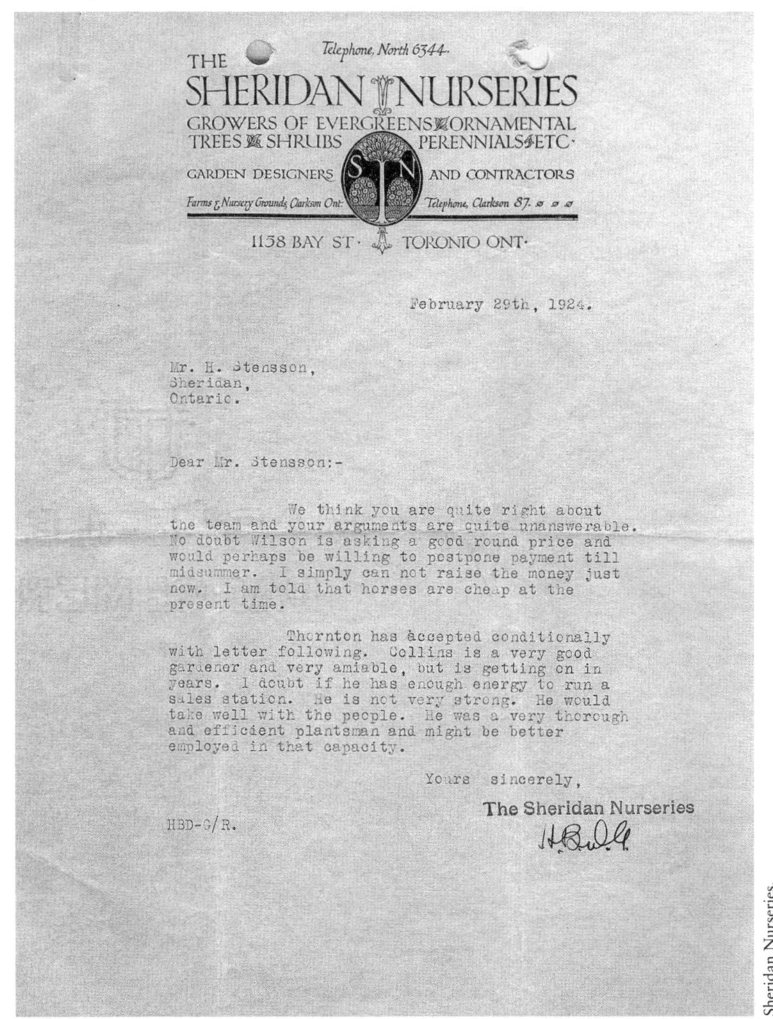

THE SHERIDAN NURSERIES
Telephone, North 6344.
GROWERS OF EVERGREENS & ORNAMENTAL TREES & SHRUBS PERENNIALS & ETC.
GARDEN DESIGNERS AND CONTRACTORS
Farms & Nursery Grounds, Clarkson Ont. Telephone, Clarkson 87.
1158 BAY ST. TORONTO ONT.

February 29th, 1924.

Mr. H. Stensson,
Sheridan,
Ontario.

Dear Mr. Stensson:-

We think you are quite right about the team and your arguments are quite unanswerable. No doubt Wilson is asking a good round price and would perhaps be willing to postpone payment till midsummer. I simply can not raise the money just now. I am told that horses are cheap at the present time.

Thornton has accepted conditionally with letter following. Collins is a very good gardener and very amiable, but is getting on in years. I doubt if he has enough energy to run a sales station. He is not very strong. He would take well with the people. He was a very thorough and efficient plantsman and might be better employed in that capacity.

Yours sincerely,

The Sheridan Nurseries

HBD-G/R.

Howard Dunington-Grubb's response to Herman Stensson, informing him that he can't afford to pay for the horses until July.

Sheridan Nurseries.

Sheridan Nurseries.

The Stensson family outside their original home in Sheridan, circa 1917. *L–R: J.V., Betty, Annie, Chris, Howard, Fred, and Herman.*

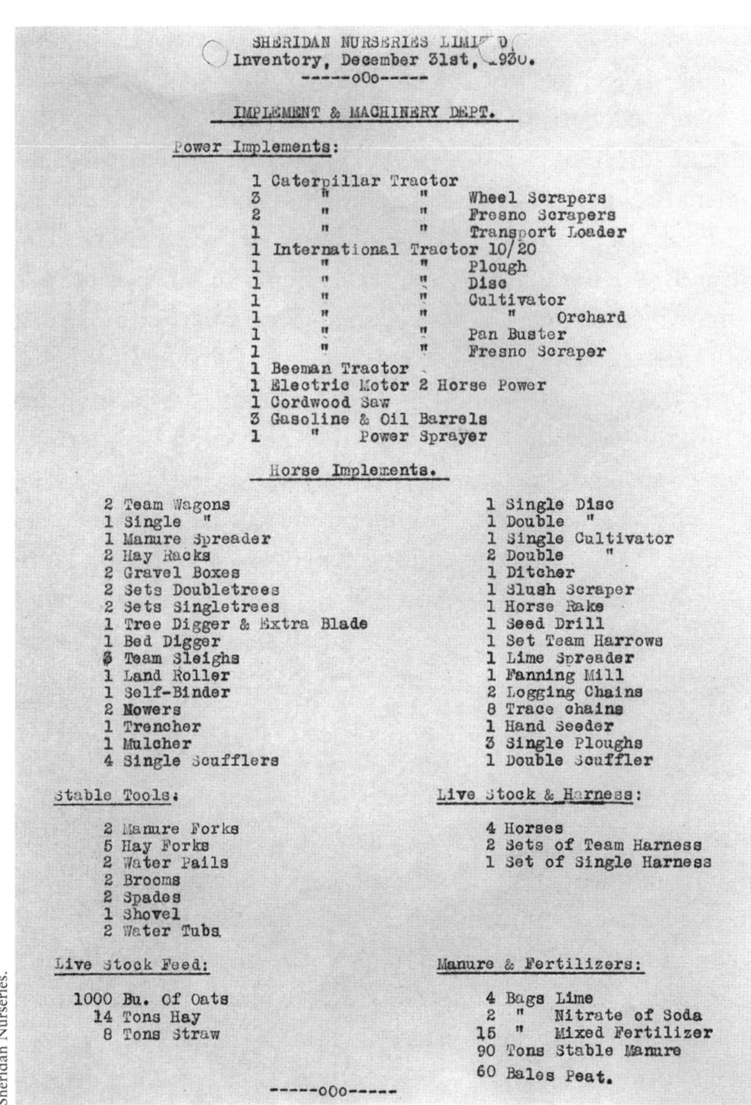

SHERIDAN NURSERIES LIMITED
Inventory, December 31st, 1930.
-----oOo-----

IMPLEMENT & MACHINERY DEPT.

Power Implements:

1 Caterpillar Tractor
3 " " Wheel Scrapers
2 " " Fresno Scrapers
1 " " Transport Loader
1 International Tractor 10/20
1 " " Plough
1 " " Disc
1 " " Cultivator
1 " " " Orchard
1 " " Pan Buster
1 " " Fresno Scraper
1 Beeman Tractor
1 Electric Motor 2 Horse Power
1 Cordwood Saw
3 Gasoline & Oil Barrels
1 " Power Sprayer

Horse Implements.

2 Team Wagons
1 Single "
1 Manure Spreader
2 Hay Racks
2 Gravel Boxes
2 Sets Doubletrees
2 Sets Singletrees
1 Tree Digger & Extra Blade
1 Bed Digger
3 Team Sleighs
1 Land Roller
1 Self-Binder
2 Mowers
1 Trencher
1 Mulcher
4 Single Scufflers

1 Single Disc
1 Double "
1 Single Cultivator
2 Double "
1 Ditcher
1 Slush Scraper
1 Horse Rake
1 Seed Drill
1 Set Team Harrows
1 Lime Spreader
1 Fanning Mill
2 Logging Chains
8 Trace chains
1 Hand Seeder
3 Single Ploughs
1 Double Scuffler

Stable Tools:

2 Manure Forks
5 Hay Forks
2 Water Pails
2 Brooms
2 Spades
1 Shovel
2 Water Tubs

Live Stock & Harness:

4 Horses
2 Sets of Team Harness
1 Set of Single Harness

Live Stock Feed:

1000 Bu. of Oats
14 Tons Hay
8 Tons Straw

Manure & Fertilizers:

4 Bags Lime
2 " Nitrate of Soda
15 " Mixed Fertilizer
90 Tons Stable Manure
60 Bales Peat.

-----oOo-----

Sheridan Nurseries.

The transition from old agricultural technology to new can be seen on this Sheridan Nurseries inventory sheet from December 31, 1930. Mechanical equipment tops the list, but farther down are items which show that horses were still being used.

snickering from other children, because she remembered it for the rest of her life. But Betty's brothers, especially Chris, would stick up for her. Betty lived in what her daughter Laurie later described as "a competitive and yet loving environment."

Being the little girl of the family did allow Betty one noteworthy comfort: bath night came once a week in the Stensson house, as it did in most rural homes. Water had to be heated on the stove, and then poured into a laundry tub. Changing the bathwater for each member of the family would have been considered impracticable, so everyone used the same water. Betty got to go first, before her dusty, muddy brothers.

Sheridan Nurseries and the young Stenssons grew up together. While Herman worked hard to make the business a success, his family became active members of the Sheridan United Church. For people in rural communities especially, membership in a congregation meant more than just attending Sunday services. Most children went to Sunday school. Picnics, musical recitals, and a variety of other "church socials" were important community activities. Herman was eventually elected to the church's Board of Stewards. He also became a member of the local Masonic Lodge. His son Fred followed in his footsteps, being a forty-year Mason. For weddings and other special occasions, the Stenssons provided flowers from the nursery free of charge to decorate the church.

SCHOOL DAYS

The Stensson children first went to the public school called S.S. #5 on the 5th Line, about two-and-a-half miles from their home. Later they changed to the 9th Line School in Oakville (now Maplegrove Public School) because it was a quarter of a mile closer to home. After graduating from elementary school, the Stenssons attended the original Oakville Trafalgar High School, located on Reynolds Street.

No doubt Herman and Annie demanded nothing less than excellence in their children's schoolwork. In many farm families, boys were expected to follow in their father's footsteps, and a little "readin', writin', and 'rithmetic" was deemed all the "schooling" they'd need. But Herman never actually said that he expected his children to work for Sheridan Nurseries when they came of age. He might have *hoped* they would, and he certainly took pains to teach them all he knew about plants. But the choice of careers would be up to them. Regardless of what those choices might be, Herman and Annie knew that a good education was vital. If any of their children *did* decide to stay with the nursery, they'd need the skills necessary to run a company. It's likely the Dunington-Grubbs also encouraged the youngsters to do well academically, especially J.V. With no children of their own, Howard and Lorrie saw in him an heir apparent to Herman.

The encouragement paid off. Chris and Howard both saw their names in the newspapers as top students in their graduating classes. That was in 1930, and for Howard it was his junior high graduation. Three years later, as a graduating senior, Howard was one of only two Peel County students to win a scholarship for the Ontario Agricultural College (OAC) in Guelph; one of the foremost centres of agricultural study in Canada. In an OAC admittance examination held in May of 1933, Howard scored an average of 87.5 in botany, zoology, and physical training.

Howard spent two years at the University of Toronto's School of Architecture, and four at the OAC. He graduated as a top student in Ornamental Horticulture. He eventually went to the Ontario College of Education, then known as Normal School, in Toronto to study to become a teacher.

Fred also studied at OAC, though only for a short time. His most memorable moment at the illustrious Guelph school came when he won a contest dancing the Charleston on the college steps. Herman sent Fred to a nursery in Brookline, Massachusetts, for some hands-on training. Chris was the only one of the brothers who didn't attend an agricultural college. Instead, he went to business school.

Betty was an award-winning athlete in high school. She went to OAC for a year and took a course in home economics. It was called the "Wedding Ring" course because it was intended to prepare young women to be good housewives. The emphasis was on cooking. Betty had a head start on the basics, thanks to Annie.

As the eldest son, J.V. was expected to do the family proud academically, and he did. J.V. attended the School of Architecture at the University of Toronto. There, in 1930, he won a scholarship to study at the School of Landscape Architecture at Harvard University in Boston. Four years later, he graduated second in his class. It was rumoured that he should have been first, but the American university was reluctant to bestow that honour on a "foreigner" from Canada. Nonetheless, J.V. was the recipient of Harvard's 1934 Charles Eliot travelling fellowship award: a six-month tour of Europe to enhance his knowledge of landscape architecture. J.V.'s impressive achievement made the Toronto newspapers. On June 27, a few days before he sailed from Quebec City, J.V. told a reporter from the *Daily*

Sheridan Nurseries.

Young Fred Stensson with his dog Mugo.

Star, "The fellowship will enable me to travel around many countries in Europe during the next six months, visiting and studying the most famous examples of garden and park design."

Like the Dunington-Grubbs, J.V. could write with great authority on gardening and landscaping. The following is an excerpt from his article "Planting for Permanence" which appeared in the October 1938, issue of *Canadian Homes and Gardens*. Howard Dunington-Grubb's influence is evident in J.V.'s journalistic style.

> Gardening is a fascinating game ... in which the rules are so mysteriously hidden that each man feels free to make his own. This confusion on the subject does not always produce happy results, judging by some of the examples which individual fancy, allowed free reign, has produced. Gardens need plenty of imagination — imagination steeped in a knowledge of history of garden design and of a kind that has not reached its limit when you have succeeded in obtaining a more spectacular shrub than the neighbours ... Speculative building and evergreen foundation planting have a certain harmony of fussiness.

In 1936, J.V. would also have a stint as a radio broadcaster. The Canadian Society of Landscape Architects, of which he was a founding member, presented a five-minute program called *The Garden Today* which aired every Saturday at 6:45 p.m. Members of the Society took turns going on air to give helpful tips to the gardening public.

CHORES AND RULES

But graduation, scholarships, trips abroad, publication, and radio talks were all still in the future when the Stensson children were growing up in Sheridan. Just like farm children, when they weren't in school they were expected to help with the work at home.

For Betty, even though she had to do some hoeing and weeding, chores meant helping her mother with the never-ending drudgery that was considered "women's work." There were no automatic appliances. Clothes were washed in a tub with a scrub board, unless the family could afford a "labour-saving" wringer-washer. Electric washing machines came out in 1908, but since the Stensson family had no electricity then, if Annie had a wringer-washer, it would have been a hand-cranked model. Operating one was an exercise in bicep development. Clothes were hung outdoors to dry. In winter they sometimes froze as stiff as boards. Since new clothes were a luxury, worn or torn garments were mended with sewing and darning needles. Younger kids wore their siblings' hand-me-downs.

For the Stensson boys, chores meant working in the nursery. Herman expected them to work harder than any of the hired men. Years later, Howard recalled how he and Chris would put in long boring hours weeding. "Dad usually came to check us at work once a day, sometimes twice. We didn't get much of a chance to dog it."

They would mark time by the passenger trains. When the work was finished, they'd take a dip in Lake Ontario to clean up. Other chores included cutting and waxing plants, and coating seeds with red lead to protect them from birds (a common practice then, but one that would horrify modern-day environmentalists and health specialists).

Even when the boys went away to college, they spent their summers working in the nursery. There was no question that Herman was the head of the household and rules were to be obeyed. On one occasion, Fred displeased his father by staying out too late at night. In the morning, a sleepy Fred was awakened early and given the job of digging up a dozen American elms and planting them along a lane adjacent to the property. It was a tough task that required hours of hard work, during which Fred could contemplate the error of his ways. The trees Fred planted that day were for many years a landmark along that road.

HOWARD'S MEMORIES

When Howard Stensson died on January 16, 2011, at the age of ninety-eight, he was the last of the pioneering family that had immigrated to Canada almost a century before; all of his siblings having pre-deceased him. Fortunately, not all of the colourful memories of that long life were lost. In 2003, he documented some anecdotal material for a talk he gave at a celebration of Sheridan Nurseries' ninetieth anniversary. In his final months, in several hours of conversation recorded at his Oakville home, Howard related many anecdotes about his family, the early days of Sheridan Nurseries, and life in the village of Sheridan. He remembered his father working with nothing but a wheelbarrow, a shovel, and a rake.

Howard was a great raconteur of boyhood misadventures. He told of the first time he and Chris went to a barbershop in

Oakville. Howard was about eight, and Chris eleven. As with many rural households, their mother had probably been the family barber. In town, the Oakville "urchins" (as Howard called them) teased the country-boy Stensson brothers because of their shaggy hair and Chris's freckles.

On one occasion Bill Pilgrim, a long-time Sheridan employee, played a practical joke that Howard never forgot. Howard was seven or eight years old.

> One day he [Pilgrim] was sent to the Sheridan store. He took me with him on the double seat of the wagon. On the way home, Bill hauled out a package, opened it, broke off a piece and started to eat it. He saw me looking at the dark brown chocolate, gave me a small chunk. I bit into it; he guffawed when I spit it out. Chewing tobacco! Cured me of that.

One of Howard's favourite stories was about the time in 1923 that Dundas Street (#5 Highway) was being paved. Howard, ten, and Chris, thirteen, came along on their bicycles and saw workmen spreading the concrete. Chris decided to drive his bike right into the wet cement. Howard didn't record what the workmen had to say about this. He did note, however, that by the time the boys got home, Chris's bike had seized up. Howard remembered the incident mainly because that was also the day the Stensson home, still the ramshackle cottage they'd moved into nine years earlier, first got electricity — long after all of the neighbours had it.

In a speech he delivered many years later, Howard provided an insight into the Stensson household. From the

Sheridan Nurseries.

Howard Stensson in his home garden. Howard was still an active gardener well into his nineties.

perspective of the twenty-first century, it's a look back into a different world:

> Sunday was usually a full day at the Stensson house. The five kids were always sent to Sunday school — walked up town line a half mile in mud (or winter snow). Dad and Mom would arrive later, for the church part. Our parsons among others were Mr. Pawson, Mr. Bellsmith, Mr. Carpenter, Mr. Lovering. I believe Mr. Pawson was a favourite of my mother's, because he seemed to be English. Mr. Carpenter was dapper, and had a good looking daughter, Irene, whose presence kept some of the young men like my brother Fred coming to church on a more frequent basis.
>
> A couple of times a year on Sundays, it would be our family's turn to have the preacher for dinner, at noon, since he had one or two more services to look after that Sunday. I recall we usually had roast lamb and batter pudding (Yorkshire).
>
> Another well-remembered event of our childhood (lifestyle) at home in the nursery was the weekly visit (at least in the summer) of Grubby and Mrs. Grubb on Sunday afternoon for tea. Of course, we did not call him Grubby. It was always Mr. and Mrs. Grubb. They spent an hour or two with my dad as he showed them around the nursery, which was small in those days, on one or two hundred acres. I believe they had spent a couple of hours at the golf club before visiting the nursery.
>
> On one occasion, Mr. Grubb left his clubs on the lawn. Us kids would take a few whacks with them. Fred being most energetic, managed to break one ... Don't believe Mr. Grubb was too angry; he didn't show it anyway. Kids [were] a soft spot for Howard and Lorrie — no kids themselves.

Everyone who knew Howard Dunington-Grubb was aware that the gruff demeanor he sometimes exhibited was an affectation. Howard Stensson recalled with considerable amusement one visit to Sheridan Nurseries when "Grubby" wanted Gus Sparre, a nursery employee, to show him around the "botanical garden." This collection of trees and conifers was Sparre's own hobby, but the Depression was on, and Dunington-Grubb, like everyone else, was looking for places where he could cut costs. Even though he knew all of the plants' names, he asked Sparre what each one was. In telling the story, Howard imitated Mr. Grubb's English accent.

"What's that, Spah?"

Sparre would reply, giving the plant's full Latin name. "*Picea excelsa aurea pendula.*"

Then Mr. Grubb would say, "Looks like hell! Burn it! What's that one, Spah?"

Sparre would respond with another long Latin name.

"Looks like hell! Burn it!"

To the Stensson children, the lanky Englishman and his prim wife — the lord and lady of the manor, as it were — must have seemed out of place. But they were benevolent

Sheridan Nurseries.

Sheridan Nurseries became involved in sports early in the company's history. Pictured here are unidentified members of the Sheridan football team.

absentee landlords who paid their Sunday visits and then returned to the big city. Many years later, Betty's daughter Laurie recalled Howard Dunington-Grubb still making his Sunday visits when she was a child. Even in his advanced years, to young Laurie the six-foot-six Englishman seemed "awesome," and she found his gruff voice intimidating. Recalling how she conducted herself in "Grubby's" presence, she said, "I behaved."

All of the Stensson children took to athletics, especially baseball and soccer. In winter they enjoyed ice-skating on the frozen ponds and on the Credit River. Chris became especially skilled at figure skating. Fred excelled at running, and once won first prize in a competition at the CNE.

Betty became a remarkably good tennis player. Family friend Ken Thornton recalled "one particular wicked stroke she possessed that did me in on every occasion." Another friend, David Langstone, remembered an incident when an acquaintance from Toronto went to Sheridan for an afternoon of tennis. He fancied himself pretty good at the sport, until he played Betty.

Howard Stensson also recalled an old water tank behind the barn where they would swim. They were probably the only family in Sheridan with a "private pool." Howard remembered himself and his brothers "running down the lane in our birthday suits in the storms. Bath water [was] scarce in those days."

In August 1959, Howard and a friend named Alex Murphy swam in all five Great Lakes in one day. They started with Lake Ontario at 5:00 a.m., and finished with Lake Superior at 8:30 p.m., having driven 646 miles. Howard always believed it to be a Canadian first.

AN ALBINO CROW AND A SPINDLESNOOT

Like most males in rural Canadian communities, Herman and his sons liked hunting and fishing. However, Fred was "the main hunter of the family." Howard Stensson wrote that Fred was "skilled at getting cottontails from brush." He knew how to sort out the maze of tracks that animals made in the snow. Sometimes Fred would take Howard along to jump on the piles of brush to flush out the rabbits. Later on, Fred's children Karen and Karl would fill the role of "ferret."

SHERWAY HUNTING GROUNDS

Fred Stensson's youthful enthusiasm for hunting continued into adulthood. He would often take his son Karl and daughter Karen with him. Karen recalls having to follow exactly in his tracks, and rustling piles of brush to flush out any rabbits that might be hiding. One of Fred's favourite hunting grounds was the Sheridan Nurseries property now occupied by the Sherway Gardens Mall. He had special permission to hunt rabbits on nursery property north of the QEW because they did a lot of damage to the plants. Today Karl and Karen can say that when people go to Sherway Gardens Mall, they are shopping at the place where they used to hunt rabbits with their dad.

Usually the men and boys who headed off into the bush in search of game weren't doing it strictly for sport. Rabbits, deer, and game birds provided meat for the table. Annie

wasn't squeamish about skinning Fred's rabbits so she could cook them up in stews or pies.

However, trophy hunting was still widely popular and unquestioned as a legitimate sport. The "politically correct" criticism of it that is heard today was practically non-existent. Mounted deer and moose heads decorated many Canadian walls, especially in rural areas.

It might have been the desire to bag an unusual prize that led fourteen-year-old Fred to stalk a rare albino crow. Fred spotted the bird on nursery property. Crows were generally considered pests, but a white one was trophy material.

According to Fred, he "crawled on his belly" for a quarter of a mile to get close enough to the bird for a clear shot. Family members say that the distance Fred crawled seemed to increase with each re-telling of the story. Whatever the circumstances, Fred shot the albino crow.

The dead bird was given to the Royal Ontario Museum in Toronto. There it was stuffed and put on display. The albino crow remained a part of the ROM's bird exhibit for many years. Fred always looked upon that as a personal claim to fame. The specimen eventually became infested and was destroyed.

Fred was also an avid fisherman. As a boy he headed off to his favourite fishing hole with his trusty pole. Later he would take his family on fishing vacations in Quebec. He also loved deep-sea fishing, and decorated his office wall with mounted trophies: sailfish, dolphin, bonita, barracuda, and lizard fish. In 1947, Fred entered a Miami fishing tournament and landed a fifty-two-and-a-half-pound sailfish, which the Toronto *Daily Star* called a "spindlesnoot." Catching that fish made Fred a record holder for nine years.

THE MUSICIAN

All of the Stensson children, with the possible exception of Fred, could play the piano, but Chris was the one who developed into a real musician. Chris learned to play the violin and the bass violin. He was the founder of the Sheridan Orchestra.

The name "orchestra" may seem somewhat pretentious, but in those days almost every community, no matter how small, had a band of some sort in which residents took pride. The Sheridan Orchestra would have played for church socials, dances, and public events such as Dominion Day (now Canada Day) celebrations. The program for the Clarkson Community Centre's 3rd Annual Variety Show, March 11–14, 1947, lists the members of the Sheridan Orchestra:

Orchestra Leader: Chris Stensson
Musical Director and Pianist: Bob Hodgson
Violins: Howard French, Nels MacMillan, Chris Stensson, Jimmy Wilson
Trumpet: Jim Pinchin
Bass: Jack Telgman

Russ Norfolk was another member of the Sheridan Orchestra. He was an accomplished musician who played trumpet. Russ also worked in the Sheridan Nurseries Oakville office as the office manager from 1949 until his retirement in 1971.

A Clarkson woman named Evelyn Hawkes Crickmore often put together variety shows using local talent as a means of raising funds for church or community projects. The Sheridan Orchestra frequently performed for her, along with

Laurie Pallett.

The Sheridan Orchestra, founded by Chris Stensson. L–R: Russ Norfolk, Chris Stensson, unidentified, Jean Stensson, unidentified.

a vocal group called the Clarkson Singers. The shows would feature everything from tap-dancing children to full-scale musical productions. Betty once had a part in *The Wizard of Oz*.

Band personnel changed over the years. Norm Abbott, who had a degree in music from the University of Toronto, played piano and cello for the Sheridan Orchestra from 1965 until the group disbanded in 1969. Years later, he recalled the orchestra playing at Christmas parties in the Sheridan Nurseries packing shed. He remembered Chris as being very outgoing. He was very good at getting musicians to join the band and would go to great pains to prepare music for the orchestra.

Norm recalled one incident in which Howard Dunington-Grubb had listened to the Sheridan Orchestra. Afterwards there was a lunch. One of the guests, trying to be polite, asked him, "Would you have another sandwich, Mr. Shrubb?" It can be safely assumed that "Grubby" took it with good humour.

In the 1940s and early 1950s, Chris also played for an orchestra leader named Bill Robinson at a place called the Music Box on St. Clair Avenue West in Toronto. Chris would go to Muskoka in the summer and play in bands on ships doing lake tours. He even spent the summer of 1944 playing in a band on the CPR Great Lakes cruise ship *Keewatin*. Chris played for the Oakville Symphony Orchestra, too.

THE HOUSE ON THE HILL

In 1929 the Stenssons finally moved out of the "cottage" and into a newly built, four-thousand-square-foot, two storey, five-bedroom brick house that cost $8,900. This was the Sheridan Nurseries "manager's house." It had *both* indoor plumbing and electricity, and was located on the west side of the Town Line (now Winston Churchill Boulevard), which marked the border between Toronto Township and Trafalgar Township. The location today is about half a mile north of Royal Windsor Drive and half a mile south of the QEW. The site is described as being a hill, but in fact was a slope that was part of the shoreline of prehistoric Lake Iroquois. The house had a beautiful view of Lake Ontario.

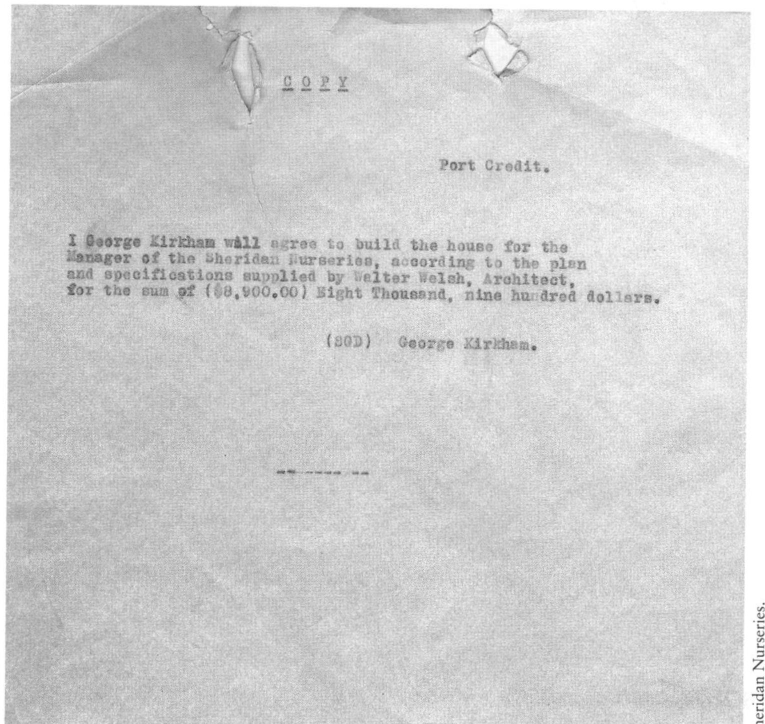

COPY

Port Credit.

I George Kirkham will agree to build the house for the Manager of the Sheridan Nurseries, according to the plan and specifications supplied by Walter Welsh, Architect, for the sum of ($8,900.00) Eight Thousand, nine hundred dollars.

(SGD) George Kirkham.

---- ---

Sheridan Nurseries.

Builder George Kirkham's 1928 contract to build a house for "the manager of the Sheridan Nurseries." Cost: $8,900!

Laurie Pallett.

The Stensson family in front of the "big house" circa 1931. *L–R: J.V., Chris, Annie, Betty, Herman, Howard, and Fred.*

Sheridan Nurseries.

The new brick house built for the manager of Sheridan Nurseries, Herman Stensson and his family. Note Fred or J.V. Stensson in the upper window just as Herman sat in the window of his home in Denmark.

HOW WINSTON CHURCHILL BOULEVARD. GOT ITS NAME

The Stensson family home was located on a country road called Town Line, which separated Toronto Township from Trafalgar Township. It was also known as Sixth Line West. Across the road was the Esperanto House; so named because it was a headquarters for the Esperanto Press, a publication for the artificially created language. According to the Stensson family, Fred's wife, Lois, saw an editorial on the Oakville Journal Record *suggesting that the Town Line be renamed Esperanto Road. That got her English United Empire Loyalist blood up. She felt that a good British name would be more appropriate, and what better than that of the man who had led her homeland through the trials of the Second World War! She wrote a letter to the editor of the* Journal Record *suggesting that the Town Line be renamed Winston Churchill Boulevard. Municipal officials always made the final decisions on such things as the naming of roads and streets, but Lois maintained that the original idea for the road's name was hers, and she was quite proud of it.*

No doubt Herman was proud to move his family into such a fine house, and Annie was happy to at last be in a place they could really call home. In a document called the Barnett Scrapbook in the archives of the Mississauga Public Library, there is a 1929 clipping from the Port Credit *News* with the brief statement: "Clarkson: Mr. Stensson is building a stone wall and a rockery in front of his house." Herman had certainly lost no time in improving the look of the new abode. He also constructed two clay tennis courts and a large sports field for the kids. This was the house where the young Stenssons grew to adulthood. It would be home to various members of the Stensson family until the property was sold in the early 1980s.

The new house and its vicinity were also the scene of the further adventures of the Stensson kids. Karl recalls a story he heard from his father, Fred.

> There was a large apple orchard in the field south of the house. It was a dry, parched summer, and the boys were working in the orchard when they came across a hornets' nest in one of the trees. Dad and Chris decided that they would burn the nest. They got a stick with a rag on the end soaked in kerosene. They lit it and approached the nest to torch it. The hornets came flying out after them. Neither one would admit who dropped the torch, but the grass caught on fire and they burned most of the orchard!

In Howard's recollection of the same incident, it was a cherry orchard, and all four Stensson brothers were involved. "George Washington was a piker compared to us," Howard said. "He only chopped down one cherry tree. We burnt down the whole orchard."

Another dramatic incident involving the young Stenssons became a family legend of the "kids, don't try this at home" variety. The hill on which the house stood had enough of an incline to make a good toboggan run in the winter. However, the steepest part of the slope — and therefore the best part

for tobogganing — had a big rock right in the middle of it. The boulder was about three feet in diameter. As tobogganing experts, Fred and Howard knew that big rocks and fast toboggans aren't a good combination, so they decided to get rid of the obstacle. Again, Karl tells the story of his father's and uncle's exploit.

> My grandfather used dynamite to clear stumps and large rocks in the nursery fields, and he was experienced with it. Fred and Howard decided that they had seen him use it enough times that they knew how to "blow" the rock. Without asking their father, they secured some dynamite from the shed and placed a couple of sticks under the rock. Of course, they did not know the details of how TNT worked (directionally), and instead of blowing it into small pieces, they cracked it in half with a good one-foot-diameter piece flying over the house and landing in the yard in front of my grandmother's kitchen window.

Annie was inside the house at the time of the blast. Miraculously, it didn't shatter any windows, but it certainly must have startled her. But even if the teacups were rattled, Annie wasn't. With calm British reserve, she remarked, "I say, what are those boys up to now?" Or so the accepted version of the story goes.

Fortunately, nobody was hurt. The boys weren't punished. The large chunk of rock that had arced over the house like a cannonball did no damage. But it was left in the spot where it landed as a reminder to all of the boys of what could have happened.

HERMAN GROWS A COMPANY

As the Stensson children grew to maturity, so did Sheridan Nurseries under Herman's stewardship. Things certainly weren't easy at the beginning. All of the work was accomplished by human labour and horse power. When Herman took the first load of trees to sell in Toronto's St. Lawrence Market, it was an all-day trip by horse and wagon. He returned to Sheridan with an empty wagon and $50.

Although Howard Dunington-Grubb was the owner of Sheridan Nurseries, he was paying himself only half the amount he was paying Herman. Even so, he was often unable to pay Herman his full wages. Not until 1923 did Herman finally receive all of his back pay — with interest. The meticulous bookkeeping of the Dunington-Grubbs is evident in the ledger that shows $62.43 deducted from Herman's back pay with the note "Less monies received from sale of vegetables."

Herman brought in new ornamental plants. He tested many, discarding those that didn't meet his standards or weren't commercially viable. Howard Stensson later said that his father selected varieties that were the easiest to grow.

By 1923 it had become clear to Herman that few of his hired workers knew much about ornamental plants. They were mostly farm hands, not nurserymen. There were, to be sure, some good, reliable people working for Herman, such as Bill Pilgrim and Charlie Barnard. But Herman felt he needed people with his own kind of expertise.

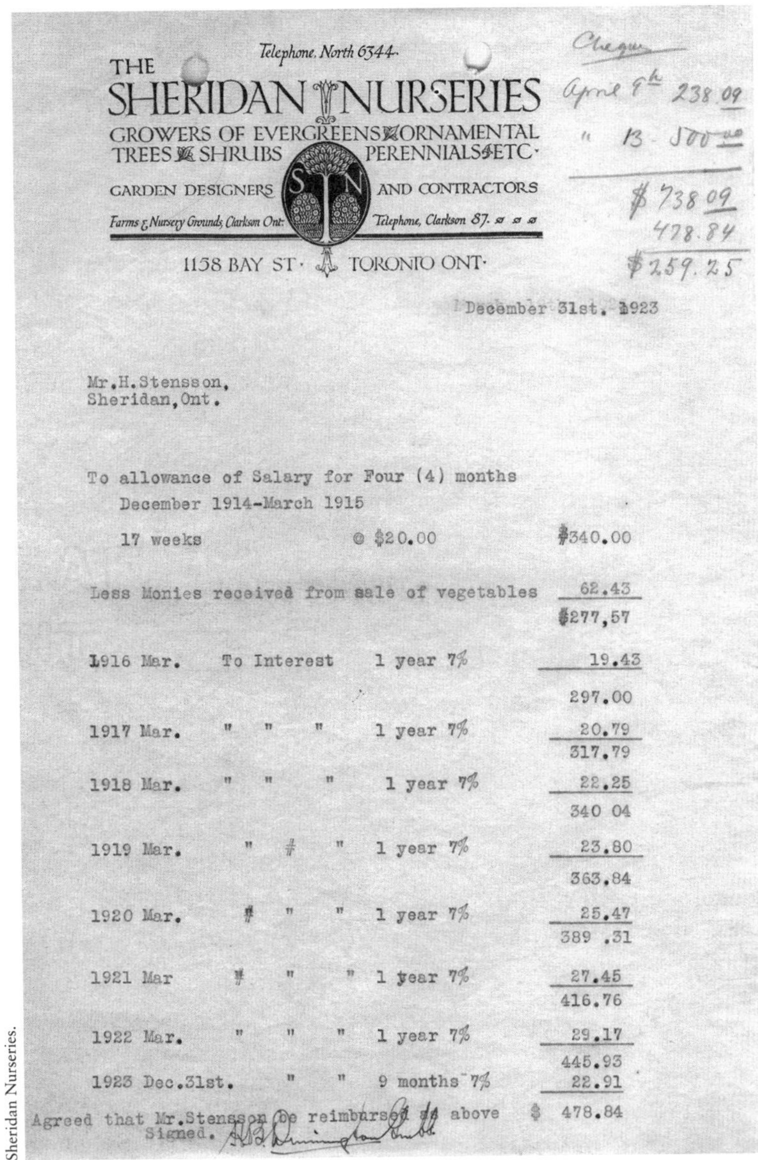

THE SHERIDAN NURSERIES — Telephone. North 6344.
GROWERS OF EVERGREENS & ORNAMENTAL TREES & SHRUBS PERENNIALS & ETC.
GARDEN DESIGNERS AND CONTRACTORS
Farms & Nursery Grounds, Clarkson Ont. — Telephone, Clarkson 87.
1158 BAY ST. TORONTO ONT.

Cheque
April 9th 238.09
" 13 500.00
$738.09
478.84
$259.25

December 31st, 1923

Mr.H.Stensson,
Sheridan,Ont.

To allowance of Salary for Four (4) months
December 1914-March 1915

17 weeks		@ $20.00	$340.00
Less Monies received from sale of vegetables			62.43
			$277,57
1916 Mar.	To Interest	1 year 7%	19.43
			297.00
1917 Mar.	" " "	1 year 7%	20.79
			317.79
1918 Mar.	" " "	1 year 7%	22.25
			340 04
1919 Mar.	" " "	1 year 7%	23.80
			363.84
1920 Mar.	" " "	1 year 7%	25.47
			389 .31
1921 Mar	" " "	1 year 7%	27.45
			416.76
1922 Mar.	" " "	1 year 7%	29.17
			445.93
1923 Dec.31st.	" "	9 months 7%	22.91

Agreed that Mr.Stensson be reimbursed as above $ 478.84
Signed. H.B. Dunington-Grubb

Sheridan Nurseries.

Howard Dunington-Grubb's signed accounting sheet for back pay owed to Herman Stensson.

After conferring with the Dunington-Grubbs, Herman embarked on a trip to Denmark to recruit workers with the kind of skills he felt Sheridan Nurseries needed. His journey can be followed thanks to a precisely itemized expense account he kept, that is now in the Sheridan Nurseries archives under *Mr. H. Stensson: Travelling Expenses to England, Denmark and Germany 1923–1924.*

After spending fifty cents on a passport photo, and two dollars for a Canadian passport, Herman took the train from Clarkson to Toronto (45 cents), and then boarded another train for St. John, New Brunswick, via Montreal ($18.61). His sea passage to Copenhagen, with a change of ships at London, cost $145. Herman recorded every expense, from taxi and bus fares in London (for which he noted that one shilling equalled 22 cents), to the money he spent on tea and tips in Germany. The total sum on Herman's recorded expense account is $514.38.

Herman's journey to Europe must have been nostalgic. Although he made no journalistic record of it, he would have seen his mother and other family members, and visited his father's grave. No doubt he returned to some of his former workplaces and saw old friends. The trip was a milestone in the development of Sheridan Nurseries, because Herman's search for qualified Danish nurserymen was a success. Kristen Buch, who came to Canada in 1924, was the first in a long line of Danes who would work for Sheridan Nurseries. Some, like Buch, would stay with the company for the rest of their working lives. The Danes would turn out to be just one of several ethnic groups to find opportunity with Sheridan Nurseries, and give the company its cosmopolitan makeup.

One of the few photos of Lorrie Dunington-Grubb, co-founder of Sheridan Nurseries.

Howard Dunington-Grubb oil painting by Bryant Fryer now hanging in the Sheridan Nurseries' head office boardroom.

Sheridan Nurseries.

New gardens at Government House, Toronto. Watercolour by A.S. Carter, 1915.

Sheridan Nurseries.

Watercolour of Gage Park, Hamilton, by S.H. Maw, 1927. Photo by Fisher Rare Book Library, University of Toronto.

Sheridan Nurseries.

Watercolour of estate of Dr. Herbert Bruce, Bayview Avenue, Toronto, by W.E Welch, 1920.

Sheridan Nurseries.

Watercolour of Graydon Hall, Toronto, by J.V. Stensson.

Sheridan Nurseries.

Watercolour of proposed entrance for the Highway Gardens and sales station on Southdown Road (formerly Lakeshore Road), Clarkson, Ontario.

Oakes Garden Theatre, Niagara Falls, Ontario.

Rainbow Gardens, Niagara Falls, Ontario.

Parterre, Rainbow Gardens, Niagara Falls, Ontario.

Sunken Garden, McMaster University, Hamilton, Ontario. Garden now removed.

University Avenue, Toronto, fountains at Queen Street intersection.

Formal hedges on University Avenue, Toronto.

Colourful planters on University Avenue, Toronto.

One of many Sheridan Nurseries inter-office summer picnics, L–R: Joerg Leiss, Lois Stensson, Alice Pokluda, Ray Grindlay (landscape designer), and Lynda Ferguson.

Former Montreal sales station on Côte-de-Liesse with long-time manager John Turnbull.

Former garden centre opened in March 1986, in Dollard-des-Ormeaux, Quebec, with manager Bob Reiter and Howard Stensson. Note large Chris Yaneff logo on the facade.

Montreal Flower Show 1971, with large original painting that had also been used earlier that year in a garden show at the Royal Ontario Museum in Toronto.

Former Sheridan Nurseries Garden Centre in Beaconsfield, on the west island of Montreal.

An early "colour" photograph of the Stensson family. Note the humorous hand-colouring. Back row (L–R): Betty, Annie, Herman. Front row (L–R): Fred, Chris, Howard, Bill (J.V.).

Sheridan Nurseries.

A Murray Stewart oil painting of the Conover barn in Oakville. This barn was dismantled and donated by Sheridan Nurseries to the Heritage Park, Britannia Farm, Mississauga, Ontario.

Until the operation was computerized in the 1970s, hundreds of thousands of nursery labels had to be written by hand. Note the different colours to denote different destinations.

Bed of Purpleleaf Sand Cherry growing in the Oakville farms.

Mrs. Koharu Sano and Mrs. Hatsue Yanoshita on a planting machine, Oakville, Ontario, 1950.

Sunburst honey-locust, growing on Sheridan's former Orr farm in Oakville, Ontario.

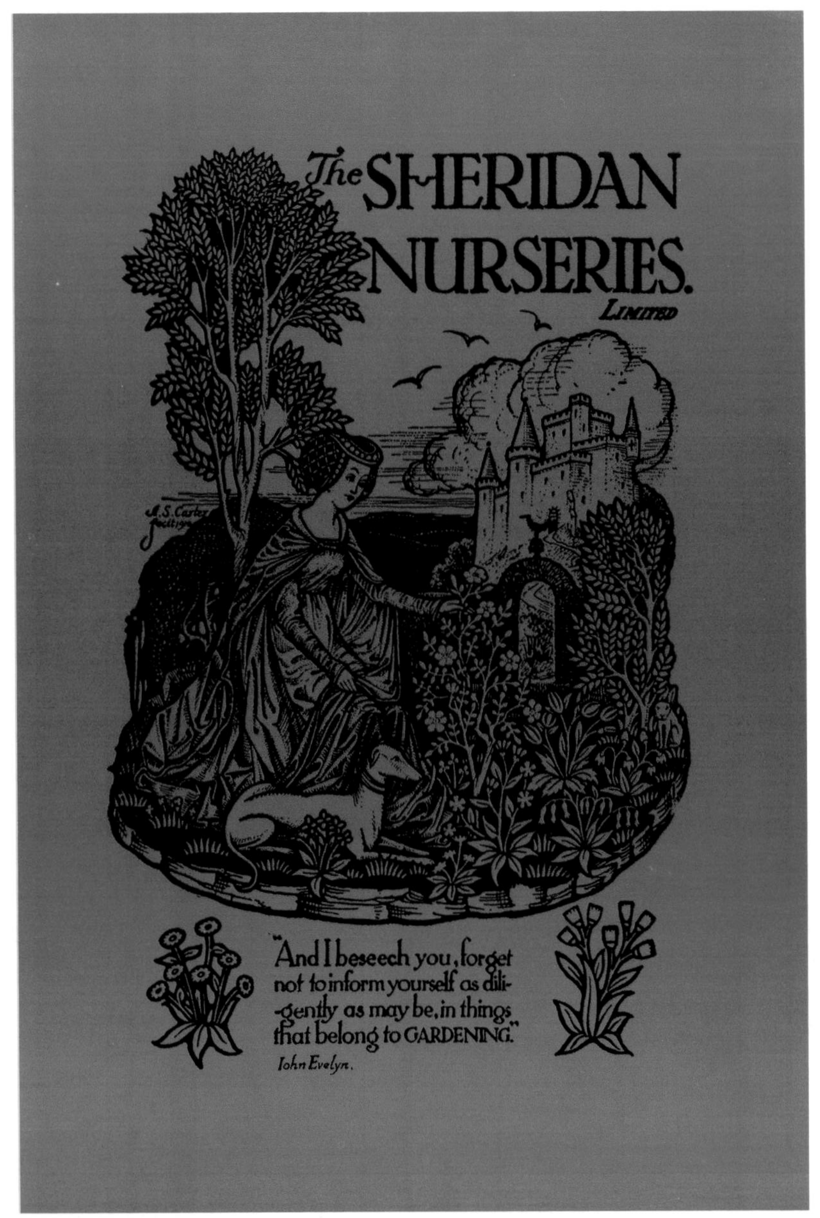

The SHERIDAN
NURSERIES.
LIMITED
A.S. Carter
"And I beseech you, forget not to inform yourself as diligently as may be, in things that belong to GARDENING."
John Evelyn.

Sheridan Nurseries catalogue for 1927 features an A.S. Carter drawing also used for 1918–19 and 1919–20.

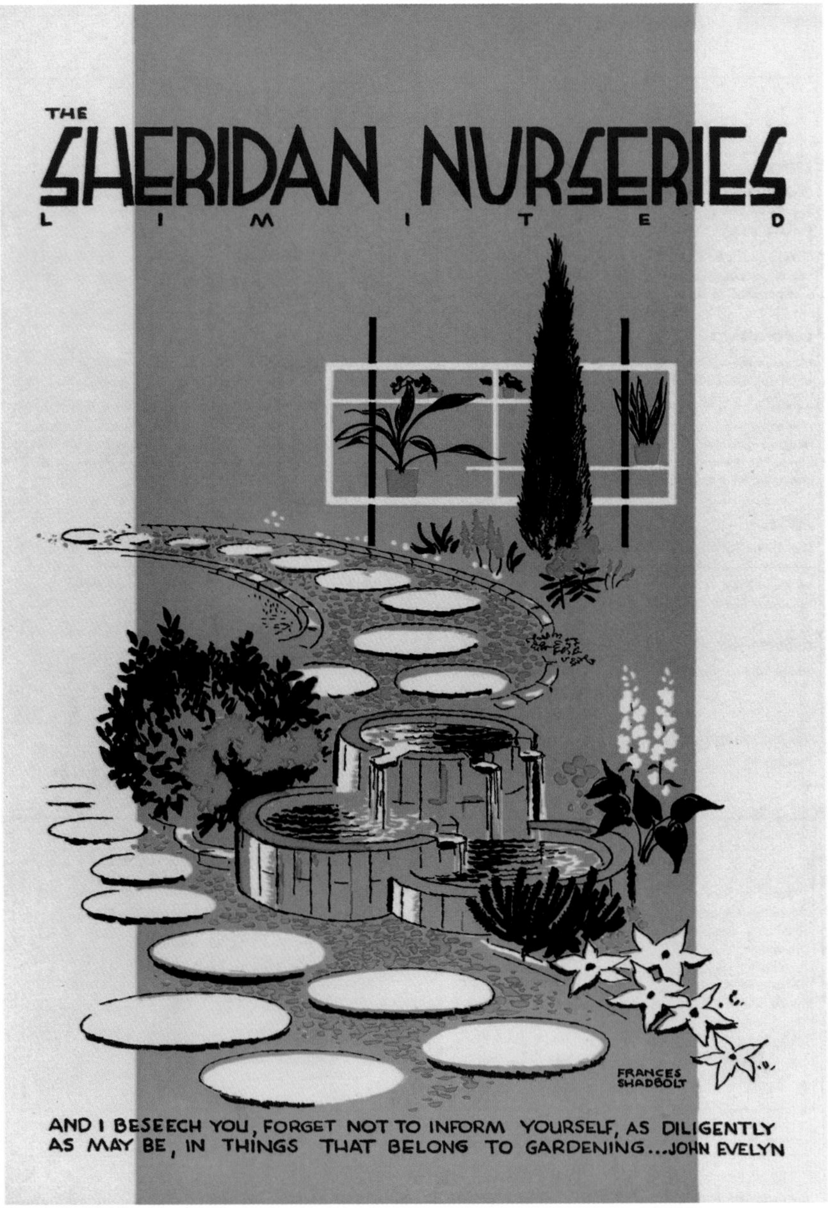
THE
SHERIDAN NURSERIES
LIMITED
FRANCES SHADBOLT
AND I BESEECH YOU, FORGET NOT TO INFORM YOURSELF, AS DILIGENTLY AS MAY BE, IN THINGS THAT BELONG TO GARDENING...JOHN EVELYN

Sheridan Nurseries catalogue for 1956.

Sunsation Rose, a Sheridan Nurseries exclusive.

75th Anniversary

CATALOGUE

1913 • 1988

$2

Sheridan Nurseries seventy-fifth anniversary catalogue for 1988 featuring Sheridan's own Sunsation Rose, still being grown today.

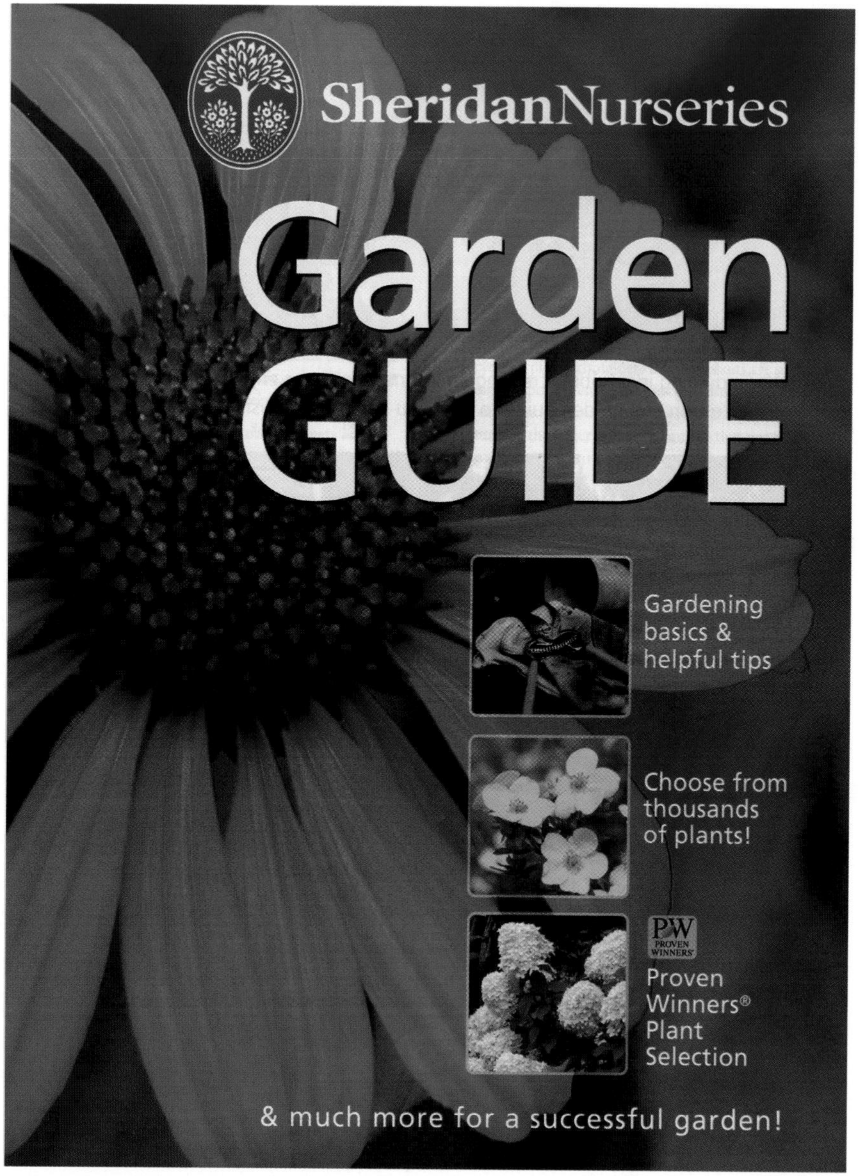

Sheridan Nurseries

Garden
GUIDE

Gardening basics & helpful tips

Choose from thousands of plants!

PW PROVEN WINNERS

Proven Winners® Plant Selection

& much more for a successful garden!

Sheridan Nurseries Garden Guide for 2011.

Sheridan Nurseries sales station on Southdown Road in Mississauga, Ontario, opened in 1964, featured a large collection of hedges and display gardens. The front of this Mississauga garden centre still features extensive display gardens.

Mr. H. STENSSON Travelling Expenses to

England, Denmark and Germany.

1923 – 1924.

Pass Photo 50¢, Passport $2.00	$2.50
Declaration	3.00
Ticket St. John-Copenhagen	145.00
Clarkson -Toronto 45¢; Toronto-St. John18.16;	18.61
Berth to Montreal, [illegible]; St. John, 4.80;	8.20
Charges on Danish draft and travelling cheques	9.35
Street cars 25¢; luggage 20¢; sleeper porter35¢	.80
Expenses in Montreal, meals 2.35 luggage,40¢	2.75
Breakfast on train	1.25
Expenses on boat, cabin steward	2.50
dining room 2.50; bath 1.50	4.00
"Montclare" luggage 25¢, stamps 10¢	.35

London expenses: 1 shilling - 22¢	sh. d.	
Room and board	28 - 9)	
Fares, taxis and bus	4 - 0)	9.82
Sleeper to Copenhagen	12 - 0)	

Expenses on Danish Steamer:$1.00 - Kr 5.80		
Expenses on steamer 7.50		
" to Copenhagen 1.00	Kr.[illegible])	
Rooms Copenhagen	10.00)	
Fare to Maribo	15.80)	
Expenses on Ferry (lunch)	1.75)	
Stamps 2.00; Nastned fares 7.10	9.10)	
Lunch, Rasmussen & self, Nastned	6.00)	53.53
Fares Nastned-Copenhagen	9.75)	
Hotel Expenses Copenhagen	[illegible].00)	
Copenhagen -Odense fares(guldager)	17.05)	
Odense-Kolding	7.20)	
Kolding hotel, 2 days	2[illegible].00)	
Kolding-Sonderborg fares	10.00)	
Sonderborg hotel	8.50)	
Sonderburg fares	21.80)	
Stamps [illegible], extra express tckt. (4.85	5.25)	

Expenses in Germany $1.00 -4.20 gold marks.		
Hotel Altona	15.00)	
Tea 2 marks; tips 4 marks	6.00)	
Fares Altona - London	98.50)	
tips to Schraders chauffeur	3.00)	
telegrams and phones	4.50)	
supper	3.00)	38.57
Hotel Weener (Hesse)	22.00)	
Expenses Weener -Rotterdam	10.00)	
carry forward		$280.23

-2-

H. Stensson's Expenses to England Denmark & Germany.

Brought forward		280.23
1 shilling - 22¢	sh. d.	
Hook of Holland, boat, breakfast	2 - 3)	
London Expenses	28 -10)	
Hitchin "	37 - 6)	
London, Hotel National	17 - 0)	38.00
" cabs and train fares	41 - 8)	
Cable to Toronto	10 - 6)	
London - St. John, £35-4-9 less £35. from office	4 - 9)	
Expenses on train	2 - 0)	
" " boat	29 - 0)	
St John to Toronto		19.20
Sleepers		8.20
Toronto - Oakville		.75
Meals on train from St. John		6.50
		$352.88
(omitted) German vise on passport		7.50
		$360.38
plus £35.00 1sh 22cts		*154.00*
700 + 22 – 154.00		*$514.38*

Sheridan Nurseries.

Expense account ledger for Herman Stensson's trip to England and the Continent in 1923–24. Herman noted everything from his passport to tea and tips.

END OF AN ERA

Even though Howard and Lorrie Dunington-Grubb were the official founders and owners of the company, and deserve full credit for their vision and their pioneering work in Canada as landscape architects, for twenty-four years Herman Stensson was the dynamo who built Sheridan Nurseries up from that small patch of sandy loam. He oversaw its expansion with the addition of more property, and its modernization with the introduction of tractors in the early 1930s. Herman orchestrated the various work crews, so that planting, growing, harvesting, and marketing plants and trees became an efficient operation. Meanwhile, he and Annie raised a family with a strong sense of ethics and moral values. He made his dream of a good life in Canada for his wife and children become a reality, along with the Dunington-Grubbs' dream of their own ornamental plant nursery.

In a sense, though, Herman didn't get to see his dream come to full fruition; he didn't live long enough to see his grandchildren. None of the Stensson children had yet married, when on March 21, 1938, Herman died of cancer just a few weeks before his sixty-first birthday. His passing was reported in a Toronto *Daily Star* obituary that noted his importance as a horticulturist.

THE NEXT GENERATION

Although Herman didn't live to see any of his children married, he did become well acquainted with a future daughter-in-law. Lois Perry was related to the Lawrence family of Sheridan. Lois's mother had a heart problem, and from the age of five Lois would be sent to visit her cousins in Sheridan so her mother could rest. Lois was the same age as Betty Stensson, so the Lawrences would invite Betty over to play with her. Lois and Betty became life-long friends. The girls would never have thought that one day they'd be sisters-in-law.

Fred Stensson first met Lois through Betty. Then in 1935, after Lois had finished business school, Herman hired her as his secretary. She was eighteen years old, and the nursery's first female office employee. Herman was surprised at how quickly she learned to identify plants by their Latin names. A Latin course Lois had taken in high school paid off. Among her various office tasks was correcting the English in Herman's business correspondence.

Lois and Fred would have seen each other practically every day. Herman was evidently fond of Lois. Because the packing shed in which the office was located was unheated, she was allowed to wear slacks to work instead of a dress or a skirt; something practically unheard of at the time.

Three years later, when Herman lay dying of cancer, he had Lois brought to his room. He told her that he had instructed the boys to raise her pay by a dollar a week. If they didn't do it, he said, she was to remind them. Herman died the next day. Lois got the raise without having to ask for it. In fact, it was she who was asked for something far more significant; her hand in marriage. Fred became the first of the young Stenssons to wed when he married Lois in 1939. Betty was maid of honour.

For their honeymoon, Fred and Lois went to Florida — on a bus! Trips with Fred often turned into adventures. The newlyweds ran out of money in Florida, and had to hitchhike

Sheridan Nurseries.

Aerial view of the Stensson house at Sheridan. The empty fields seen here are now occupied by subdivisions. The road at the right is now Winston Churchill Boulevard.

Sheridan Nurseries.

The Stensson family circa *1935.*

home. More memorable, perhaps, than the run-of-the-mill honeymoon in Niagara Falls.

Betty married Ronald Stewart on July 12, 1941. Ron had been Howard's roommate at OAC. He met Betty when Howard took him home on a visit. Ron might have met Herman. Ron had a beautiful singing voice, and when he became a resident of Sheridan, he joined the United Church choir. He soon became the choir's lead tenor, and would often sing solo. Ron won prizes for singing at music festivals. The distinguished Canadian composer Wilfred Pelletier encouraged him to study for an operatic career.

Unfortunately, Ron's desire for a career in music, combined with other issues, placed a strain on the marriage. Betty and Ron were divorced in 1955. Thirty-one years later, Betty married Ron's brother Ross on June 6, 1986. Marrying one's former brother-in-law was a bit controversial, but Betty wasn't always one to follow the narrow path of convention. Both Ron and Ross predeceased her.

On October 6, 1947, Chris married Jeanne Munro Scott of New Toronto. The wedding made the social pages. Betty was a bridesmaid, and her daughter Laurie was the flower girl.

Music had brought Jean and Chris together. She was an accomplished pianist, and she and Chris were both active in musical circles. She often accompanied Ron Stewart on the piano when he sang. Jean would spend many summers as a music teacher at the Banff School of Fine Arts. Jean and Chris did not have any children. They were, however, popular with their nieces and nephews, who recall them as being full of a love for life.

Fortunate circumstance also led Howard Stensson to romance and marriage. After graduation, he didn't immediately go to work for Sheridan Nurseries. Instead, he went into business for himself, surveying land for tobacco farmers in southwestern Ontario. Howard would travel around the region, renting rooms in the communities in which he was working.

In the town of Norwich in Oxford County, Howard stayed in a boarding house run by the Nethercott family. The Nethercotts had a daughter, Maurine, who worked as a secretary for Stelco Steel in Hamilton. She would go home on the weekends. During one visit she met Howard. As their son Bill puts it, "The rest is history." Howard and Maurine were married in 1946. Besides Bill, they had two daughters, Gay and Janice.

J.V., though the oldest of the Stensson siblings, was the last to take a spouse. In 1958 he married Janina Korkuc, a

Sheridan Nurseries.

L–R: J.V., Howard, Lois, Chris, unknown, on a farm vehicle nicknamed Beelzebub.

landscape architect from Poland whom he had met at a conference in Switzerland. J.V. and Janina were childless. But J.V. loved kids, and his nieces and nephews fondly remember his quiet ways and his dry sense of humour.

MR. SHERIDAN

At the time of Herman's death, J.V. was working as a landscape architect, having gone into partnership with the Dunington-Grubbs in 1935. When he had to devote his energy to running the nursery, they officially terminated the partnership. However, Howard and Lorrie kept the name "Dunington-Grubb & Stensson" for the landscape-design business.

J.V. succeeded Herman as manager of Sheridan Nurseries, officially becoming managing director in March of 1939. For the next thirty-four years, to his employees and colleagues in the industry, J.V. Stensson *was* Sheridan Nurseries. The staff at the sales stations said that customers who were unaware of the company's actual ownership and management hierarchy would often ask, "Who is Mr. Sheridan?" They didn't reply, "Howard Dunington-Grubb." They said, "J.V. (or Bill) Stensson."

J.V. was generally a quiet, reserved person; shy, in fact. People who knew him well said he didn't make close friends quickly, but that he also never lost a friend. Other people who knew J.V., but not well, thought he didn't seem to get much fun out of life, because he worked day and night, rarely taking a vacation. Most agreed that J.V.'s work was his life, and his life was his work.

According to his friend Keith Laver, J.V.'s joy in life came from carrying on his father's work. "His love of plants and design and creation of beauty became his hobby and recreation. The work that tired him was public speaking and directing policies of his large company."

Under J.V.'s direction, Sheridan Nurseries expanded to over a thousand acres. At one time there were forty-seven houses on nursery property, serving as homes for employees. Most of the houses were on the smaller farms Sheridan Nurseries

Olive Mahon.

This picture of J.V. Stensson was taken by Olive Mahon, one of the Farmerettes from the Ontario Farm Service, who worked for Sheridan Nurseries during the Second World War. She wrote on the back, "'The Big Boss' but nice."

bought over the years, while a few were designed and built specifically for the staff. J.V. designed the interior details for the new houses, and he renovated older houses. He hired a carpenter, a paper hanger, and a painter to maintain them. J.V. also designed the detailed plans for garden centres and the new head office building at Sherway. Some of this was done in collaboration with Howard Dunington-Grubb as well as various staff members. J.V. was always willing to listen to suggestions from the garden centre managers, and kept an open mind for new ideas.

Credit: Sheridan Nurseries.

The Stewart farmhouse; example of the housing Sheridan Nurseries provided for employees.

In the autumn of 1971, J.V. saw an item in the *Toronto Star* in which Erik Jorgensen, a professor of forestry at the University of Toronto, was critical of tree-planting policies in the city. J.V. didn't agree with everything he read in the article. The following is from his response that appeared in the *Star* on October 21.

> Professor Jorgensen is critical of the use of European and Asiatic species of trees on Toronto Streets. They have been used for the simple reason that experience and practice over many years has proved them more successful in putting up with uncongenial city environment than their native counterparts. That is why we find on Toronto streets and parks, to name three examples, European linden instead of the native basswood, Norway maple instead of sugar, and Austrian pine instead of red pine. Even the much maligned tree of heaven is an exotic from China ... Examine the lindens on Queen St. just east of Spadina. These 28 trees, the product of a Canadian nursery, were planted seven years ago and, in spite of sidewalks and salt, are doing quite well. The local merchants take great pride in them.

A few months after writing this letter, J.V. suddenly took ill. He died at the age of sixty-four in Queensway Hospital on March 8, 1972. In the words of Robert J. Hilton, director of the University of Guelph Arboretum, "News of the recent death of J. Vilhelm Stensson has brought a rarely equalled sense of profound shock to all those Ontario citizens who, even in a humble way, are connected with horticulture."

THE SALESMAN

Fred Stensson became Sheridan Nurseries' first salesman in 1932. It was he who built up the company's wholesale business. He started by selling plants at Toronto's St. Lawrence Market. Fred was the perfect man for the job. The cowboy philosopher Will Rogers once said, "I never met a man I didn't like." One could invert that and say that everybody who met Fred liked him. Fred was an outgoing person who enjoyed mixing with people and making new acquaintances. He disliked sitting in an office, but loved going on the road with the back of his car packed with sample plants.

Previously, Sheridan's orders had all come in by mail or phone. Now the company had Fred driving all over Ontario, as well as regions of the United States that were within easy reach of his home base. Fred never flew. If he had to go to some distant city such as Chicago for a convention, he'd take the train.

Fred would visit stores, cemeteries, and any institution that might be a potential customer. He knew how to talk to people. Having grown up in the nursery, he knew his product well. Fred was as professional as he was congenial; always dressed in a long-sleeved white shirt with cufflinks, a tie, suit jacket, dress pants, and fedora. You'd never catch Fred wearing blue jeans and sneakers, not even when he went on his famous fishing trips. The concession that he made for those occasions was that he removed the tie and jacket! Like many a travelling salesman who enjoyed his work and the places he visited, Fred often took his family along.

A STENSSON FISHING BALLAD

Fred Stensson's love of fishing was legendary within the family, the company, and the nursery industry. In his years of deep-sea fishing, among his many catches Fred landed nine sailfish, one of them a record-breaker. The story of one exploit was humorously memorialized in verse by Fred's colleague and fishing pal, Ted Johnson of Johnson's Nurseries in Kingston, Ontario.

The Nurserymen and The Fish

It was midway on the ocean,
Not a pine tree was in sight,
When Fred and Ted went fishing,
For a sailfish that would bite.

They started through the Inlet,
Where the seas got really rough,
The Southern Comfort *pitched and rolled,*
And they got feeling tough.

So Freddie looked at Teddy,
And said, "Now don't you think,
We would feel a little better,
If we had a little drink?"

So they up and "spliced the mainbrace,"
Then they had a couple more,
Till they didn't mind the pitching,
And the rolling or the roar.

Then came action on the sternline,
And the Captain called "Ahoy!"
The Mate said, "Hold her steady!"
What a sailfish Freddie boy!

The big fish broke the surface,
What a battle, such a sight,
To see that leaping beauty,
And Freddie in a fight.

The fishing soon was over,
And they headed for the shore,
They would have had another,
But there wasn't anymore.

The rest is now on record,
And I've told you nearly all,
If you want to see the sailfish,
Look on K.F. Stensson's wall.

Fred would invite customers to visit Sheridan, and have them come to his home for supper and an overnight stay. He'd take them right out to the fields to select plants. Karen and Karl recall a steady stream of visitors that included heads of municipal parks departments and even the occasional celebrity. Fred once brought home the Toronto Maple Leafs hockey star Charlie "the Big Bomber" Conacher.

Fred was a great supporter of social clubs and organizations. He would go to local bazaars and buy all of the ladies' homemade jams. For forty years he was a member of the Oakville Lions Club, and was their champion ticket seller. The tickets were sold to support charitable causes. It would be difficult to find a Sheridan Nurseries employee, business associate, or customer from Fred's time, to whom he didn't sell a ticket. He even sold one to Toronto Maple Leafs owner Harold Ballard. Over the years, Fred sold an estimated 250,000 Lions Club tickets. That he accomplished this as a volunteer speaks highly of Fred's social commitment.

Sometimes Fred's connections could lead to extraordinary situations. Lois got to participate in the inaugural flight of the Air Canada Boeing 747 because Fred knew the pilot. Her invitation came on such short notice that she didn't have a chance to dress properly for the occasion. She just pulled a trench coat over her old housedress. Lois found herself sipping champagne with dignitaries, still in the trench coat, while the big plane circled over Niagara Falls.

Fred was once asked to be a judge for the inmates' gardens at the Kingston Penitentiary. There, at Canada's most notorious prison, was a flea market where the inmates sold their own arts and crafts. Fred bought a pair of hand-knitted socks from Evelyn Dick, who had been convicted of killing and dismembering her husband in Hamilton's gruesome Torso Murder case. Every time Lois washed those socks, she got the shivers.

Fred liked the racetrack, too. Because of his love of horse racing, May 26, 1951, became a special date in Stensson family history. Fred was all set to attend the King's Plate at Woodbine Racetrack in Toronto. He intended to bet on a horse called Major Factor. Fred couldn't go to the track that day, because Lois went into labour. While Fred was at the hospital awaiting the birth of his son Karl, jockey Alf Bavington rode Major Factor to victory. Because Karl's arrival was a "major factor," the name became a family catchphrase.

Although Fred was in his element as a salesman, he nonetheless made other noteworthy contributions to Sheridan Nurseries. Fred was credited with getting permission from Lord Mountbatten to name a new juniper after him. Fred's brother Howard also credited him with the development of the three-stem birch, although it isn't certain if that idea actually originated with Sheridan.

Every Sunday Fred would drive around the nursery to inspect the inventory. Both Karen and Karl learned to drive by chauffeuring their dad around looking at the plants. Karl remembers one of the "big lessons" in his life when his dad used to say, "Each one of those plants is a five dollar bill." It put things in perspective and instantly taught Karl a great respect for each plant on the farms.

Fred and Lois always insisted on proper family meals. On Sundays that invariably meant roast beef. Karl and Karen never tasted Kraft Dinner until they went to university. Often, when Howard Dunington-Grubb visited Sheridan, J.V. would take him out to Fred's house for coffee or tea. Howard was especially fond of Lois's homemade cookies.

After his retirement in the early 1970s, Fred remained on the Sheridan Nurseries board of directors. In his last years, health problems put an end to his favourite activities, hunting and fishing. He no longer sold Lions Club tickets.

But nothing could totally dampen Fred's humour and good-spirited outlook on life. He still managed to make an occasional trip to the racetrack. Whenever an article about Sheridan Nurseries appeared in the *Horticultural Review*, editor Rita Weerdenburg knew she'd get a phone call from Fred, offering thanks and a compliment.

When Fred passed away on March 7, 1991, at the age of eighty-one from the effects of Parkinson's disease, condolences poured in from friends and colleagues all over Canada and the United States. The following July, the *Horticultural Review* published a selection of memorials. All were gracious and carried fond thoughts of Fred. One in particular, from Paul Coughlin, former owner of Toronto York Nurseries, had an anecdote that captured Fred's spirit in plain eloquence. Paul reminisced about Fred as a fine businessman and about the Lion's Club tickets. Then he said, "I'm in the horse race business, and Fred was always a race track fan. The Saturday before he passed away I had a message that there was someone in the balcony who wanted to see me. I was pleasantly surprised to see Fred there with his granddaughter. He gave me $30 to bet on a horse, and the horse won $300 for him, so to me, Fred was a winner right up to the very end."

Those last words would make a fitting epitaph.

***

Lois worked in the office until 1944, when Karen was born. After that she devoted herself to running the household and raising her family. With Fred away much of the time, that was a full-time job. However, Lois was still part of the team of women who did the tedious but necessary task of writing labels. In her later years, Lois lived in a senior's residence in Georgetown, and then a nursing home in Burlington. She passed away on July 16, 2008, in her ninety-first year.

THE TEACHER

Howard Stensson's son Bill thinks his father might have gone into teaching because no position was available at the nursery, but there was a shortage of teachers during the Second World War. Howard had been rejected by the Canadian Army because his eyesight wasn't good enough. He contributed to the war effort by establishing a high school cadet corps.

Howard began teaching in Norwich about 1941. He was a modern-day Renaissance man, and it showed in the wide range of subjects in which he was an exceptional teacher: history, physics, physical education, chemistry, and math. Even though Howard could be a disciplinarian when necessary, his sense of humour made him popular.

One year, Bill had his father for homeroom teacher. If Bill expected preferential treatment, he was disappointed. Dad would give him detentions if he got out of line.

Howard's students especially liked his field trips. These were great learning experiences for the boys, most of whom came from farm families. Howard took them out to the countryside. He taught them surveying and how to identify native plants. The highlight of the year was the trip to the artificial insemination unit in Woodstock. This was a breeding centre for Holstein cattle. A statue of a cow named Snow Countess, the world-champion butterfat producer, was unveiled in 1937 and is still a Woodstock landmark. The boys in Howard's class were more impressed with the three-foot-long condom that was used to collect bull semen.

Howard began his teaching career at a time when one didn't necessarily require a university degree to be a teacher. Howard had a degree, but one of his colleagues didn't. Eventually the provincial government insisted that teachers have post-secondary degrees. Howard's colleague, who taught typing, took a night course at McMaster University to get his BA. Howard drove him to Hamilton for the night classes, and decided to take a Spanish course to fill time. Howard completed the course at the top of his class, while his friend just barely managed to pass.

Howard ran a small nursery in his back yard. He grew apple trees and did custom budding for local farmers. He always took his family to Sheridan at Easter and Christmas, and for summer vacations. They stayed at the big house with Annie. Bill recalls that he looked forward to those visits because he always found the nursery interesting. He particularly recalls the pleasant aroma of the packing shed. There were return visits, too, and Howard took the kids fishing at Turkey Point or Port Rowan on Lake Erie.

In 1964, Howard returned to Sheridan as nursery manager. With J.V.'s passing in 1972, Howard became president. That same year, Howard was made president of the Ontario Nursery Trades Association. From 1986 to 1987 he was president of the Canadian Ornamental Plant Foundation.

Howard finally went into semi-retirement in June 1992 at the age of eighty. He still worked, but only for eight hours a day. On many occasions, Howard would be found travelling the fields to tell Bill and Karl "what needed to be done." On May 20, 2006, Maurine passed away. In spite of his advanced years, Howard remained bright and active for the rest of his life. He died on January 16, 2011, a little over a month into his ninety-ninth year.

By the time Howard Stensson died in 2011, the next generation of the family had ably taken the helm of Sheridan Nurseries. The company that had been a one-hundred-acre farm when Herman took charge had grown into the largest horticultural company in Canada; a major corporation. But it remained in essence a family business in which his traditions of hard work, good service, and fairness would be carried on by his grandchildren. However, not all of the younger Stenssons would stay with the nursery. Howard's daughter Gay (Stensson) Haddon went to work as a secretary in the nursery office in 1980, succeeding Kay Pleasants who was retiring. She left in 1982 when she moved to Toronto. His other daughter, Janice (Stensson) Fozard, worked for Sheridan Nurseries during summer vacations, including two summers taking inventory with Mitzi Iwasaki, and another as cashier at the Southdown sales station.

THE MUSICIAN: ENCORE

Although Chris's passion in life was music and he continued to play in bands, he worked for Sheridan Nurseries for most of his life. He was a familiar figure in the head office on St.

Thomas Street in Toronto. Then he went to Oakville to assist J.V. as office manager. Chris oversaw payroll and personnel records for the entire company until his retirement in 1970.

Chris was a whiz at handling "modern" office equipment. There were no computers or electronic calculators. Sitting on the right corner of his desk was a large box with seventy-two buttons on it and a large pull-handle on the side. It was called a *comptometer*. The noise from his office of this "calculator" was constant all day long.

Chris also had a passion for English sports cars. He owned many different models, including a number of Triumph Spitfires and TR3 convertibles, as well as a couple of Rovers which never seemed to be out of the garage.

Chris's wife Jean passed away in 1989. Chris died in his eighty-sixth year on March 6, 1995.

Laurie Pallett.

Besides music, Chris Stensson loved fine cars. Note the bass violin in the front seat.

SWEETHEART OF THE FLOWERS

In 1951, Betty began a career with Sheridan Nurseries that would last forty-five years. To her, the company and its people were like family. For many years she worked in the Oakville office. One of her principal jobs was writing labels by hand. When that tedious chore was computerized, Betty took charge of the Oakville farm's payroll department. All she needed was a pencil and paper; she could do most of the math in her head. Betty remained in that position until her retirement in 1987 at the age of seventy.

Betty had a lifelong love of flowers, and kept a beautiful garden at her home. As her nephew Jon Stewart put it, "We all know she had a green thumb, as her lawn and gardens were about as close to perfect as close can get." Family friend Bill Mason recalled that for Betty, a visit to the garden centre on Southdown Road was like a child's trip to a candy store. In the early spring when the first shoots were coming up through the last scraps of snow, she would say excitedly, "The pansies are in, Billy!" Bill Mason dubbed Betty "the Sweetheart of the Flowers."

There are many intangibles that go into the making of a successful company. Among them are a strong sense of hospitality to visitors, and a natural ability to make employees feel good about their workplace. Therein, perhaps, lay Betty's most substantial and memorable contribution to Sheridan Nurseries.

Betty was a great organizer. For a company party at Christmas or any other special occasion, she was the person who could be relied upon to bring people together and get things done. It didn't matter if the event was to be held in the shipping shed (as so many get-togethers were), or in a hall; with Betty in charge, it was guaranteed that a good time would be had by all.

Betty was a gourmet cook whose culinary creations were famous. She had style. If a dish called for pistachios, the ordinary red-dyed pistachios weren't good enough. She had to have premium natural pistachios. Her punch was legendary.

Betty's "people skills" as a hostess went well beyond her ability to organize a good party. She had a way of making everyone feel at home. Young European nurserymen who came to Canada to spend a summer in training at Sheridan Nurseries would be taken out to Betty's home to see her showpiece garden and enjoy her hospitality, and some boarded there. In a sense, Betty took over her father's role as a diplomat maintaining good relations with representatives from foreign nurseries.

Sheridan Nurseries.

A Sheridan Nurseries Christmas party. L–R: Kay Pleasants, Mary Iwasaki, Elsie Herod, Doris Laflin, Betty Stewart.

Art Drysdale, who was Sheridan's first horticulturist in the 1960s, recalled that Betty's house was like a second home to him. To quote Art, Betty's home was "always the place to enjoy the best of unique foods and cooking — especially at Christmas when I was known to take to stretching out on the floor for an hour or so after the dinner! Her grasshopper pie was absolutely wonderful, and I always volunteered to pick up [at a Toronto liquor store] the liqueurs that it contained, because they weren't stocked in Oakville or Mississauga."

Betty died on August 30, 2006, at the age of eighty-nine. In his eulogy, Jon Stewart said, "I remember Aunt Betty as being clearly dedicated to things that mattered to her family, her home, gardening, and of course Sheridan Nurseries."

THE LITTLE STENSSON JOURNAL

In the Dunington-Grubb Collection in the archives of the University of Guelph's McLaughlin Library, there is a pocket-sized notebook full of hand-written entries made by J.V. and Howard Stensson. This rare "primary source" document is a small gem of Stensson family history. Unfortunately, not all of the entries are legible. Some were hastily scrawled and others, written in pencil, have faded.

The first entries are J.V.'s, beginning when he was nineteen. They are brief, chronologically sporadic, and are mostly about baseball, social events, and school. The entry for May 30, 1928, says "Peggy Brand arrives." That was eighteen-year-old Margaret, a cousin on his mother's side, visiting from England.

When J.V. wasn't at school, he was obliged to do his share of work at Sheridan Nurseries. He also occasionally hired out

to do agricultural work elsewhere. His feelings are reflected in a few terse notes and introspective comments.

> Thurs. Oct 13. Like work very much.
>
> March 8. Know what you have to do and do it.
>
> July Frid 13. Up at Ancaster. rotten work and rotten pay. 30c p.b. [30 cents per bushel]
>
> July 23rd 1928. 21 years [his birthday]. Spent day in Ancaster shoveling dirt 10 hours. getting tanned! Like work for a change but prefer to use my brains[?] to brawn. Be Broad-minded, Brave and Unselfish.

J.V.'s last entry is for May 4, 1930. He won a first prize of $40 dollars in a competition, but the words naming the event are illegible. J.V.'s total journalistic input for a period of almost three years fills only thirteen pages. The little book then went unused for almost four years. It was probably tossed into a drawer and forgotten.

"*Howard Herman Stensson 1934*," flashily underlined, marks the beginning of Howard's section of the little book. It is an itinerary of a trip he and J.V., aged twenty-one and twenty-six respectively, took to England and the continent, starting on June 29, 1934.

Howard's entries cover sixty-one pages and a period of about ten weeks. He made notes about the ocean crossing, which apparently was rough:

> July 2. Foggy in morning and cold … ship rolling more.
>
> July 3. More roll than yesterday … Missed lunch.

Upon reaching Southampton on July 5, Howard became more earnest in his observations, which from time to time are underlined by the humour of a young man facing new experiences far from home. For their tour of England, Howard and J.V. bought an old car they called a "Beazle" (possibly a BSA) for six pounds. The frequency of the word "rain" in Howard's notes is matched only by the many references to car troubles. In the course of their adventures in English driving, the brothers experienced a clogged carburetor, a broken piston, and a broken axle. They had numerous flat tires; as many as five in one day. A day that was free of car trouble was significant enough for Howard to note in his book, "Car running okay."

They ran out of gas once, "but spare can does the trick and we fill up at Newport." On an occasion when they were lost, Howard blamed J.V., who got "mixed up in the roads."

For a side trip to London they left the Beazle behind and took a bus. Their tour of the capital took in Westminster Abbey, the Tower of London, St. Paul's Cathedral, and Buckingham Palace, and they had lunch in Hyde Park. But on the return trip the bus "went bum," to use Howard's expression, and they had to walk three miles to Ascot.

Howard and J.V. toured many of England's most famous sites: Windsor Castle, Stonehenge, the Eddystone Lighthouse, and Blenheim Palace. At Stratford-on-Avon they visited

"Shakey's theatre, house, etc." Howard's impression of Leeds, Sheffield, Barnsley, and Wakefield was: "Scruffy factory towns, coal mines, etc. First sight of Leeds is nothing but smoke and chimneys. Drive right through to Moortown."

At Hever Castle, once the home of Anne Boleyn, Howard noted that in addition to seeing many relics of King Henry VIII, they also explored, "a maze of clipped yew trees in garden — have a hard time finding way out. Gigantic floral garden with a lot of marble work ... quite beautiful."

One of the main reasons the brothers were in England was to visit gardens. Their father thought they would benefit from some exposure to the classical gardens and landscaping of "Olde England." Howard's reactions were mixed.

"Not much to look at," Howard wrote of an estate they visited at Cullompton. Nor did he seem to be impressed with some old clipped yew specimens he saw in the Adams Garden in Bradfield. The gardens they visited at an estate near Taunton were "nice but rather dilapidated as usual." However, Howard did record seeing "a fine garden at St. Catherine Court." The only things he found noteworthy about the famous formal gardens at Athelhampton were the yew trees. At a place called Saxons Hill they saw, "a garden of a queer old bozo with long hair."

On July 22, Howard and J.V. visited Kew Gardens, where their father had once worked. Howard's only remark was, "Very interesting." The next two days' events were more memorable.

> Monday July 23. Start off for Reading. Decided not to change weak-looking tire. Change it five minutes later. Proceed to Sonning-on-Thames. Then to Sutton Seed Trials. Reading. Very beautiful show. Then to Folly Farm, Sulhamstead, fine formal gardens. Back to Henley & have peek at Friar Park. See Lord Devonport's estate where pop used to work. Very pretty & beautiful herbaceous borders. On to Marlow & change another tire in about half mile. Celebrate Bill's birthday by 2 good blowouts. Have supper up in Quarry Woods & so to bed."
>
> Tuesday July 24 — & on top of that Bill is sick in the middle of the night, all over the window & street. To Guildford in a.m. & see Duke of Sutherland's. Two nice flowerbeds. Proceed to Liphook & book room for night. Rain heavily on & off in afternoon.

During their stay in England, Howard and Bill met several relatives, including "Aunty Lil" (Annie's sister Lily), "Uncle Ted" (Lily's husband Edward Duke), and an assortment of cousins. One evening, after the usual rain, Howard and Bill had a chance to "play cricket in the field with uncle & the lads." They also met "Uncle Jess and Aunty Blanche" (Jesse Benning was Annie's brother). On August 2, they went to Hitchen where they visited the house in which Howard had been born. Shortly after that they met a Mrs. Gray, who had once been a nurse to the Stensson children. Howard noted that she was "delighted to see her old babies."

On August 3, the brothers went to Letchworth to meet Edward and Emma, Howard Dunington-Grubb's parents. "Like them very much," Howard wrote. "Mr. Grubb shows

us the [Quaker] Friends Meeting House. Mrs. Grubb gives us a book of Edward's to give to Mother." Howard and J.V. were also shown the remains of a rockery Herman had built.

Howard and J.V. sold the old Beazle for twenty-five shillings on August 15, after removing its clock for a souvenir. Three days later they sailed for Denmark, where they met more relatives: "Uncle Bill" (Vilhelm, Herman's brother), "Aunty Inga" and "Aunty Emma" (Herman's sisters), and their grandmother, Christiane. They went to Knutenborg Park and saw "pop's old house" and "grand pop's grave." (Nils Stensson had died in 1911.)

The brothers enjoyed a swim in the Baltic Sea, and Howard commented on sleeping in a Danish bed: "funny affair, with clothes all in one piece." He also noted, "Things cheap in Denmark."

On August 28, after just a few days in Denmark, the brothers boarded a train for Paris. Howard was impressed with the Eiffel Tower, Versailles, Napoleon's Tomb, the Louvre, and Les Invalides. They visited several French gardens, but Howard commented at length on only one.

> Tuesday Sept. 4. Take train to station about 25 miles S. of Paris, then taxi 4 miles to Vaux le Vicomte [a magnificent seventeenth-century estate]. To our surprise see the best garden we have seen yet in Europe. Large scale, formal, simple, well kept up. Very nice chateau, luxurious inside.

Overall, the brothers enjoyed France. But Howard did have one complaint:

> Never get butter in France, except a little bit for breakfast. Grapes are good, especially one kind, blue, with distinct flavour. French apparently don't eat as much as English, Danish, etc. Maybe that's why they are such little runts.

For September 7, Howard wrote, "Up early for a change." This was a big day on the European journey because he and J.V. were parting company. J.V. boarded a train for Turin, Italy. The next day, after a "Self-wander around the city," Howard caught a train to Cherbourg where he boarded a ship for home.

Howard's final entry, "Leave Cherbourg about 6:30" isn't the last in the little book. Long before he used it to make notes about the trip to Europe, nineteen-year-old J.V. had jotted a few thoughts on the last page in his clear cursive style:

> *Landscape Architecture*
> *For the welfare of mankind and betterment of the masses.*
> *Incidentals*
> *Livelihood*
> *Pleasure*
>
> *To do*
>
> *Study*
> *Read*
> *Travel*
> *Think of Others*
> *Exercise*
> *Drink more water*

THE SHERIDAN YEAR BOOK

In the early twentieth century it was common for the residents of rural communities like Sheridan to mark the arrival of a new year with the publication of a small year book. This was a chronological summary of supposed "important events" from the old year. Most of the entries were folksy hyperbole and light, good-natured jokes made at the expense of local residents and businesses, and would be immediately understood in a small community where everybody knew everybody else. The 1928 Sheridan Year Book contains numerous references to the Stensson family and to Sheridan Nurseries. Of course, the prominence of the Stensson name might be because a Stensson was one of the main contributors. Evelyn Bullied, a longtime Sheridan resident, believed the humour in the book gave away one of the authors as J.V. Stensson.

> *January 26th*
> Chris Stensson is taking lessons on the fiddle. His father has fixed up a sound proof room in the basement for him to practise in. Howard Lawrence is also taking lessons on the same instrument. His mother sent him down to the barn for his practise, but Mr. Lawrence would not have him there, as the hens were dancing the Two Step instead of laying eggs. Now the poor lad has to hike down to the old implement shed every time. Mr. Wilson sent John across there the other day as he thought his pigs had got loose.

March 18th
A dance was held on Saturday evening at the Stensson's new house. The Hostess assisted by Mrs. Lawrence and Mrs. Morris received the guests. They were dressed in charming Gorgette, trimmed with Muresco, with necklaces and ear-rings to match. (Dresses supplied by Swanky Tailors, necklaces from Woolworth.) The guests were received in the main hall, but on account of the small proportions of this, and the rather large proportions of some of the hostesses, the visitors had to be admitted one at the time. The young people spent most of the evening trying to wear out the new hardwood floor. (Hardwood by Bert Hill.) Excellent music was provided. (Piano suppl. By Screechman & Co.) Refreshments were served during the evening (Caterers Ham & Slam Ltd.) Everybody had an enjoyable time, but as it was thought advisable to leave sufficient of the flooring to hold another dance next year, the party closed at 11:59 p.m.

April 23rd
John Jessen, the shipper at the Sheridan Nurseries made a huge packing box, which when packed weighed just six-and-a-half tons. As the railway people refused to handle it, it was brought back, and K. Buch set it up behind his house as a combined garage and

chicken house. Well, it is an ill packing box which blows nobody any good.

May 9th

A man called on Mr. Stensson today and wanted him to replace a tree, which he bought two years ago. He also called on Mr. Wilson to get another cow for nothing, as the one he bought from him twelve-month ago died last week. What is the world coming to? In both cases this not unreasonable request was refused.

June 15th

The Boss at Sheridan Nurseries has got a new Ford. He is great at figures and has already estimated as he will now be able to tear about at the rate of 50 miles per hour instead of the old Lizzie's puny 25 miles, he will be able to get through twice as much work, speed up production 100 percent and reduce the cost another 100 percent. I have been doing a little figuring myself, and I calculate that the Boss going at that rate be getting two grey hairs in his head for each one he would have had if he had stuck to the old Lizzie. May be that I am wrong. I ain't no scholar like the Boss.

July 7th

The weeds at the Nurseries are said to have reached an enormous size. Hoes have been discarded by Mr. Buck and his gang, and pickaxes have taken their place. Buck reports that the men are not looking upon this change very favourably, as the picks are so short in the handle and very uncomfortable to lean on.

July 19th

This day may well go down on record as being the blackest day in the history of Sheridan. Blinds are down and flags are at half mast. The reason is not far to seek. The load of stone going down the Town Line was not for the road at all, but delivered to Sheridan nurseries who are building a new packing shed.

August 16th

22 travellers called on Mr. Stensson to canvas for orders for materials for the new packing shed. Needless to say, each representative carried the very best line of goods obtainable in the market. The list of firms represented is too long to enumerate, but we give a few of the more important firms for the benefit of those contemplating new buildings in the near future.

Jack & Douglas, Lumber
The Hammerem Nail Co.
I. Leak & CO. Ready Roofing
Smear Brothers, Paints
The Never-Shut Door Company
Bright & Spark, Electricians
The Cheatem Scale Co.

August 22nd

Mr. C. DeGroot, the nursery foreman, has invented a new mouthpiece for his old pipe. He approached the manager to find out if the nurseries were willing to pay for this, as he claims he only smokes to keep the Aphids off the plants. Mr. Stensson could not see his way to grant this, as he is afraid it would cause a precedent, and probably Bob Holliday would want to be supplied with Bachelor Cigars just to keep the flies away from the horses.

September 29th

The Phlox in the Nurseries are looking fine just now. The weeds are lookin' pretty middlin' too, considerin'.

October 26th

Threshing at the Nurseries went off without a hitch. Fred Brown's separator only broke down 14 times. This was considered extremely lucky, as it might easily have stopped at 13. It is rumoured that the outfit which is said to be of pre-historic origin has been acquired by Professor Currelly, shortly to be placed in the National Museum, Toronto.

November 7th

Allan Hughes was on time in the Nurseries this morning. Pilgrim says this is the third time this year, and constitutes a record. The other employees have decided to award him a prize if he can make it five times for the year. Allan says he will make a bid for the prize, or die in the attempt.

December 31st

A VERY HAPPY NEW YEAR

Sheridanitis Poeticus var. Nonsensicus

This is the aristocratic name given to a new Perennial which originated last year at Sheridan. It differs from all other Perennials in that it comes into bloom very early, generally about the first week in January, and is therefore extremely hardy. It has proved very popular with most people, though a few consider it too rank. Belonging to the Nightshade Family, it has the characteristic of most of the narcotic plants, that of having a soothing effect on the nerves, and only in a few isolated cases where the person has taken an extra good sniff at it has it been known to cause irritation. Dr. Burton St. Claire who was called in to attend one very obstinate case, ordered the patient to take the leaves of the aforesaid Sheridanitis, tear them up, and put them in his pipe and smoke them. This acted as an antidote, and an immediate cure was effected.

CHAPTER 3

The Projects: "Eternal Aspects of the Landscape Art"

With Sheridan Nurseries in the very capable hands of Herman Stensson, Howard and Lorrie could concentrate on landscape design. That didn't mean they looked upon the nursery as a mere sideline. In the early years, the money they earned as landscape architects kept the nursery going. Nonetheless, Howard and Lorrie *were* first and foremost landscape architects — with a mission!

Although the Dunington-Grubbs were involved in many large public projects, most of their clients were private homeowners. They worked in Toronto's exclusive Rosedale district, in the expanding suburbs, and in the countryside. They designed the beautiful grounds of such estates as Wynnstay, the residence of Mrs. Frederick Fenner Dalley in Ancaster (now the Mount Mary Immaculate Retreat Centre), and Randwood in Niagara-on-the-Lake.

Like all artists, Howard and Lorrie had personal ideas about aesthetics and beauty. They were not always in agreement with their colleagues, and sometimes not even with each other. There has even been speculation that Lorrie was a better designer than Howard. She sometimes worked independently. For example, Lorrie alone designed the garden for historic Barnum House, near Cobourg, Ontario

Nonetheless, Howard and Lorrie made a remarkably good team. The Dunington-Grubbs' friend and colleague Humphrey Carver reflected in the May 1989 issue of *Landscape Architectural Review*:

> Perhaps they represent two eternal aspects of the landscape art: the structure of the design and the content. Howard, the 18th century

> man, who knew how to lead you into the landscape scene by the terraces, pathways and avenues, the spaces and vistas, the whole structure of the landscape picture. And Lorrie, the 19th century flower lady who knew all the richness, variety, color and habit of plants and flowers in their seasons — an art passed on to her by Gertrude Jekyll.

Carver was one of the few to give Lorrie equal space in professional assessments of the Dunington-Grubbs' work. However much Lorrie may have been credited with being Howard's full partner during her lifetime, in posterity she has been somewhat in his shadow. This is evident in the writings of critics and admirers alike. According to horticulturist Ann Milovsoroff, author of a biographical study of the Dunington-Grubbs in a Canadian Horticultural History booklet in 1990:

> Howard Dunington-Grubb was neither innovative nor particularly imaginative in his designs ... but he was very good at tastefully amalgamating eclectic design elements ... His importance, however, lies not in his design work itself, but in the amount and variety that he accomplished ... and in his enthusiastic participation in all facets of the profession.

The study from which this passage is taken provides some information on Lorrie's life and her relationship with Howard, and acknowledges her talents. But the bulk of the text is about Howard. Helen Skinner, in contradiction to some of Milovsoroff's points, wrote in the April-May 1989 issue of *Century Home*:

> Howard Dunington-Grubb was never a static designer. It is interesting to observe the changing styles in his garden plans. In the early days they have an English flavour with wide borders and formal plantings. But soon an Art Nouveau influence emerged with the clean, curving lines so typical of that period ... Ever adaptable, he was in the forefront of the planning movement.

The article credits Lorrie with having great ability as a garden designer, but she is more or less mentioned in passing. Skinner describes Howard as "a pioneer in the Canadian landscape architectural profession whose innovative designs gained national acclaim." Then Skinner acknowledges Lorrie as Howard's collaborator.

Modernism, with its spare, functional approach to design in art and architecture, was coming into vogue. But Howard preferred the older beaux-arts style. That neo-classical movement, which dates back to seventeenth-century France, emphasized the human enhancement of the environment. It subscribed to a marriage of the architecture of buildings to their surroundings to form a controlled and ornamental scene that was more of a human stage than a natural theatre. As Ann Milovsoroff explains, "He [Howard] was devoted to the values expressed in fine gardening, ornament and attention to detail, and was willing to defend them in lively debate."

The concept of "decorative nature under the control of art" was a cornerstone of beaux arts philosophy, and one that Howard embraced. "Design has always been based on functionalism," he wrote. "The modernist's interpretation of functionalism may reduce our houses to the barren bleakness of an orphans' home." He believed that the landscape architect should furnish the important artistic link between a building and the landscape surrounding it.

Humphrey Carver was of a different mind. He had been working for another designer, Carl Borgstrom (for whom a modern-day environmental award has been named). Carver wrote in *Compassionate Landscape: Places and People in a Man's Life*:

> If making gardens is an essential part of a nation's culture, Canada owes a lot to the Dunington-Grubbs, not only because they designed and built gardens but because it was from their Sheridan Nurseries that the suburban population of Toronto first learned to carry home triumphant all the blue spruces and pfitzer's junipers and Chinese elms to make a garden out of the desert they had bought from the speculative dealer.
>
> I think Borgstrom was a better landscape artist than Howard Grubb because he wanted the trees and the ground to develop in their own natural way, whereas Grubb couldn't forget that he was a designer, highly trained in the "beaux-arts style," and he wanted to dominate the pattern and impose on the planting material his own view of how they ought to grow. It's like the difference between a permissive and an authoritarian parent … In spite of any differences of artistic opinion, I had a relationship with Howard Grubb that I can only describe as one of affection.

Howard dismissed the modernist garden as being made "of such severity, or such grotesqueness, as to have little resemblance to anything that we should recognize as a garden." In a *Canadian Homes and Gardens* article titled "The Modernist in the Garden" Howard gave his own tongue-in-cheek description of a Humphrey Carver garden:

> As an example of virile decoration, suitable for his he-man pleasuance, we see an illustration of a garden consisting of two tennis rackets, an umbrella, and a glass of whiskey and soda. Gone are our finials, our tubs, and our garden pots. Surely our flower bed, our herbaceous border, and our roses, having no possible practical value must be overboard also.

Howard didn't think pure functionalism would be popular for long. He believed the chief purpose of a garden is "to delight the eye and soothe the spirit," and the best way to achieve that was through an artistically harmonized landscape. If an inconveniently located tree didn't fit in with his design, then it had to go. Today that would be considered heresy. In Howard's own time it drew critical fire from colleagues who believed in an ecological balance between human activities and natural ecosystems.

By the 1950s, Howard admitted that the principals of modern art as applied to garden design were beyond him. He didn't feel that tradition should be abandoned solely for the sake of originality, or that stability and a sense of permanence should be sacrificed for some elusive sense of artistic freedom. As a result of his faithful (some would say stubborn) defence of the ideal landscape as an artificial but humanistic image "full of variety and surprise and delightful detail," Howard came to be viewed as a member of an outdated old guard.

This conflict of opinion with their colleagues didn't alter the fact that the socially conscious Dunington-Grubbs believed they had a mission. In the early twentieth century, large Canadian cities like Montreal and Toronto certainly had their unsightly and unsanitary slums, but not on the same scale as the worst parts of London, Manchester, and Liverpool. Smaller Canadian population centres had only recently begun to break out of their frontier-town confines. To Howard and Lorrie, newly arrived from England, there was still hope for the Canadians.

In 1912 Howard went to Calgary, apparently as an associate of Thomas Mawson, to study the site of a proposed university. He had ambitious ideas, and drew up impressive plans. They were published in the university's "Preliminary Announcement." To Howard's disappointment, the Alberta provincial government denied the would-be university permission to grant degrees. The project was abandoned, and Howard's plans were never used.

In 1914 the Parks Commission of Brantford, Ontario, approached the Dunington-Grubbs for their expert advice on how to "make Brantford convenient, healthy and beautiful." In their preliminary report, made after "many months of thought and study," Howard and Lorrie stressed the importance of making long-range plans rather than short-term ones. Their report deplored the fact that potential parkland along the Grand River had been taken over by railways. It presented proposals for the development of a street plan, and ideas for the Bell Homestead Park and the Ontario School for the Blind. Unfortunately, like so many other civic projects of the time, this one was postponed indefinitely due to the Great War's monumental drain on money and other resources. There are no known records as to whether any of the Dunington-Grubbs' plans were ever used in Brantford.

In 1913, Howard and Lorrie were commissioned to draw up a full set of landscape plans and garden designs for Wymilwood, the estate of financier Edward Rogers Wood and his wife Agnes. (Later re-named Falconer Hall, it is now part of the University of Toronto). They worked on the project for two years. The plans and drawing contained many features that were typical of the Dunington-Grubb style.

In 1924, the Woods moved to a new estate called Glendon Hall (now a part of York University). This time they decided to design their own landscaping. However, there is strong evidence that they were greatly influenced by the designs Howard and Lorrie had drawn for Wymilwood. There has even been testimony that Howard actually worked on Glendon himself. But without documented support, Glendon can't officially be listed as a Dunington-Grubb project.

GAGE PARK: A TRIP ON A TIME MACHINE

One of the most energetic proponents behind the movement for civic beautification and the social gospel in southern Ontario in the early twentieth century was a Hamilton politician named Thomas B. McQuesten. His staunch Presbyterian upbringing instilled in him a strong sense of social responsibility. He and such colleagues as Nicholas Cauchon, Hamilton's city engineer; and C.V. Langs (QC), chairman of the Hamilton Parks Board, believed in the theory that green spaces in the midst of urban sprawl would be beneficial to the physical and spiritual well-being of the working-class and the poor. McQuesten was instrumental in the development of dozens of parks, especially in the booming industrial region at the western end of Lake Ontario, from Toronto to Niagara-on-the-Lake and along the Niagara River to Fort Erie. It was through his tireless efforts, often opposed by conservative city fathers, that Hamilton came to have the largest, most scenic, most thematically varied, and best-planned-and-executed developed park acreage of any city in Canada.

In 1917, McQuesten was an alderman and chairman of the Hamilton Public Works Committee. He was one of the principal advocates for the acquisition of almost sixty-four acres of land at the foot of the Niagara Escarpment, east of the downtown core. This property was owned by the prominent Gage family. Shortly before his death in 1918, Robert Russell Gage made the land available to the city for about half its retail market value. In January 1922, the land officially became city property. McQuesten then hired the Dunington-Grubbs to design the new park.

The master plan that Howard and Lorrie created called for a rich combination of open spaces, gardens, playing fields, and tree-lined pathways. Lorrie's beloved herbaceous borders were set against lush hedges and dense woodlots. The flora was an eclectic mixture of roses, evergreens, and carpet beddings that a visiting American landscape architect called the finest he had ever seen. The bedding plans were actually carried out by an eighty-three-year-old gardener named William Duncan who had been a Hamilton parks employee for forty-three years.

From a central promenade, pathways branched off to the park's various features; tennis courts, a bowling green, a cricket pitch, and a pergola — another favourite decoration of Lorrie's. The original plan included a conservatory, but it was never built. Instead, there were greenhouses. One observer who visited in the winter wrote of them:

> Those twin magicians of the twentieth century, the goddess of electricity and the genie of gasoline, can transport the lover of the beauty of nature to a corner of paradise, fragrant with perfume, glowing with glorious colour, vibrant with the humming of bees, a touch of sweet summer time set in the drab tones of yet unawakened nature … a visit to the conservatory of Gage park is like a trip on [H.G.] Wells' time machine into the month of June.

The greenhouses, which the observer called a conservatory, were not the Dunington-Grubbs' idea, but were incorporated into the plan under their supervision. There was, in fact, much that was new and innovative about the whole project. At Gage Park, Howard and Lorrie were pioneers in adapting the ideals of a formal English garden to a large park setting, while considering the imposition of automobile traffic. The gradual transformation of the old Gage property into a new park was considered worthy enough of public interest to keep its progress in the newspapers throughout the mid-1920s.

One story concerned a fountain that Robert Gage's daughter Euginia had erected as a memorial to her parents. She contracted the work to John W. Lyle, an architect and sculptor who was best known for designing Toronto's Royal Alexandra Theatre and Union Station. Lyle created a three-tiered basin fountain that featured turtles, geese, and an inscription. It was to be installed in a central location and framed by herbaceous borders. But the fountain wasn't part of the Dunington-Grubbs' plan, and they didn't like it!

Lyle and the Dunington-Grubbs knew each other and respected each other's work, but in the case of the Gage Park Memorial Fountain, Howard and Lorrie believed an artistic mistake had been made. Lorrie didn't take it quietly. She wrote in an article titled "The Value of Water as a Garden Feature" that appeared in *Canadian Homes and Gardens* in October 1926: "To place a large handsome wall fountain, the work of a noted sculptor, out in the middle of a park, with no better backing than a group of deciduous trees, is to commit an unforgivable crime; yet, alas, I have seen it done."

The official opening of Gage Park on June 22, 1927, was a red-letter day for the Dunington-Grubbs and Sheridan Nurseries. It had been carefully planned and among the dignitaries and several hundred other invited guests were Governor General of Canada Viscount Willingdon and his wife. However, the formal occasion would be more memorable for a few unintentionally comedic mishaps.

A platform had been erected for the Willingdons and other notables. Most of the ticket-holding guests sat in a roped-off enclosure south of the fountain. All around, on the beautifully groomed Dunington-Grubb lawns, and amidst the gardens resplendent with Sheridan Nurseries plants, milled the curious public.

After a few preliminary formalities, Chairman C.V. Langs gave a short speech. He concluded with a request for Mayor Freeman Treleaven's daughter Jane to present Lady Willingdon with a bouquet of flowers. At that point, the governor general was to call for the fountain to be "unveiled." Thomas B. McQuesten would raise a handkerchief. That was the signal for an attendant to turn on the water.

Before Willingdon could say a word, one of the dignitaries on the platform — perhaps in anticipation of a sneaking sneeze — pulled out his handkerchief. The attendant took that as his signal. He turned the fountain on at full volume. At the same moment, a strong wind swept north across the park and carried the water from the fountain like rain. The guests in the roped-off enclosure were soaked before the fountain could be turned off.

To make matters worse, someone had forgotten to bring the bouquet that Jane Treleaven was to present to Lady Willingdon. After an embarrassing pause in the formalities, Lady Willingdon graciously saved the day by asking that Jane be presented to her instead. She later received the flowers at tea in the club house.

Today much of the original Dunington-Grubb design of Gage Park is still evident, in spite of changes that have been made over the years. However, time and vandalism have taken their toll. A major project to restore the park to its former glory began in 2008, to be completed in 2012.

PARKWOOD: HERITAGE SITE

The Parkwood estate in Oshawa was the palatial home of Colonel Robert Samuel McLaughlin and his wife Adelaide Louise Mowbray. Colonel Sam was the founder of the McLaughlin Motor Company, which eventually became General Motors of Canada. He had purchased Parkwood in 1915 and wanted to develop it into an ostentatious showpiece. The project, which would take years to complete, centered on the fifty-five-room mansion. During the Depression, Colonel Sam employed GM workers to finish the house instead of laying them off. In those days of car-building, craftsmen skilled at woodworking for the dashboard and wheels, as well as metal workers for the body, ended up making ornate iron grills for the windows and doors, as well as intricate wooden fences for the estate's Italian Garden. In its glory years, Parkwood was one of Canada's most famous estates. Colonel Sam and Adelaide could boast that they entertained royalty.

The Dunington-Grubbs became involved with Parkwood about 1925. They had ample space in which to apply the principals of estate design established by Gertrude Jekyll and Thomas Mawson. Parkwood would reflect Howard and Lorrie's ideals of the creative and subjective elements of landscape design.

The location of the mansion allowed them room to maximize the sense of space with sweeping lawns and walks. Windows and terraces provided excellent vantage points from which to view the grounds. A screen of spruces, pines, maples, and chestnuts ensured privacy. Cedar hedges enclosed the estate, and divided it into compartments. This was in keeping with Howard's belief that, "Privacy, enclosure, and simplicity are the first principals of garden design."

Sheridan Nurseries.

Patio garden sketch for Parkwood Estate, designed by Howard Dunington-Grubb. Drawn by H.S. Maw. Note the misspelled Dunnington. *This is a frequently made error that appears even in publications today.*

Sheridan Nurseries.

Colonel Sam McLaughlin's Parkwood Estate as Howard and Lorrie knew it. It is now a National Historic Site where some of the original landscaping can still be seen. Unfortunately the statue, Hebe, *was destroyed by vandals.*

Sheridan Nurseries.

The patio garden at Parkwood shown in the S.H. Maw illustration.

A formal sunken garden was enclosed by what is believed to be the first Japanese yew hedge used in Canada. The central feature of this garden was *Hebe*, a classically inspired statue of a woman in flowing draperies. She stood on a rectangle of grass, surrounded by neat, flat flowerbeds. This was entirely in keeping with Howard's belief that, "Statues never look as well as when placed against a background of formally clipped evergreens or a group of stately pyramidal cedars." Unfortunately, *Hebe* was destroyed by vandals in 1999.

The lily pond in the Italian garden was probably Lorrie's contribution. She loved water features, and once wrote that the "lily tank ... should be part of an architectural layout, either in connection with the house proper, or some subsidiary, such as a garden pavilion." Lorrie was also responsible for the presence in the Italian garden of Florence Wyle's small sculpture *Baby With Dolphin* and Frances Loring's *Girl With Squirrel*.

The most formal section of Parkwood included the terrace and sundial gardens to the south of the house. This was also the area that presented Lorrie and Howard with one of their biggest challenges. Howard wrote, "In all the departments of garden planning, none calls for greater skill on the part of the designer than the terrace ... Many a fine piece of architecture has been ruined by an inappropriate setting."

Photographs and plans show how the vision for this part of Parkwood evolved from 1919 to 1929. In the creative process, key elements remain the same, while details are altered. The scope of the terrace becomes grander, while the use of potted plants diminishes. The low stone retaining walls so favoured by Howard and Lorrie help to create severely formal geometric flower beds framed in box and symmetrically positioned around an antique European sundial. The most dominant structure is a summer house.

The McLaughlins had a tennis court laid out to the west of the house. In Howard's opinion, "Tennis courts, though part of the pleasure grounds, should be more or less screened, as they are usually unsightly." He screened Parkwood's tennis court on all sides with cedars and spruces.

Parkwood today is an official National Historic Site and is open to the public. Thanks to the McLaughlins and the Parkwood Foundation, much of the original landscape architecture designed by the Dunington-Grubbs is still intact. Sheridan Nurseries has made significant commitments in contributions to the restoration of the gardens over the late twentieth and early twenty-first centuriues. This gives the estate a special artistic value as a historic site.

SHADOWBROOK: PICTURESQUE SERENITY

Shadowbrook, the Willowdale estate of industrialist Hamilton B. Wills, was one of the most ambitious private projects Howard and Lorrie undertook. They designed the landscaping, and for eight years directed the work, most of which was done by Wills's own staff of gardeners. Around a lovely Italian Renaissance-style mansion, they created what gardening writer J. Herbert Hodgins called in a 1929 edition of *Canadian Homes and Gardens* "as serene a bit of beauty as I have ever seen ... *Shadowbrook* is one of the most highly developed estates on the environs of Toronto."

A tributary of the Don River flowed through the length of the property. This was dammed to create a miniature lake and a ten-foot spillway. It also provided water for streamlets around which a Japanese garden was constructed. Oriental bridges spanned the waters, and the view from a Japanese teahouse was "altogether enchanting." Hodgins praised the Japanese garden as "the most nearly authentic of any similar garden that I know of in Canada."

Across the facade of the house was a circular, flagged terrace of weathered grey and terra cotta flagstones. There was a low balustrade intersected with twelve Italian urns. The terrace was built up in the manner of a rock garden.

Hodgins was especially impressed with the lawn. "One might properly refer to it as *The Lawn*, in true English manner. It is the serene parkland of the estate ... a splendid stretch of unbroken green."

Throughout the estate, Howard and Lorrie skillfully placed rose gardens, clipped hedges, and an assortment of conifers and perennials. There was a tennis court, a summer

Sheridan Nurseries.

Caruthers Estate, one of the many fine gardens in Toronto designed by the Dunington-Grubbs.

house, a beautifully bordered promenade, and even a "kitchen garden to delight the practical chatelaine." Every aspect of the flora was precise, from mosses to giant elms. This masterpiece of landscaping had as its backdrop, "the untouched woods which offer the elements of intrigue that Nature reserves for herself, and for Peter Pan."

Even before the landscaping at Shadowbrook was completed, Howard and Lorrie realized the potential of the project as a showpiece for their work. In 1927, 1928, and 1930 such features as perennial borders, strategically placed urns, the Japanese Garden, and the rock garden were photographed. The pictures appeared in *Canadian Homes and Gardens* as publicity for Sheridan Nurseries. In later years, Howard Stensson would recall that once a year his family would drive out to Shadowbrook for a picnic.

OAKES GARDEN THEATRE AND RAINBOW GARDENS: A LEGEND OF NIAGARA

Niagara Falls has had an amazingly colourful history. It is associated with many legends, dating back to the Native tale of the Maid of the Mist. In the nineteenth century, Niagara Falls became a major tourist attraction, and by the early twentieth century it was the "Honeymoon Capital" of North America.

The Canadian side of Niagara was by far the more popular because it had the better vantage points from which to view the falls. Thousands of American tourists crossed over every week. Local businessmen wanted the Americans to stay a while and spend their money, so they established the "attractions" associated with tacky tourist traps. Niagara Falls became something like a carnival midway lined with sideshows, bowling alleys, pool halls, low-brow amusement parlours, and souvenir shops where tourists could buy everything from cheap paintings of the falls, to naughty postcards with cartoon images of blushing, buxom brides and panting grooms. It was a decision to do something about this tawdry image and beautify the community that resulted in Howard Dunington-Grubb becoming part of the history and lore of Niagara Falls.

In December 1932, the Clifton Inn, one of the most famous hotels in Canada, burned down. The elegant structure had occupied one of the most advantageous sites in Niagara Falls. It had a magnificent view of the whole Niagara panorama. Across the road was the Canadian terminus of the Honeymoon Bridge.

The Great Depression had severely hurt Niagara's tourist business, so the hotel's owners didn't rebuild. They decided instead to dispose of the property. On an adjacent property another landmark, the Hotel Lafayette, was about to be torn down. It, too, had suffered from the Depression, and had been sitting vacant. The entire piece of ground that was now available measured about 460 feet by 330 feet.

Thomas B. McQuesten was now chairman of the Niagara Parks Commission (NPC), Ontario minister of Public Works, and minister of the Department of Highways. He believed the location was perfect for a park development that would be a welcoming point of entry into Canada for American visitors. However, the value of the real estate put it beyond the NPC's budget. Then the legendary Harry Oakes stepped in.

Oakes was an American-born adventurer who became a multi-millionaire when he struck gold at Kirkland Lake in northern Ontario. He became a naturalized Canadian citizen and bought a palatial home in Niagara Falls. Oakes took a

Sheridan Nurseries.

Photo of a model of Oakes Garden Theatre in Niagara Falls, a major Dunington-Grubb and Stensson project.

great interest in the community, and was more than generous with his newfound wealth.

Among other things, Oakes bought the Clifton and Lafayette properties. He hated developers, and didn't want them getting their hands on such beautifully situated real estate. He also purchased a five-acre strip of land along the Niagara River between Chippewa and Usher's Creek. Then Oakes gave all of this property to the NPC in exchange for a small plot of land near Queen Victoria Park.

Oakes first discussed plans for a new project to be called the Oakes Garden Theatre with Humphrey Carver and Carl Borgstrom. They envisioned an informal, naturalistic setting like that of Queen Victoria Park. It would take advantage of the topography of the Clifton/Lafayette site, and would be a relaxing place from which to view the falls.

Meanwhile, Oakes felt he was being unfairly taxed by the Canadian government. In 1935, he moved to the Bahamas. However, he still provided the lion's share of the funding for the development of Oakes Garden Theatre. In 1939, as a reward for his many good works, Oakes received a knighthood from King George VI. Then in 1943, under very strange circumstances, Sir Harry Oakes was murdered in his Nassau home. The crime has never been solved.

After Oakes left Canada, Commissioner Thomas B. McQuesten decided to hire his favourite landscape architect, Howard Dunington-Grubb. He asked Carver and Borgstrom to collaborate with Howard. They felt insulted, and rejected the invitation. Years later, in his autobiography, Carver wrote that he had explained his and Borgstrom's plans to Oakes, but, "about a year later the job had somehow passed into the hands of Dunington-Grubb."

Work on the project began in 1935. Some six hundred men who had been forced on to relief (welfare) by the Depression were contracted by the NPC as labourers. By this time Lorrie was in poor health, and probably contributed little, if anything, to the project. The plans for Oakes Garden Theatre and the Rainbow Gardens were principally the work of Howard and J.V. Stensson. Even though Oakes Garden Theatre formally opened in 1937, the destruction of the Honeymoon Bridge by ice in January 1938 meant that a new structure — the Rainbow Bridge — would have to be built. That also meant plans had to be altered. The entire project was not completed until 1944.

Howard and J.V. brought the principles of the beaux-arts style into the layout of Oakes Garden Theatre, though art deco would be the style for the Rainbow Gardens. Oakes Garden Theatre was to be an enclosed garden that would take advantage of the site's various levels. It would be made up of numerous separate spaces, some of which would be obvious to the park viewer, while others would provide surprising encounters. The stage would be the basis for the axis within the park, with pavilions and the Horseshoe and American falls as the ends to the axes.

The whole plan differed drastically from the one Carver and Borgstrom had prepared. Their concept allowed nature to take precedence, while Howard's emphasized human control over nature. Carver described Howard's design for Oakes Garden Theatre as "a dainty and almost feminine arrangement of steps, little clipped hedges, balustrades, garden ornaments, and interlacing patterns of flowerbeds. That was Grubb's vocabulary and trademark."

Howard wanted to create an air of mystery and charm, and he was meticulous in his planning. He made exquisitely

Sheridan Nurseries.

Rainbow Gardens, Niagara Falls, looking toward the Rainbow Bridge.

detailed drawings for the Niagara projects, and could be as painstaking in making the design for a bench as he was in plotting a section of the garden. He prepared all of his drawings in pencil on trace paper, and scoffed at the notion that future generations would study his designs.

To assist Howard and J.V., McQuesten hired a Hamilton-based architect named William Lyon Somerville. He had worked with McQuesten on such projects as McMaster University and the McNab Street Presbyterian Church. The large number of architectural features within Oakes Garden Theatre made someone with his abilities essential to the project, but there were rumours that he was given the job for political reasons.

McQuesten felt strongly that Canadian art should be incorporated into the project. Florence Wyle, Frances Loring, and Elizabeth Wyn Wood were commissioned to design fountains and architectural ornamentation. Among their contributions are the eight bas-reliefs of Canadian birdlife that decorate the arches leading from the pergola to the pavilions, the bas-relief Canadian scenes on one wall of the Rainbow Gardens, the animated fountain of fish in the formal Rainbow Gardens, and the wall fountain within the Rainbow Gardens.

Wood designed all three of the Gardens' fountains. She had wanted to use white marble, cast glass, and mosaic. Under electric lights at night, their colour would have softened the sternness of Howard's formal parterres. But because of the Second World War, the materials she required couldn't be imported, and she had to substitute Queenston limestone.

Wartime conditions also meant that a little subterfuge was involved in the project's funding. Frances Loring said that her payment was "sneaked in sort of as construction work." The government was afraid that the opposition might take a dim view of money being spent on art in a time of war.

If Lorrie was unable to directly participate in the project, her influence was nonetheless apparent in Howard and J.V.'s designs. Her trademark herbaceous borders were there. The lily pond with a bridge and a rock garden were reminiscent of her early association with Selfe-Leonard.

Today the fan-shaped Oakes Garden Theatre with its classical Greco-Roman amphitheatre is one of the most popular sites in Niagara Falls. Because Oakes Garden Theatre has not changed dramatically over the years, it is one of the few surviving examples of early Canadian landscape architecture.

On January 14, 1948, Thomas B. McQuesten died of cancer. If there were any feelings of resentment still lingering from some of the controversies surrounding Oakes Garden Theatre, they were put aside out of respect for his memory. Three of the honorary pall-bearers at McQuesten's funeral were Carl Borgstrom, William Lyon Somerville, and Howard Dunington-Grubb.

GRAYDON HALL: A SPORTSMAN'S PARADISE

Toronto's magnificent Graydon Hall estate was the dream home of a man whose financial success was equalled only by his love for sports. Rupert Bain was a successful businessman, and made a fortune during the Great Depression by financing the Pickle Crow gold mine in northwestern Ontario. By 1934, Bain was a millionaire. He purchased a

hundred acres of farmland on a concession east of Yonge Street. This would be the site of a home befitting a millionaire, as well as Bain's idea of a "sportsman's paradise."

Bain hired architects Allan George and Walter Moorehouse to build his twenty-nine-room Georgian manor house. It cost a quarter of a million dollars — an extraordinary sum in Depression-strangled Canada — and was completed in 1936. Then Bain turned to Howard Dunington-Grubb to do the landscaping. This would be a significant project for Dunington-Grubb & Stensson. It was one of the first major projects on which J.V. participated as a full-fledged landscape architect.

Bain had his own nine-hole course designed by George Cumming, the "Dean of Canadian Golf." He also played polo, and was master of the fox hounds for the Eglinton Hunt Club. The Dunington-Grubb/Stensson plans for the estate had to include stables for the horses and a riding track. Bain also wanted a swimming pool; something different for architects accustomed to designing pools that were strictly decorative. Bain was more interested in recreation and parties than he was in aesthetics. Nonetheless, like F. Scott Fitzgerald's Jay Gatsby, he wanted to display his wealth with a show of ostentation.

The Dunington-Grubbs and J.V. worked on the Bain estate from 1936 until 1941. J.V., fresh out of Harvard and brimming with new ideas and youthful energy, was a very able partner for Howard. They rose admirably to the challenges Rupert Bain presented.

Evergreens and gardens surrounded the house. The curving driveway passed through parkland much like that of an eighteenth-century English manor. Trees and mounded earth created fairways in the long green that was the golf course. Although the course was laid out by George Cumming, Howard and J.V. almost certainly built its landscape. The foundation plantings of the driveway and the walled-in forecourt of the manor house were designed in a formal style that looked attractive the year round. They included some of Howard's favourites: yews, pyramidal cedars, junipers, and spruce.

A TREASURE DISCOVERED

Sometimes treasure is "hidden" in plain view. While researching and giving shape to this book, Larry Sherk and Ed Butts consulted many times at Sheridan Nurseries' head office in Georgetown, using whatever rooms were available. One day they had the use of a lower floor office which neither man had previously been in. They noticed a striking watercolour hanging on a wall. It was an impressively detailed illustration of a magnificent estate. The feature that caught their attention was a swimming pool. They knew that Howard Dunington-Grubb had noted the fact that he had to include a swimming pool in his design for Graydon Hall, the vast estate Rupert Bain built in Toronto.

Closer inspection revealed that the subject of the watercolour was indeed Graydon Hall. Moreover, the artist was none other than J.V. Stensson! This meticulously executed painting, which might well be representative of J.V.'s best work, had been hanging in that office for years, but its origin and importance had been forgotten. The restored watercolour will have a more conspicuous place among Sheridan's collection of important works of art.

The gardens were enclosed in a series of compartments that became gradually less formal as they blended into the landscape farther from the house. To reach them, a visitor had to go through the house and onto a terrace shaded by lime trees. The gardens were described in a May 1939, article in *Canadian Homes and Gardens* as: "… three separate garden developments parallel to the length of the house, swimming pool, canal, lower formal pool garden, and at each end, water escapes into an informal rock-ringed pool."

The central feature was the fountain court. It was paved with a combination of Queenston limestone and Credit Valley sandstone, a favourite of the Dunington-Grubbs. The design for the staircases and the cascades was simple, yet clearly modern — perhaps reflecting J.V.'s influence.

Overlooking the court was a fountain piece by Florence Wyle that Bain had specially commissioned. Carved from Indiana limestone, it was a graceful figure of a woman spilling water from a basin. Lorrie was undoubtedly influential in bringing Wyle's work to Bain's attention. The sculpture is now the property of the Art Gallery of Ontario.

Graydon Hall and its grounds constituted an architectural landscaping masterpiece. In 1948, the *Journal of the Royal Architectural Institute of Canada* praised Graydon Hall as "one of the few houses to be harmoniously planned with its landscape and gardens."

Unfortunately, as with so many examples of artistic landscaping, Graydon Hall's glory was fleeting. In 1950, Bain sold a large part of the property to business tycoon E.P. Taylor. This included the stables, kennels, polo field, and racetrack. In 1951, Bain sold the mansion and its grounds to Nelson Morgan Davis of Intercity Forwarders. Later that year, Bain suffered a cerebral hemorrhage in a riding accident. He died in March 1952, at the age of fifty-four.

In 1964, Davis sold Graydon Hall Manor to developers, one of whom was future Edmonton Oilers owner Peter Pocklington. The site of Bain's sportsman's paradise was soon occupied by apartment buildings. Today what remains of the gardens and stonework Howard and J.V. created has fallen into decay.

UNIVERSITY AVENUE: TORONTO'S CHAMPS ÉLYSÉES — OR NOT?

> *The opportunity of designing the most important street in a city of one and a half million people does not often arise. When it does arise, we can expect considerable interest on the part of several classes of citizens. Many ideas as to the most suitable style of approach will be put forward. Groups of public spirited citizens will give up their time to attend meetings and present ideas. Busy committees of architects will be appointed to urge the adoption of some particular program for University Avenue.*
>
> — HOWARD DUNINGTON-GRUBB

The late author Pierre Berton once criticized University Avenue as "that pretentious boulevard" and complained that it was "rendered antiseptic by the presence of hospitals and insurance offices … the pristine display of wall to wall concrete that ran from Front Street to Queen's Park." However, others have called it Toronto's most prestigious street, and

one of the finest thoroughfares in all of North America. Regardless of which point of view one takes, a stroll up the avenue from the South African War monument to Queen's Park offers an outdoor gallery of Canadian art, much of it inspired by history; and an opportunity to appreciate one of Howard Dunington-Grubb's most significant projects.

In 1842, Charles Dickens visited Toronto during his first North American tour. The novelist had been bitterly disappointed with much of what he had seen in the United States, but he was impressed with Toronto. Dickens especially liked "a long avenue [University] which is already planted and made available as a public walk."

Dickens's favourable views of Toronto appeared in his *American Notes*. Toronto's city fathers were delighted. They had always thought that the "long avenue" might one day become Toronto's own version of the legendary Champs Élysées in Paris.

In the latter part of the nineteenth century and the first decades of the twentieth century, there was a concerted effort to make this vision a reality. It was extended south to Front Street, and north beyond Queen's Park to the location of Upper Canada College. It was also widened. The old King's College building was torn down to make room for the provincial government building. As automobiles and trucks replaced horse-drawn buggies and wagons, the avenue was transformed from a pleasant promenade to a major traffic artery. Its fine old trees were sacrificed to "progress," but the first of the monuments were put in place, giving the avenue a stately appearance.

According to Allsopp Hillier Du Toit, author of *The Art of the Avenue: A University Avenue Public Art Study*, "Through the 1950's, numerous proposals were debated regarding the decorative treatment of the newly realigned Avenue; in the same period plans were begun for a new subway line up the Avenue." However, an article published in the *Globe and Mail* on April 8, 1948, shows that the municipal government had been in consultation with Howard Dunington-Grubb even earlier.

> Plans which would make University Ave. one of the continent's finest thoroughfares were before a conference of Toronto's city planning board, works committee and board of control yesterday. With water-color sketches and pencil drawings, landscape artist H.B. Dunington Grubb showed what may be done with respect to the street. The conference, viewing the sketches favorably, approved in principle and directed the planning board to bring in more detailed plans and cost estimates.

The article went on to outline Howard's plan. "Cost would be about $200,000 or $300,000, the architect thought." Those figures made the planning board uneasy.

Alderman Allan Lamport said, "I'm in favor, but I'm thinking of the taxes. It's a lot of dough. If this can be done as a capital item, and the cost spread over a number of years, I'm agreeable; if not, put it off for a while."

Seven months later, Howard apparently was still hopeful that the University Avenue project would get underway. On November 16, 1948, he wrote a letter to the Toronto City Planning Board:

Sheridan Nurseries.

Howard Dunington-Grubb on University Avenue, Toronto, in 1964. University Avenue was the last major landscaping project undertaken by Dunington-Grubb & Stensson.

> University Avenue is almost the only wide street in Toronto. Connecting the Union Station with the Parliament Buildings, the University, and the north, its location makes it inevitably, not only a great traffic artery, but also a monumental street providing sites for many of the City's most important buildings. Adequately developed, it could become the most famous street in the Dominion of Canada.

Howard was optimistic, but there was still that matter of "a lot of dough." Dressing up University Avenue was going to be expensive, and the people who held the purse strings weren't about to loosen them. In fact, it would be another thirteen years before a design for the avenue went past the planning stage.

In October 1961, Dunington-Grubb and Stensson presented the board with an ambitious plan. From the point of view of the landscape designers, the civic squares and open spaces of a great metropolis should be treated with the emphasis on the architectural rather than the horticultural layout. For the mile-long stretch of University Avenue from Front Street to Queen's Park, they visualized a series of twelve sculptured islands, each with trees, grass, and hedges, but all dominated by sweeping paved areas where the public would be invited to stroll.

According to this plan, each of the islands would be distinctively different in design. The most impressive would be the one dominated by the South African War Memorial. It would have a pool with three fountains at one end, and a sunken central area at the other. The Sir Adam Beck Memorial would have a sunken court surrounded by beds raised on walls. There would also be a small pool. Other islands would have varying displays of tree boxes, pots, grass, and paving, with progressively ascending steps and raised garden beds.

Two striking proposals in the plan called for multicoloured pavements and underwater lighting for the pool and fountains. The monuments would be illuminated by already-existing light standards in the outer boulevards. The middle parts of the islands would be lit by recessed lighting fixtures in the interior walls. Seasonal Christmas lighting would make the avenue's islands sparkle. Air vents servicing the subway line below University Avenue were treated in such a way as to make them as inconspicuous as possible. A specially designed wall would protect vegetation and pedestrians' shoes from road splash, which was full of the calcium chloride used to melt ice.

When Howard put his design before the Toronto City Planning Board, he was sure that it would be accepted. Instead, as was reported in the *Globe & Mail*,

> Few proposals for beautifying Toronto have been kicked downstairs so speedily as a plan by a firm of landscape architects for improving the boulevard of University Avenue. In mid-October the City Planning Board rejected almost in its entirety a stylized and imaginative scheme by consultants Dunington-Grubb and Stensson in favour of an unspecified but starkly simple treatment along traditional lines.

The city planners and the landscape designers differed on a fundamental point: the planners wanted to see a design that emphasized a horticultural layout. Trees and grass, they said, were the city's principal amenities, even on such a distinctive route as the avenue. Metro Parks Commissioner Thomas Thompson said that it would be impossible to make an "arid street" like University Avenue into a Champs Élysées.

The city planners felt that the plan was inappropriate because its complexity and variety would detract from the unity of the avenue. They also thought it unlikely that University Avenue could be made attractive to pedestrians and that even if it could, heavy pedestrian movement between the islands would interfere with vehicular traffic. They requested that Howard and J.V. review their plan, and consider suggestions made by other officials and architects.

Of course, Howard was disappointed, but he revised his design. In December, the city planners approved a much simplified plan. On September 10, 1962, the Toronto *Daily Star* published a brief article.

> Metro is calling for tenders for a $500,000 parkway-promenade for the centre of University Ave. between College and Front Sts. Plans by architects Dunington-Grubb and Stensson provide for construction of 11 islands, including two pools and five fountains. The larger of the two pools will contain four fountains and will be located near the South African war memorial. The scheme is designed to brighten up the drab University Ave. median which has been torn up for subway construction for the past two years. Most of the islands will be circled by planter beds and small shrub hedges to protect the area from salt spray in the winter. Tenders will be received until Sept. 25. Construction is expected to begin before winter.

Howard and J.V. completed the University Avenue project within budget and without fanfare. There was no ribbon-cutting ceremony. The final trees and potted plants were installed amidst traffic and daily bustle. The opening of the new subway extension attracted much more media attention.

University Avenue did not become Toronto's Champs Élysées, and Howard's critics have called it one of his least successful designs. But he could hardly be blamed for the office buildings that made a utilitarian canyon of the avenue. He was proud of what he and J.V. had accomplished with a narrow space and limited funds. On January 25, 1965 — just a month before he died — Howard wrote a brief autobiographical entry for the CSLA files. The only one of his many projects that he mentioned in it was University Avenue.

In an interesting turn of events, at the time of this writing in 2012, the City of Toronto was tendering out the complete refurbishment of the four fountains in the South African War Memorial for an estimated $700,000. That sum is $200,000 more than the original cost of the entire University Avenue project!

THE BATTLE OF THE REFINERY

In 1941, Sheridan Nurseries became involved in a political war over one of the loveliest parts of Lake Ontario's Canadian shore. The "Checkerboard," as the area between Clarkson and Oakville was called, was made up of farms and beautiful rural residences. Sheridan Nurseries was one of the principal property owners.

Petroleum was essential to the Allied war effort, and the British-American Oil Company wanted to build a refinery at Clarkson. Oakville municipal council was in favour because the refinery would create jobs and attract industry. But many people, including Howard Dunington-Grubb, were hotly opposed. They formed the United Counties Property Owners' Protective Association. "I am co-operating with the organization formed to protest the establishment of the refinery," Howard told the *Toronto Star*.

Association members argued that there were many other places to put a refinery, such as the Toronto waterfront. They expressed concern about the pollution of air and water, and the effects the refinery would have on local agriculture and property values. "Once industrial plants creep into a district, they grow like measles," said lakeshore resident John Ross.

Howard and his fellow opponents brought American experts into the fray. An engineer and planning officer from New York stated that in the United States, a refinery was looked upon as a "nuisance industry" because of noise, smoke, and odours. The head of the U.S. National Society of City Planning said of refineries, "They are fit neighbours only for slaughter houses, tanneries, junk yards and garbage dumps." The chairman of a Chicago zoning committee added, "To permit an oil refinery to go close to a suburb of fine houses would be like inviting a skunk into a living room."

Throughout the spring, summer, and fall of 1941, the battle raged in community council meetings and in the newspapers. In spite of a valiant effort, the association couldn't prevail against Big Oil. In November, the oil tanks began to rise. A beautiful piece of countryside and Lake Ontario shoreline became a victim of the war. The refinery is still in operation across the road from the Mississauga Garden Centre.

CHAPTER 4

The People: Sheridan's Heroes of Horticulture

On February 19, 1988, Sheridan Nurseries celebrated its seventy-fifth anniversary with the unveiling of the *Sheridan Nurseries Story and Collection and Memorabilia* at Hamilton's Royal Botanical Gardens. Many people from across the spectrum of the horticultural industry, along with their families and employees, attended the event. Howard Stensson delivered the welcoming speech.

Howard acknowledged the vision of Howard and Lorrie Dunington-Grubb. He paid tribute to his father and the long years of hard work Herman had devoted to the company. He spoke about the difficult early years the Stensson family had experienced as they worked to build something out of next to nothing, while living in a house that was "a mere hovel by present day standards." Then Howard came to the part in which he addressed the contributions of the many people who had worked for Sheridan Nurseries over the years.

> Sheridan Nurseries has been fortunate over the years to have a great number of loyal employees. Some stayed all their working lives; others moved on to start their own businesses. We owe a debt to every one of them for their faithful service. Some of the names are noted in the exhibit displays. Others appear only in our payroll records. A few names that come to mind, in no particular order …

Howard then read off sixty-two names, including those of his siblings, and concluded by saying, "… and hundreds more."

Howard's list of names reveals the cosmopolitan mix that has been part of the company's employee make-up for the better part of a century. Among the many nationalities represented are the Danes, Japanese, Dutch, and Portuguese. In the same manner that cities and regions of North America experienced influxes of immigration due to social upheavals caused by war and economic crises, Sheridan Nurseries experienced waves of people from diverse ethnic backgrounds. It is an extraordinary story that continues to this day.

Certain names on Howard's list stand out. They were the people who began working with Herman in the early days, and stayed on for years. They helped lay the foundations not only of Sheridan Nurseries, but also of ornamental plant horticulture in Canada. They were the pioneers. Unfortunately, documented information on most of them is sketchy.

THE SHERIDAN PIONEERS

Charlie Barnard was from London, England. At the time that the First World War broke out, he was living in Oakville, and was probably employed on the estate of the financier Herbert Cox. Charlie enlisted with the Canadian Expeditionary Force on February 3, 1916. He gave his occupation as "chauffeur."

Charlie was gassed in France, and though he survived, he came home in poor health. In 1919, he was hired by Sheridan Nurseries. He did general work around the farm. When Sheridan finally bought a pair of trucks, Charlie became the driver of the larger one.

Driving was what Charlie did best, and in busy times he put in ten-hour work days. Roads then were not what they are now. When the QEW was first built, it wasn't a true freeway. The 401 wasn't built until after the Second World War. For much of the time that Charlie was driving for Sheridan, Montreal was an overnight trip along old Highway 2.

Originally from Nottingham, England, Bill Pilgrim also started working for Herman in 1915. Because horses were still used for heavy work, a man like Bill was necessary for daily operations. Bill knew horses.

Bill also answered Canada's call for volunteers. On February 18, 1916, fifteen days after Charlie Barnard went off to war, Bill enlisted in the CEF. He listed his occupation as "farmer" on his Attestation Paper. As a skilled horseman, Bill was placed in a cavalry unit.

The mechanization of warfare and the extensive use of trenches in the First World War had all but rendered cavalry obsolete, and most cavalrymen wound up crawling in the mud alongside infantrymen. But there were occasions

Sheridan Nurseries.

Workers loading trees into the first Sheridan truck.

Sheridan Nurseries.

Only a few of the men in this photo have been identified. Front row: far left, KK Buch; far right, Joseph Roberts; second from right, Charlie Barnard. Middle row: (standing behind Buch) Bob Nielsen. Back row: (standing in doorway behind Nielsen) C. Sorensen, (standing with back to the wall of the house, second from right) Ejnar Johnson.

Sheridan Nurseries.

In this illustration from the 1918–19 Sheridan Nurseries catalogue, women are hoeing. There was a shortage of male labourers because of the First World War.

in which mounted soldiers engaged in combat. Bill participated in one such clash, in which most of his companions were lost. After the war, Bill returned to the less dramatic but much safer job of driving teams for Sheridan Nurseries, and caring for the animals.

Frank Shepherd was yet another Englishman who was a Sheridan pioneer. Frank was the first manager of Highway Gardens, which later became the Southdown sales station, and today is known as the Sheridan Mississauga Garden Centre. The "garden centre" started out as a strawberry shed; strawberries being an important crop in the Clarkson area. Howard Stensson recalled that Frank always showed up for work wearing a shirt, collar, and tie. He also remembered going with Annie to the old house where Frank lived with his wife, and having tea with Mrs. Shepherd. Frank managed the Clarkson store well into the 1940s.

Walter Clark was one of Sheridan Nurseries' Canadian pioneers. He was a local man who earned what Howard Stensson described as a "hard scrabble living" on his farm. The site of the Clark farm eventually became the location of the Ford Motor Company's head office.

Walter had a wife and several small children to support, so even after Sheridan hired him, he continued to work his own farm. It must have been a tough routine, dividing his time between his fields and the nursery. But Howard remembered Walter as a reliable worker who became a foreman. His son William also worked for the nursery.

Over Sheridan Nurseries' first twenty-five years, other Canadians, both local or from distant communities, worked for Herman. Some stayed for only a short time; others for many years. Charles William Munn signed on in 1916, left, and then came back in 1936. Karl Kay and Stanley Osborne, who both started in 1934, left to fight in the Second World War.

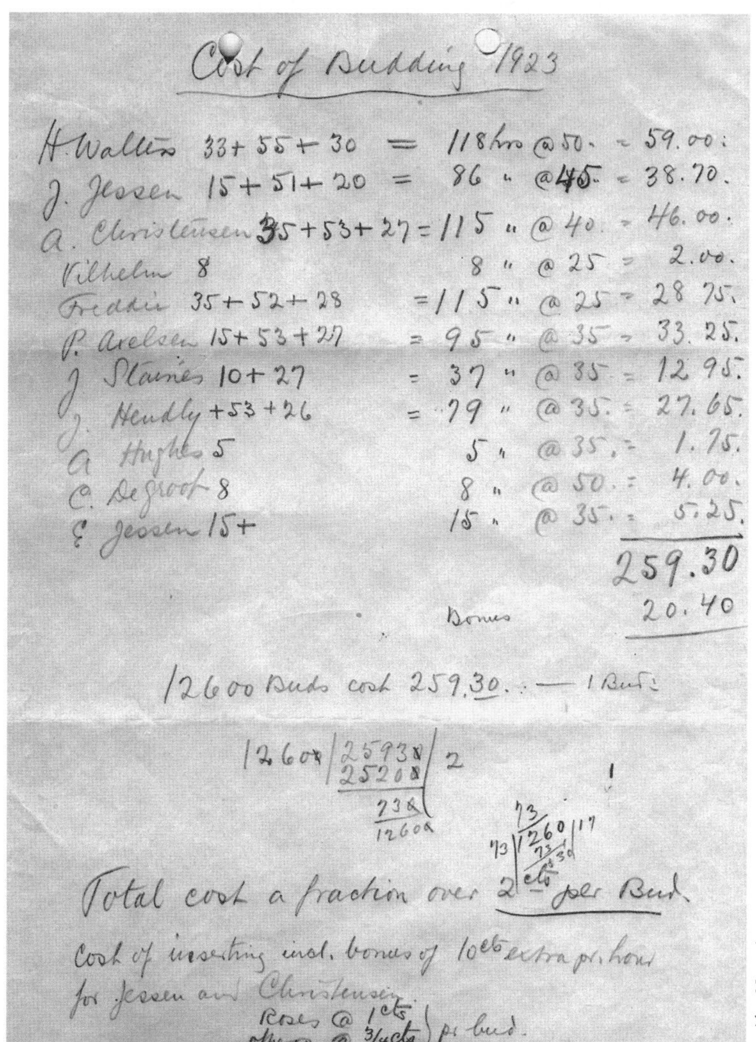

Cost of Budding 1923

H. Walters 33 + 55 + 30 = 118 hrs @ 50 = 59.00
J. Jessen 15 + 51 + 20 = 86 " @ 45 = 38.70
A. Christensen 35 + 53 + 27 = 115 " @ 40 = 46.00
Vilhelm 8 8 " @ 25 = 2.00
Freddie 35 + 52 + 28 = 115 " @ 25 = 28.75
P. Axelsen 15 + 53 + 27 = 95 " @ 35 = 33.25
J. Slaines 10 + 27 = 37 " @ 35 = 12.95
J. Hendly + 53 + 26 = 79 " @ 35 = 27.65
A. Hughes 5 5 " @ 35 = 1.75
C. Degroot 8 8 " @ 50 = 4.00
E. Jessen 15 + 15 " @ 35 = 5.25

259.30

Bonus 20.40

12600 Buds cost 259.30 — 1 Bud:

Total cost a fraction over 2 cts per Bud.

Cost of inserting incl. bonus of 10 cts extra per hour for Jessen and Christensen.
Roses @ 1 cts, others @ 3/4 cts per bud.

This 1923 ledger sheet shows an analysis of the cost of budding roses by employee.

Most of the Canadians who were employed at Sheridan in those years were general workers. Their names can still be seen on records in company archives: Allan Hall (1935); Vernon Wood, William Ripley, and Donald McCauley (1936); and Edgar Alfred Devlin (1937). However, James Arthur "Jimmy" Staines, who started in 1926, was a well-known nurseryman. So was Joseph Roberts, who was hired in 1937 and worked for Sheridan for many years.

Olive Mahon.

Accountant and office manager Harry Walters poses with Olive Mahon, one of Sheridan's wartime "Farmerettes," August 13, 1945.

Sheridan Nurseries.

Some of Sheridan's longest-serving employees on the stairway of the Sherway head office at the 1963 fiftieth anniversary celebration. L–R: Les Windmill, twenty-three years; C. Madsen, thirty-nine years; A. Girtssen, thirty-five years; K. Buch, thirty-nine years; Mitzi Iwasaki, twenty-two years; Charlie Barnard, forty-four years; Constant DeGroot, forty-one years; Chris Sorensen, thirty-three years.

John Turnbull came to Canada from England early in 1925. He joined Sheridan Nurseries in April of that year, working at the sales station at Bay and Bloor. In 1929 he moved to Montreal to manage the outlet on Greene Avenue in Westmount. He then opened the new location on Côte-des-Neiges in 1934. He moved again in 1956 to open the Côte-de-Liesse location near Dorval Airport. However, health problems forced John to retire. He moved back to the Clarkson area, and continued to work seasonally at the Sherway sales station until 1970.

Henry Baranachi started at Sheridan in 1927. He was a Canadian of Ukrainian background who came to Ontario with his parents, Harry and Lucy, and brother Peter to escape the dust bowl of Saskatchewan. Henry worked with Kehlet Kreston (KK) Buch's crew, hoeing fields of shrubs. Keeping the weeds at bay was back-breaking work. Weed killers didn't come into use until 1945. Peter might also have worked for Sheridan. At some point the family name was changed to Barnicke. That was the name Peter used when he joined the Royal Canadian Air Force during the Second World War. He was killed in 1944 at the age of nineteen. Henry's son Joseph became famous as J.J. Barnicke, the millionaire real-estate magnate.

Les Windmill came from England, and started working for the nursery on a temporary basis in 1939. He became part of the permanent staff in 1940. Les started in the field, but worked for many years in the shop, keeping the trucks, tractors, and other mechanical equipment in good repair. He also repaired household appliances for friends. Les retired in 1981, and at that time he was "head of the garage."

For years Les supervised the manufacture of chromestones in Sheridan's Oakville facilities. Chromestone paving was introduced in 1950 as an inexpensive alternative to natural quarried flagstone. Sheridan manufactured them as a means of keeping field crews employed during the winter months. For a few years they were also made in Montreal. They were made in greased steel pans from cement, gravel, and water, and came in as many as fifteen different colours. The were 1 and 3/8 of an inch thick, and weighed sixteen pounds per square foot. Four patterns, including one with a centennial symbol, were introduced in 1967. By the early 1970s, only two patterns,

Sheridan Nurseries.

Four examples of patterns for chromestone including 1967 Centennial symbol.

Sheridan Nurseries.

Chromestone produced in Sheridan Nurseries' Oakville packing shed

pebbled and smooth, and one colour, Desert Buff, were available. The 1977 Sheridan catalogue saw the first reference to the new KNR-Durastone Interlocking Paving Stones, smaller and much easier to handle, ending over twenty-five years of production at Sheridan Nurseries.

THE DANES: WHY EJNAR FAERGE FELT RIGHT AT HOME

In 1953, Ejnar Faerge, who had recently arrived in Canada from Denmark, went to Sheridan Nurseries in search of a job. The first person he saw on the property was a man who

Sheridan Nurseries.

Sheridan Nurseries garden at the 1968 Garden Club of Toronto show at the O'Keefe Centre (now the Sony Centre).

was polishing a car. Ejnar didn't speak any English. Not knowing what else to do, he spoke to the man in Danish. To his surprise, the man answered him in Danish. By happy coincidence, Ejnar had run into Viggo Pedersen, a fellow Dane. Ejnar was hired, and went on to open up the first fields at Glen Williams. He stayed with Sheridan until 1960.

It wasn't by mere coincidence that Ejnar had met a fellow Dane at Sheridan. In the history of Sheridan Nurseries, Herman Stensson's trip to Europe in 1923–24 was a milestone. Herman went to Denmark in search of qualified nurserymen to help him turn Howard and Lorrie Dunington-Grubb's patch of ground into a real nursery. Herman's journey resulted in the first "wave" of people from specific ethnic backgrounds who made their mark on Sheridan Nurseries; the Danes.

KK Buch was a Danish nurseryman who had been planning to go to Argentina to work on a cattle ranch when he met Herman Stensson. He came to Canada in 1924, intending to work for Sheridan for a year before continuing on to South America. KK stayed with Sheridan for more than fifty years. Howard Stensson recalled him as "a big, strong fella."

Ejnar Faerge.

Early post–Second World War tractors used on the Sheridan Nurseries farms.

Sheridan Nurseries.

Kehlet (KK) Buch, pictured here in 1965, came from Denmark to work for Sheridan for a year, and stayed with the nursery for more than fifty years.

KK became one of Sheridan's best foremen, and was often in charge of the hoeing gangs, the teams of horses, and later the tractors and planting equipment. He died in 1984.

KK Buch led the vanguard of Danes who came to Sheridan. Some of them, like C. Sigurd Christenson and his brother Aage, who came in 1926, were expert nurserymen. But not all came from nursery-related backgrounds. Jens "Pop" Madsen, for example, had been a fisherman before he left Denmark in 1929 to come to Canada. But he learned the nursery trade well enough to become a top Sheridan foreman. He was also a good carpenter who looked after the houses and spent the winter months making shipping boxes. Jens's old fishing skills came in handy when he made the goal nets for the soccer matches in which Sheridan teams competed. He retired in the late 1960s.

Many of the Danes, like Chris Larson, John Martin Juul, Chris Mickleson, Max Sorensen, and Kjelb Nielsen, stayed with Sheridan for only a few years and then went back to Denmark. A few, such as Henry Fuglesang, worked for Sheridan for a while and then went on to start their own nursery businesses. Henry must have known that one day he would be a businessman, because even when he worked in the fields he wore a collar and tie. Then there were those who stayed on for years.

Hans Gertsen joined Sheridan in 1928 and worked in the perennial department. He retired in 1974. Jens Christian Jensen was hired in 1927. He drove machinery, and stayed with Sheridan all his life.

Jens Pedersen joined Sheridan in 1931 and worked year-round for the nursery until 1946 when he left to establish Rose Arbour Nurseries on Royal Windsor Drive near Sheridan Nurseries. His wife Joan, "Pop" Madsen's daughter, also worked seasonally during the Second World War. Their son Paul worked for Sheridan as a student.

Anders (Chris) Sorensen started in 1934 and became the manager of the Ryrie farm on the Lakeshore in Oakville. Chris lived in a house on Sheridan property, and when the

Sheridan Nurseries Limited

NAME G. Sparre WEEK ENDING Dec. 3th 41

		Hours
Thurs.	Making changes back of Palisstation	9
Fri.	Planting Box in Rosegarden	9
Sat.	" " "	4
Mon.	Mixed work	9
Tues.	Digging Orders 5 other work 4	9
Wed.	" " 2 " " 7	9
Thurs.	Making changes back of Palisstation	9
Fri.	Digging Orders 2 levling Border 7	9
Sat.	" " 2 " " 4	6
Mon.	Levling and planting Borders	9
Tues.	" Borders 5 Digging Orders 4	9
Wed.	Digging and levling Borders	9
	TOTAL	100

Sheridan Nurseries.

Sheridan employee Gus Sparre's worksheet, dated December 3, 1941, lists the jobs he did and the hours he put in. Sparre's worksheet was chosen for an illustration because it was one of the few with legible handwriting.

property was sold, the company decided to move the house to another Sheridan location so Chris would still have his home. They accomplished the not-so-easy task of relocating the house, only to learn after the job was done that they had to have a permit. Sheridan had to pay $75 after the fact. Unfortunately, Chris was killed while crossing Royal Windsor Drive when he was in his nineties.

Kristian Westergaard joined Sheridan in 1931 and drove trucks for many years. His son-in-law eventually started a nursery in Ballinafad, Ontario. Ejnar Johnson was another Dane whom Howard remembered as a "big, strong guy." He came to Sheridan in 1928 and stayed for many years, usually working with the digging gangs.

Gustave Sparre was one of the nurserymen Herman recruited in 1924. At first he worked for Sheridan Nurseries only during the summer. The rest of the year he was employed as a gardener at the George Allan estate in Hamilton.

Bertha Sparre.

Trucks like this one were Sheridan's workhorses, delivering plants across southern Ontario and into Quebec.

In 1929, Gus became a full-time Sheridan employee for $30 a week and free use of a cottage. Herman made him foreman of Sheridan's Highway Garden in Clarkson. He kept that position for fourteen years.

Gus had a special talent for developing new plants, particularly chrysanthemums. This proved to be of great importance to Sheridan Nurseries. Among the successful varieties Gus developed were Karen Stensson, Mrs. Dunington-Grubb, and Mrs. E. Sparre. Gus signed an agreement with Wayside Gardens in the United States for the American rights to some of the Sheridan mums, including one that they renamed Madame Chiang Kai Shek and released in their 1945 catalogue.

In a letter dated October 19, 1938, in which he addressed Gus as "My dear Sparre," Howard Dunington-Grubb wrote, "I discussed the matter of your new Chrysanthemums yesterday with Mr. Stensson and suggested to him that we ought to give up most of the old varieties we have been growing and concentrate largely on your new varieties as I have never seen anything quite like them. I told him that you ought to be properly paid for the wonderful work you have done."

The death of Gus's wife in 1939 left him a widower with a daughter, Bertha, to raise. Bertha would have fond memories of her childhood years at the cottage in Clarkson. She swam and tobogganed with the Stensson kids, and sometimes worked at the nursery, doing such jobs as tying roses. She found that picking Japanese yew fruit at McMaster University and various estates was "a cold and gooey job, but necessary." Bertha was especially proud when her schoolmates were given tours of the nursery.

Sheridan Nurseries.

Gus Sparre and his daughter Bertha. Gus developed the extensive range of hardy garden chrysanthemums for Sheridan Nurseries in the 1930s and 1940s. Bertha remembers working during the summer months for Sheridan Nurseries during the Second World War and having to go to McMaster University to collect scarce Japanese yew seeds that could not be imported from Japan at that time.

Gus left Sheridan Nurseries in 1943 to work for Clarkson Greenhouses. He retired in 1969 and died in 1972.

Thomas Frank grew up on a farm in Denmark. After the Second World War he worked for several years in a greenhouse in Norway. In 1953, he travelled to Toronto where he saw a job ad for Sheridan Nurseries in Union Station. Thomas took a bus to Sheridan, and the next day he was pulling bare-root roses with KK Buch's crew.

Over the next few years, Thomas became familiar with many nursery duties, from making softwood cuttings to making chromestones. He worked in the shipping department for a while, and then in 1958 he took over as foreman of KK Buch's digging crew. When Sheridan Nurseries started the farm at Glen Williams, Thomas and his men were kept busy both there and Oakville, sometimes working at night in the beams of the headlights on their bus.

In 1960 Thomas married a Swedish girl named Luville (Susie) Karlson. For the first year of their marriage, Susie cooked for sixteen people living in the Clarkson bunkhouse. Thomas moved to the Glen Williams farm in 1986, but he commuted back to Oakville to oversee the last year of Sheridan's operations there. On January 1, 1988, he became the manager at Glen Williams. In 1990 he was made field crop manager at the Glen. Thomas retired in 1995.

THE JAPANESE: FROM INTERNMENT CAMPS TO CAREERS

In December of 1941, the armed forces of Imperial Japan attacked the American naval base at Pearl Harbor, Hawaii,

April 30, 1943

Mr. G.E. Trueman,
The British Columbia Security Commission,
~~330 Bay Street~~, Toronto

Dear Mr. Trueman:

We list herewith, the names and registration numbers of the Japanese now employed by The Sheridan Nurseries Limited:

Name	Registration Number	Previous Occupation
Akase, Misao	05175	Student
Akiyama, Kaye	00959	Hardware store
Inamoto, Tsugio	09343	Carpenter
Inouye, Kazuyoshi	10214	Farm
Iwasaki, Mitsuhiko	09616	Paper Mill
Kagayama, Shinobu	09508	Mill hand
Kato, Kazud	09236	Mill
Kimura, Masajiro	01699	Gardener
Kimura, Katsuko	04429	Housewife
Koyonaga, Kitaji	06470	Mill
Kobayashi, Seitaro	10030	Pulp mill
Kobayashi, Toyojiro	00738	Salesman
Kondo, Hisao	05988	Fruit Store
Kondo, Kinue	01610	Housewife
Koyanagi, Tadatoshi	03989	Fisherman
Maede, Shizuo	12147	Fisherman
Nagai, Susumu	09435	Gardener
Nakata, Takeo	12071	Fisherman
Negoro, Hiroshi	02345	Fisherman
Nishino, Bob T.	01600	Elevator
Uchimaru, Iwao	13535	Mill
Wakisaka, Minoru	11277	Mill Hotel

Yours very truly,

KVS/LS

Nursery Manager

Sheridan Nurseries.

Letter from Sheridan Nurseries to the British Columbia Security Commission, listing the names of ethnic Japanese employees. Many Canadians of Japanese background who were unjustly interned during the Second World War, came to work for Sheridan Nurseries.

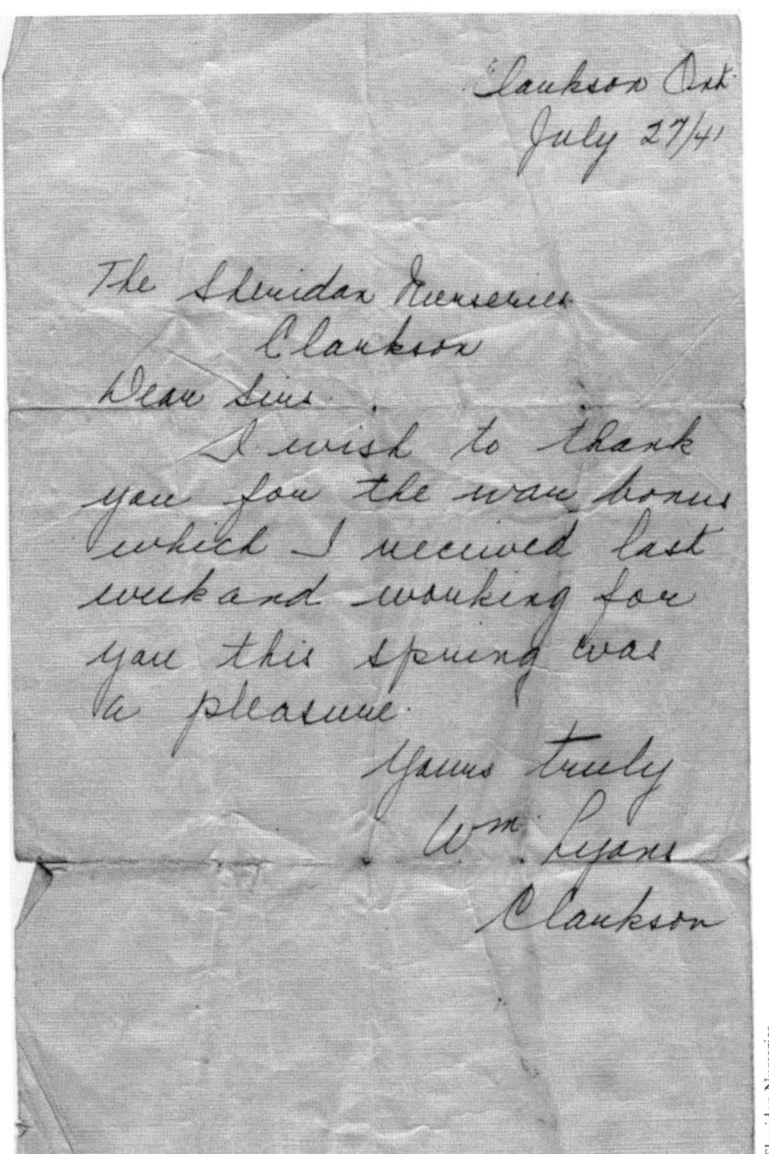

Clarkson Ont.
July 27/41

The Sheridan Nurseries
Clarkson

Dear Sirs

I wish to thank you for the war bonus which I received last weekand working for you this spring was a pleasure.

Yours truly
Wm. Lyons
Clarkson

Sheridan Nurseries.

Letter from employee, dated July 27, 1941, expressing gratitude for bonus pay during war years.

and the British colony of Hong Kong. Two thousand Canadian soldiers who had been sent to defend Hong Kong were killed or became prisoners of war. The Canadian government imposed the War Measures Act, and came down hard on British Columbia's Japanese community. Most of these people were naturalized Canadian citizens or had been born in Canada. Nonetheless, there was fear that they would be spies or saboteurs.

Schools in the Japanese community were closed. A dusk-to-dawn curfew was imposed. Anyone caught outside after dark without a permit would be arrested. The RCMP confiscated boats, cars, radios, cameras, homes, and businesses. Then came the evacuation of all able-bodied Japanese males between the ages of eighteen and forty-five to inland internment camps. Eventually, many wives and children were sent to join the men.

Most of the internment camps were in fact labour camps. The inmates were used for roadwork and agricultural work. Living conditions were disgraceful. The two worst were Petawawa and Angler in Ontario. These camps were reserved for men who had allegedly resisted evacuation. They were classified as prisoner of war camps.

Mitzi Iwasaki was born in Vancouver to Japanese immigrants on July 8, 1920. His father and an older brother were fishermen. At the time of the attack on Pearl Harbor, Mitzi was working in a paper mill in Ocean Falls. When the evacuation order came, Mitzi's father was ill and was allowed to remain in Vancouver with his wife. Mitzi was granted permission to stay with them. However, one morning Mitzi made the mistake of going outside before dawn. He was arrested by the RCMP because he didn't have a permit.

Mitzi was sent to Angler, an isolated location on the north shore of Lake Superior. His parents had no idea where he was. To escape the boredom of camp life, Mitzi would go

THE SHERIDAN NURSERIES LIMITED

NURSERY DEPARTMENT PAYROLL............WEEK ENDING August 25, 1943

NAME	N. D. T.					OVERTIME		EARNINGS	Deductions N. D. T.	NET PAYMENT	REMARKS
	MSW	Dp.	%	Time	Rate	Hours	Rate				
C. De Groot								72.00	5.25	66.75	
S. Christensen						6	.75	67.50	.80	66.70	
K. Buch								58.00	1.00	57.00	
H. Walters								55.00	8.20	46.80	
W. Pilgrim								60.00	3.07	56.93	
F. Shepperd								52.00	2.80	49.20	
R. Holliday								46.00	.90	45.10	
L. Stensson								40.00	6.80	33.20	
H. Fuglsang				100	.56			56.00	.80	55.20	
C. Madsen				100	.54			54.00	2.50	51.50	
J. Pedersen				90				48.60	.60	48.00	
J. Herod Jr.				100		2	.75	55.50	.40	55.10	
W. Clark				91		1	.75	49.89	.60	49.29	
C. Sorenson				100	.50			50.00	10.50	39.50	
W. Jalowcza				91				45.50	8.60	36.90	
L. Windmill				97	.48	4½	.72	49.80	.65	49.15	
C. Barnard				100		3		50.16	.10	50.06	
M. Werstuck				95				45.60	8.60	37.00	
N. Jensen				58				27.84	1.35	26.49	
H. Baranachi				59	.46			27.14		27.14	
P. Smith				102				46.92		46.92	
A. McNeillie				100				46.00	6.96	39.04	
J. Kuzyk				72				33.12		33.12	
J. Herod				100	.44			44.00	.28	43.72	
H. Anderson				95				41.80		41.80	
M. Faint				95				41.80		41.80	
L. Homer				41	.34			13.94		13.94	
Joan Pedersen				62				21.08		21.08	
W. Savage				100				34.00		34.00 ?	# 9177 Cancelled see 9188
N. Christensen				77	.28	2	.42	22.40		22.40	
G. Buch				93½				26.18		26.18	
R. Moodie				21				5.88		5.88	
M[illegible]een Barnard				106	.26			27.56		27.56	
D. Barnard				103				26.78		26.78	
Mona Barnard				107				27.82		27.82	
P. Snider				73				18.98		18.98	
M. Kimura				98½	.24			23.64		23.64	
B. McKettrick				60				14.40		14.40	
T. Crossman				62				14.88		14.88	
H. Groocock				71				17.04		17.04	
R. Crossman				71				17.04		17.04	
D. Crossman				62				14.88		14.88	
P. Golding				69				16.56		16.56	
J. Schreiber				55				13.20		13.20	
J. Kuzyk, bonus				304	.06	plus	$4.	22.24	1.56	20.68	
J. Bronee, bonus								14.00		14.00	
								$1656.67	$72.32	$1584.35	

General Distribution: Hoeing and weeding, scuffling, harvesting, budding roses, pruning, planting perennials, tearing down old pergola and fixing dining hall at Brown's Line for men, spreading manure, digging orders and trucking
$1656.67

Sheridan Nurseries.

Sample of a weekly payroll statement, dated August 25, 1943, showing hours worked and hourly rate.

ice-fishing. This also provided a supplement to the inmates' insufficient food rations.

Mitzi had been in the camp for about a year when the opportunity came for him to escape the cold and dreary North Superior Shore and go to work for Sheridan Nurseries in the much more hospitable climate of southern Ontario. Because of the war, there was a labour shortage. One account of the story says that the nursery asked the federal government for farm help. Another claims that the government asked Sheridan to hire Japanese internment-camp inmates. Whatever the case, Mitzi was with a group of twenty-two men and women who were sent from Angler to Sheridan.

Lois Stensson was working in the office when she learned the Japanese workers were coming. Writing about it in later years, she said, "Before their arrival, I had to get a bunkhouse outfitted for them. They required beds, linens, furniture, kitchen utensils, food, etc., and last but not least, a sauna! I remember the day they arrived I phoned Clarkson General Store and ordered a *ton* of rice. They thought we had gone crazy."

PETTY CASH ACCOUNT FOR THE WEEK ENDING MARCH 10, 1943

Special Delivery (office)	.10	
Martin Transport	.99	
J.V.S. Gas	3.15	
125 One cent stamps	1.25	
100 Three cent stamps	3.00	
Dodge II, 3 gas	.98	
Building Permit, Bunk House	1.00	
Cat's food (9 of them)	.50	
'phone call, Oakville	.20	
2 Record Books, A. Guild	.50	
		$11.67
Dr. E.G. Vernon account ([illegible])	15.50	
Bank charges, January	4.95	
" " February	4.00	
Finlay Fish & Storage Co. ([illegible])	41.25	
J.E. Sinclair, gas	12.60	
Oakville Hardware	19.12	
Oil Controller Coupons	4.10	
Jerry's Garage	17.20	
Dominion Hardware	9.25	
Trafalgar Public Utilities [illegible]	2.72	
		$130.69
		$142.36

Sheridan Nurseries.

Petty cash accounting sheet, March 10, 1943. Note the entry for cat food. Cats in the barn kept the mouse population in check.

The Japanese arrived on April 19, 1943. They found living conditions at Sheridan a great improvement over what they'd experienced at Angler. Their quarters, in a renovated farmhouse known as the Hammond House, were clean and comfortable. They had good meals. Moreover, they were paid forty cents an hour.

Mitzi Iwasaki entered Sheridan Nurseries company history as a name on a list, with a government registration number: 09616. Beside that, his occupation was listed as "Paper Mill." It's interesting to note that in that original group of twenty-two Japanese workers, only two had their occupations listed as "gardener," and one as "farm." Most of the others were fishermen or mill hands. Katsuko Kimura and Kinue Kondo were each listed as "Housewife." There were in addition a student, a hardware store worker, a carpenter, a salesman, a fruit store employee, and an elevator operator.

At the time, Mitzi could hardly have imagined that his unfortunate arrest in Vancouver would result in a lifetime career with a nursery in Ontario. He began in the shipping area, working under the supervision of Sigurd Christensen. Mitzi so impressed management with his good work and reliability that when Christensen retired, he was made head shipper.

For many years, Mitzi — or "Curly," as he was known to fellow employees — made out the morning work sheets for the truck drivers. He was also responsible for taking stock of the entire growing inventory. He became an expert on plants, and

Sheridan Nurseries.

J.V. Stensson and Lois Stensson taking inventory.

could identify many species from a distance of a hundred yards. However, as a stock-taker in the field, he ran into problems when big-tree-digging machinery was brought into operation. He occasionally fell into the holes they made.

Ironically, Mitzi's misfortune in Vancouver led him to the woman he would marry. The romance came about almost by accident. The Japanese bunkhouse needed a cook. The job went to a married couple named Morikawa. They had a sixteen-year-old daughter named Mary who soon caught Mitzi's attention. They were married in 1953.

Years later, Mary recalled that the Japanese were well received by the other Sheridan workers, who generally regarded them just as fellow employees. She said many Japanese internees worked at Sheridan, but only a few like her husband stayed on after the war. Most of the others left for Toronto.

Mitzi worked for Sheridan Nurseries for forty-five years. Mary worked many of the summers, tying roses. Mitzi was well liked by the other Sheridan employees, and at Sheridan Nurseries social functions his bartending skills made him even more popular. Anybody who ever attended a Sheridan party knew about the famous punch he created, which at Sheridan was affectionately called the "velvet hammer."

Mitzi wasn't afraid to speak his mind about work-related matters. He once confronted Howard Stensson about the lack of machinery in the shipping department, where most of the labour was manual. Mitzi actually said he was quitting. There is no official record of the conversation between Mitzi and Howard, but Sheridan did become a leader in modernizing the industry.

Mitzi became close friends with many colleagues, including Jim Herod. Mitzi and Jim would go ice-fishing off Fox Island

Sheridan Nurseries

The Japanese bunkhouse. The accommodations Sheridan Nurseries provided for Japanese-Canadian workers was an improvement over what some of them had experienced in internment camps.

in Lake Simcoe, sometimes accompanied by Howard Stensson. As he and his fishing buddies sat in a hut on the Lake Simcoe ice, Mitzi might well have recalled the days when he fished through the Lake Superior ice, within sight of the guards at Angler.

THE JAPANESE LEGACY

Dozens more people of Japanese background came to work at Sheridan Nurseries. Not all of them arrived by way of the internment camps. Many came in the postwar years, because they had heard it was a good place to work, free of the prejudices that had existed in other places even before the war.

Jessie Ebata was born in 1943 in the internment camp at Slocan, British Columbia. Her parents, Gene and Chiyoko, moved to Oakville in 1946. Jessie recalled how her father worked for Sheridan for forty-five years, until he retired in 1991 at the age of eighty-one. He operated a planting machine, and according to Jessie, was very good at it. "The rows were very straight," she said. In fact, everyone at Sheridan used to remark on the rows that were as straight as an arrow without any guidance except a steady hand. Before the coming of tractors, Gene also worked with horses at the Anderson farm, under the supervision of Ken Dickison. Gene eventually graduated to tractors. Jessie's mother was a Sheridan employee, too. Jessie herself worked at the nursery during the summers.

Takeo Nakata, a former fisherman, arrived at Sheridan Nurseries with Mitzi Iwasaki. He worked primarily in the propagation and perennial departments. Tak stayed with Sheridan for forty years, until his retirement in 1982. His colleague Mike Ujihara worked in the same department from 1942 until 1986.

Isamu (Sam) Kayama was born in Prince Rupert, British Columbia, in 1922. He arrived at Sheridan with his family in 1947. Sam had been working as a carpenter's apprentice for $5 a week. He could hardly believe it when he was told he'd be paid fifty-eight cents an hour at Sheridan.

Sam's brother Akira (Harry) was already with Sheridan. He'd started the previous year after the British Columbia lumber mill where he'd been employed burned down. He worked, as he later put it, "at just about everything"; digging, cutting, and eventually driving. Harry would recall the poker games that were the nightly pastime in the Japanese bunkhouse. He left Sheridan after just a few years.

Sam worked as a shipper and a carpenter until his retirement in 1987. One of his first carpentry jobs was to add a room to a building at the Clarkson Sales Station known as the Old Pig Pen. In 1949, he and Jack Scott, Chris Stensson's father-in-law, built Chris's house on the Town Line in Sheridan.

Sam was an expert carpenter. It was said that if he built your kitchen cabinets, you could be sure the drawers wouldn't squeak. Sam helped build, repair, and modify many of Sheridan Nurseries' buildings, including the "Apartments" at Sheridan. These residential units were home to many Sheridan employees and their families over the years. When Sheridan Nurseries relocated its headquarters to Glen Williams, near Georgetown, Sam worked on the head office and lunch room. He constructed many Sheridan Nurseries exhibits for the Canadian National Exhibition, as well as for flower shows and trade shows such as Landscape Ontario.

J.V. Stensson hired Sam's father Yotaro (known at the nursery as "Y"), his mother Susuma, and his brother Hiroshi (Walter). They lived for many years in accommodations Sam had built at the Mississauga Garden Centre, next door to the home of Sam and his wife Mary. Mary Kayama never worked for Sheridan, but with her friend Mary Iwasaki, during an interview she recalled the many good years she'd had there with Sam, and reflected on the Japanese legacy that had helped to shape the company.

Mike Ujihara was another Japanese Canadian who stayed with Sheridan for his entire career. He became skilled

Sheridan Nurseries.

Gene Ebata, shown here plowing with a horse, was noted for his perfectly straight furrows.

SPECIAL NOTICE

Owing to wartime conditions, it is essential that this box be used again.

OPEN CAREFULLY,

by undoing the wire twists and gently prying the two nails holding centre of lid. Return

IN GOOD CONDITION

for full credit, freight collect to:

The Sheridan Nurseries Ltd.

CLARKSON, ONTARIO

Sheridan Nurseries.

During the Second World War, many things were in short supply, including the materials needed to make boxes. This notice offers the customer credit for returning the box in good condition.

Kayama Family.

Boxed plants being loaded for shipment. Sam Kayama is at lower right.

Kayama Family.

Mike Ujihara wrapping bare root trees for shipment.

Kayama Family.

First two men unidentified, then Mike Ujihara and Jens "Pop" Madsen.

Sheridan Nurseries.

L–R: Ben deBoer, Fred Stensson, Lou Sato, and Jim Herod mark Sheridan's fiftieth anniversary in 1963.

at propagation and was a fixture in the "boiler room" where he would be seen sitting on a wooden chair (made by Sam Kayama) cushioned by a bundle of burlap. He was never without his budding knife and an unfiltered cigarette! Mike retired in 1985 at the age of seventy-five.

Seizu (Lou) and Takeo (Kim) Sato came to Sheridan Nurseries by a somewhat different route. Before the war, Kim was living with her parents and brothers in British Columbia. She first met Lou Sato there. When she was about sixteen, she moved with her family to the Toronto area. Several years would pass before she saw Lou again.

The war came, and with it the spectre of forced relocation. Kim's parents were going to return to Japan, while she stayed in Canada with an aunt. However, changing circumstances allowed her mother and father to remain in Canada.

While her parents worked on a farm, Kim went to school and completed grade twelve. Then she went looking for work. At that time it was almost impossible for Japanese-Canadians to find good jobs. Kim took whatever she could get, no matter how difficult.

After the war, Lou moved to Ontario. He must have kept in touch with members of Kim's family, because he began visiting her brothers. Lou and Kim renewed the relationship that had begun in British Columbia. They were married in 1953. Lou found a job with Sheridan Nurseries. He eventually became the manager of the Toronto Garden Centre, and later of the Unionville store.

Kim stayed home to raise their children, but when they were grown, she worked in the store with Lou. They were a team for twenty-two years. Even after retirement, Kim stayed on for five more years as part-time help at Unionville.

During the war and the postwar period, anti-Japanese sentiments ran high in many Canadian communities. However, the Japanese-Canadians at Sheridan Nurseries experienced relatively little hostility from local residents. The neighbours recognized them as ordinary people who had been unfortunate victims of war.

Every New Year's Eve and Day, it seemed that the Japanese would rotate an open house, and the Stensson family members were always included on the guest list. The Japanese were always considered part of the "family," and vice versa. It was here that the Stenssons were introduced to such delicacies as squid, eel, and fried grasshoppers!

THE PORTUGUESE: THE AZORIAN CONNECTION

The Azores Archipelago is a province of Portugal. Agriculture is the principal economic activity of these islands. Since 1952, about six hundred people from the Azores have worked for Sheridan Nurseries. The first two were Jose Augusto Fria and Manuel Vargas. The third was Manuel Sobrinho, who was sixteen when he arrived in Canada in 1956. As Manuel explains it:

> A few thousand Azorians came to Canada because Canadian farmers needed farm hands. Many of them went to Quebec, including my brother-in-law, but the wages there were low. Some went to the railroad, some went to the bush for the lumber, and some for Leaver Mushrooms, and then some to Sheridan Nurseries. Sheridan Nurseries was quite

> popular at that time. My brother-in-law had a friend that started a few months before, and then he came, and soon after sponsored me.

Manuel started in the fields, digging euonymus while there was still snow on the ground. "You can imagine. My fingers felt like they were falling off." After that numbing experience, Manuel moved on to a wide range of other tasks, and a long, commendable career with Sheridan Nurseries.

The first lightweight, asbestos-cement containers were imported from Switzerland in 1957. In 1960, arrangements were made with Reff Brothers for their manufacture in Canada.

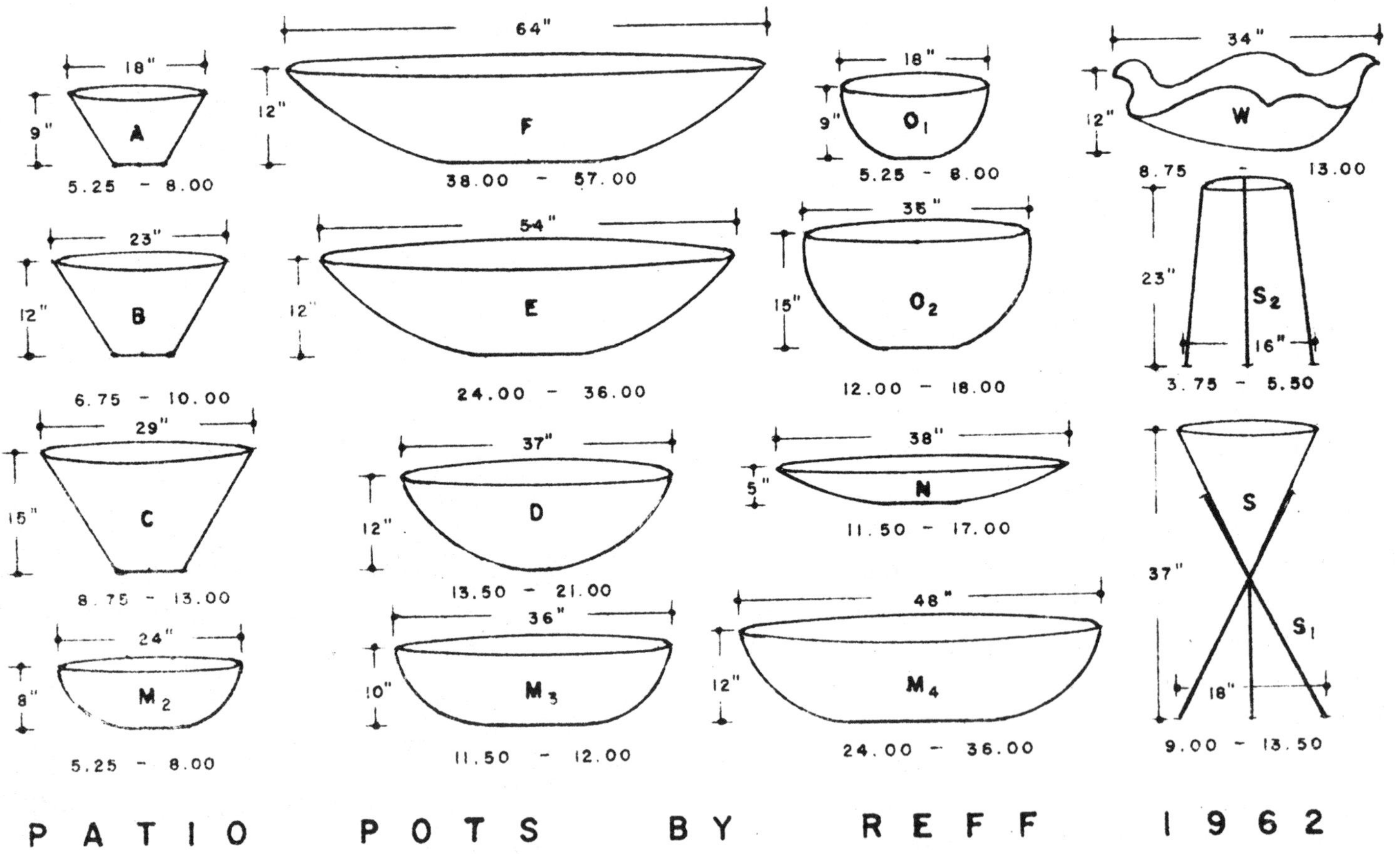

Sheridan Nurseries.

Drawings used in catalogues to show the many shapes and designs of patio pots.

In 1965, Sheridan purchased the machinery, moulds, and technological know-how from Reff. Sheridan began making the nursery's own pots. Manuel took over direction of pot-making, and in the winter of 1965–66, his crew made 3,500 of them. The pot-making operation was discontinued in the 1970s.

In 1997, Manuel was promoted to vice-president of nursery sales. He celebrated his fiftieth anniversary with Sheridan in 2006, becoming the third member of the Sheridan family to reach that milestone, after Howard Dunington-Grubb and Albert Brown. Manuel has now worked for Sheridan Nurseries longer than any other person.

Raul Cordiero was twenty-two years old when he came to Canada from the Azores in 1956. In the spring of 1957 he went to work for Sheridan Nurseries. His first task was digging hemlocks on the Oakville farm.

Joerg Leiss observed that Raul was a hard worker and a quick learner. A perfectionist like Joerg wasn't easily impressed, so it was certainly a mark in Raul's favour when Joerg asked Constant DeGroot to transfer him to his own crew. Raul did a variety of jobs for Joerg, and was soon promoted to foreman. He became involved in production-oriented work such as field digging, packing roses, the propagation of shrubs and evergreens, grafting, and budding. Raul supervised work crews, and during the winter he made chromestones and cut burlap. Raul worked in the container department for fifteen years, while at the same time he was involved in propagation and perennial growing.

In 1987 and 1988, the Oakville farm had been sold for development and was winding down its operation. The propagation unit was being moved to the new farm at Norval, which was purchased specifically to house the department. Raul had shown such talent at propagation, that he was sent there to help the new production manager, Fraser Hancock, get the farm up and running.

Jose "Joe" De Lima came to Canada on April 7, 1956, with several other Azorians, and started work on April 11 at the Oakville farm. Joe's first job was working in the fields with Joerg Leiss's crew "digging B&B" [evergreens or shrubs with a ball of soil wrapped in burlap]. He later went to the shipping department and worked there until 1987 when Sheridan Nurseries moved to Glen Williams.

Joe continued to work in the shipping department until his retirement in November 1999. He loved plants, and in

Sheridan Nurseries.

Long-time Sheridan employees L–R: Herman Maiato, Joe Lima, Ronald Campbell, Mitzi Iwasaki, Thomas Frank.

his off-hours he would earn extra money by working in private gardens. Manuel Sobrinho recalls spending many hours working alongside Joe in other people's gardens on weekends and evenings. Most of the money they made from moonlighting went to their families in the Azores. By the time Joe retired, he'd put in forty-three years with Sheridan. Joe died in 2009.

Tony Viana was a seventeen-year-old fisherman when he came to Canada in 1963. By that time the Portuguese connection at Sheridan Nurseries was well established. He came directly to Ontario, and began making cuttings at the Oakville farm the day after his arrival.

Tony worked for a long time with Thomas Frank's digging crew. Then for six years he was a shipper for Mitzi Iwasaki. There, Tony worked with Les Windmill, who was in charge of the Sheridan garage, and mechanic Bjarne Henanger. Thanks to Bjarne's encouragement, Tony obtained his mechanic's licence.

Tony was a mechanic, welder, plumber, and carpenter all in one. He did everything from irrigation to roofing, and worked at most of Sheridan's locations at one time or another. He was always ready to answer an emergency call, even if it came at night or on the weekend or a holiday. Tony retired in September 2011, after forty-seven years with Sheridan.

The Maiato family was Sheridan's largest family group. Herman Maiato came to Canada from the Azores in 1960 and started with Sheridan Nurseries in 1966. In 2012, he completed forty-six years with Sheridan. He first worked in the fields in Oakville, then in the shipping department. He moved to Glen Williams when Oakville was closed down, continuing to work in shipping and also driving trucks when there was a shortage of drivers. After forty-six years, Herman Maiato is still working for Sheridan.

Other Maiato brothers who worked for Sheridan Nurseries included Gill, a truck driver who started in Oakville and then moved to Glen Williams. He was with Sheridan for twenty-one years. Edward worked in Oakville and the Mississauga Garden Centre for twenty-five years. Manuel worked in Oakville for one year, in 1969, and Antonio worked for Sheridan's Landscape department in Etobicoke for two years starting in 1969. Joe worked in Oakville for eighteen years, followed by sixteen years at the Mississauga Garden Centre.

Two sisters, Fernanda and Esperanca, worked in Oakville, as did their husbands Edward Pascoal and Joe Faria. Joe's son Kevin worked at the Mississauga Garden Centre for a few years. Antonio's son Eddie is continuing the family tradition and has completed over nineteen years with Sheridan.

Limited space allows the inclusion here of just a few of the stories of the Portuguese who helped build Sheridan Nurseries. However, an observation from Manuel Sobrinho gives an indication of their work ethic. In the hard task of "balling" Japanese yews, the Portuguese prided themselves on their ability to make perfect balls. As they worked, they would compete to see who could make the greatest number of perfect balls in an hour. There is certainly something admirable about a race for perfection.

THE DUTCH:
TO CANADA FROM THE LAND OF FLOWERS

The Netherlands has long been famous for its flowers. After the Second World War, many Dutch horticulturists and nurserymen left their homeland to seek new lives in Canada.

Not surprisingly, some of them found opportunity with Sheridan Nurseries.

Len Vermaas was eighteen years old when he left the Netherlands for Canada in 1954. After he secured a job with Sheridan's landscaping department, one of his first assignments was landscaping around the new head office on Evans Avenue in Etobicoke. Len also worked on the grounds of the Oakville Ford plant. When Sheridan Nurseries went through a slow period, Len found work as head gardener for the Hospital for Sick Children.

In 1960, Len returned to Sheridan's landscaping department and worked his way up to foreman, then supervisor,

Sheridan Nurseries.

Moving a maple tree in full leaf to the new Oakville Ford plant in July.

and finally manager. He kept that position until the department closed in 1993. Len was then transferred to the container department, where he was eventually promoted to container farm supervisor. Len retired in 2000, but in February 2001 he did an autobiographical article for the employee profile column of the Sheridan Nurseries *News*, and looked back over his years with the company:

> In the early days, I remember working with Mr. Grubb and Mr. J.V. Stensson at such places as Casa Loma and the O'Keefe Centre [flower shows]. I also remember a skinny kid named Manuel Sobrinho (of course, I was a skinny kid myself in those days) working for Mitzi Iwasaki in the barn at Oakville. In those early days, Andy Weiss, who worked for me at that time, managed to roll, with the help of another young fellow, a stump from the roof of the truck onto my head. That is the only time that I was ever knocked out and the first words I remember hearing was one of the men saying, "He's a goner." Fortunately he was wrong ... My dad also worked for the Sheridan Landscape Department until his death in 1969 ... Sheridan has been a family tradition with us.

All of Len's children worked summers at Sheridan to pay for their university education. His son Jeff also worked for Sheridan as shipping manager, and Len's wife Lynda often helped with office work.

Ben deBoer learned all about plants in his father's nursery in the Dutch city of Boskoop, a community famous for its woody plants and perennials. In 1953 he moved to Canada. He had $200 in his pocket and no prospects for employment. Ben had no luck finding a job until his landlord put him in touch with Sheridan Nurseries. He was hired immediately and put to work making cuttings.

It didn't take long for management to see that Ben loved plants and knew them well. He had been with the company for less than a year, when he was asked to manage the Clarkson sales station. He was offered the use of a house on the property. His four children were born there: Adrian, Paul, Joan, and Janet.

Ben managed the Clarkson store for sixteen years. He was a superb salesman. Although he could be gruff with employees, he was always big-hearted. He knew what it was like to be a newcomer in a strange country. His wife Florence recalled an occurrence when Ben was still unfamiliar with some English figures of speech. His supervisor at Sheridan Nurseries had asked him to "give the roses a shot." Ben wasn't sure what to do. Was he supposed to shoot the roses? He finally asked a co-worker what the expression meant. The man handed him a can of insecticide and told him to spray the roses.

Manuel Sobrinho, who became Ben's assistant manager in 1966, recalled, "Ben taught me how to successfully deal with people, how to buy and sell nursery stock and also how to hunt rabbits."

In 1969, Ben left Sheridan Nurseries to go into business for himself. He bought a farm in Uxbridge, Ontario, in 1972, where he established Uxbridge Nurseries. Ben died on New Year's Day, 2009.

Bill Kegel immigrated to Canada from the Netherlands in 1952. As a boy he had grown vegetables and sunflowers with his father. He'd also seen Rotterdam in flames during the Nazi invasion of 1940. Bill's brother Hank had come to Canada the year before he did, and found work with Sheridan Nurseries. Bill therefore had a job waiting for him when he got off the train in Clarkson. He began work the very next day.

Bill spent his first months hoeing, and then picking up shrubs and making cuttings and grafting. Then he was a planter for Harry Kayama, which was hard because, "You had to work on your haunches all the time."

Bill's big break came one day when he was sent to the Clarkson sales station. It started out as a "spring job" only. However, it led to a twelve-year learning experience in salesmanship under Ben deBoer. After working with the indomitable Ben for so long, Bill was considered the right man to manage the Sheridan sales station on Yonge Street in Toronto.

When he took charge of the store in 1966, Bill immediately thought the building was too small. J.V. Stensson offered to have the walls extended, but Bill said that wasn't good enough. He drew up a plan which he submitted to J.V. The entire building was renovated according to Bill's ideas.

Bill ran the Yonge Street store for eight years. One problem he encountered was parking. The store had only three parking spaces, and he had to use one himself. Customers who had been ticketed for parking on the street often demanded that Sheridan pay the fines. Bill told them he couldn't do that. But, being resourceful, he found a way to at least partly resolve the problem. Bill got permission to park his car in a neighbour's garage, thus freeing up a spot.

Many of Bill's customers came from Orangeville, his wife Geraldine's hometown. These customers were disappointed that Orangeville was too far away for Bill to provide home delivery service. Asked why they didn't buy locally, they said there was no garden centre in Orangeville.

Sensing opportunity, Bill and Geraldine purchased a ten-acre lot. In 1974, Bill left Sheridan to start Dufferin Garden Centre near Orangeville. He and Sheridan parted on good terms. J.V., he recalled, "was very good to me."

JAMAICA AND MEXICO: HEADING NORTH FOR THE SEASON

In 1972, Sheridan Nurseries became involved in the Seasonal Agricultural Worker Program, which provides seasonal employment opportunities in Canada for workers from other countries. Over the years, hundreds of people from Mexico and Jamaica have come to Sheridan through this program. Some worked for the nursery for only a season or two, while others have made Sheridan their home away from home for many successive seasons.

Miquel Quiroz Gomez, from Miacatlán, Mexico, worked for Sheridan as an equipment operator. He was also very knowledgeable in ornamental plant production. Arturo Escamilla-Corrales, from Guanajuato, worked at harvesting and plant maintenance, and became one of Sheridan's main topiary persons.

Eulice Walters and Jeffrey Pommells joined the contingent of Jamaicans that has become part of Sheridan's cosmopolitan make-up. Eulice worked in shipping, and Jeffrey at the Glen Williams nursery. In 1998, Sheridan honoured both men for twenty-five years of service and loyalty. Jeffrey Pommells is still with Sheridan, and is the second-longest-serving offshore employee at thirty-eight years.

Ron Campbell came to Oakville from Jamaica in 1973. For the first few years he worked with field crews; digging, planting, and pruning. Then he was transferred to shipping. He demonstrated a talent for operating forklifts and other equipment, and became supervisor Herman Maiato's right-hand man. In 1988, when the head office was moved from Oakville to Georgetown, Ron went, too. Among the duties in which he took pride was grounds maintenance. Ron is Sheridan's longest-serving Jamaican employee, celebrating forty years in 2013.

CANADA AND THE WORLD

People have come to Sheridan Nurseries from many nations besides those already mentioned. The homelands of the Sheridan family are as far flung as Belgium and Tanzania. Of course, many of the company's most exceptional individuals were born and raised in Canada.

Constant DeGroot was a Belgian nurseryman who served in his country's army during the First World War. He received the Belgian Croix de Guerre after being wounded in action. He met his wife, Jesse, an English army nurse, while recuperating in a British hospital.

Constant and Jesse immigrated to Canada in 1920. In 1922, Constant joined Sheridan Nurseries. One of his first jobs was in Niagara Falls, working on a garden project for Howard Dunington-Grubb. It was the beginning of a long and illustrious career.

Constant was in charge of propagation and production. He was instrumental in the development of many new and improved plants that Sheridan introduced to the trade.

Constant DeGroot, one of the Sheridan Nurseries pioneers, worked for the nursery from 1922 to 1971.

Thomas Frank.

The workers here are weeding by hand. The slats are for shade. Repairing them provided winter work.

Sheridan Nurseries.

Seedling and cutting beds under shade in Oakville.

Sheridan Nurseries.

Aerial view of Sheridan Nurseries in the post–Second World War era. The background area in the upper right is now occupied by the Ford plant.

Among them were the DeGroot linden, Sheridan's Red barberry, Unicorn white cedar, and the famous Sheridan hybrid boxwoods. According to his son John, Constant claimed to have originated ninety-two varieties of plants. However, like other nurserymen of the time, Constant didn't keep records, so it's impossible to verify his total.

One of Sheridan's most popular plants was the Mountbatten Juniper. Constant found the juniper in a field, and in 1948 Fred Stensson approached Lord Mountbatten when he was on a visit to Canada, and got his permission to give the plant his name. Fred then marketed the plant very successfully.

Constant worked for Sheridan Nurseries for forty-nine years, retiring in 1971. On January 19, 1965, he was the recipient of the Trillium Award, the Ontario Nursery Trades Association's highest honour. He died in Cambridge on July 10, 1989, at the age of ninety-seven.

When Jim Herod Jr. died on May 31, 1991, at the age of eighty-one, an era lasting three generations came to a close at Sheridan Nurseries. Jim's family personified the strong bonds that were often forged between the company and the people who helped to build it. Jim was the son and grandson of Sheridan Nurseries pioneers.

Jim's grandfather, Harry Walters, began with Sheridan as an accountant and office manager in 1915. He was from England, and it seemed there was a skeleton in the family closet. Harry kept what was later described as a "silver pistol" in his desk. He was allegedly concerned that a black sheep brother might one day walk through the door. Herman Stensson's granddaughter Karen recalls that her mother, Lois, spoke about seeing the gun. It was her most vivid memory of Harry Walters. Harry left Sheridan Nurseries in 1928, but came back four years later. He was still working at the age of seventy-seven.

James Herod Sr., from Mimico, was a First World War veteran who began working for Sheridan in 1919. He married Harry Walters's daughter Winifred. Howard Stensson recalled that Jim Sr. drove the smaller of the two trucks that made up Sheridan Nurseries' first fleet. Jim chewed tobacco, and he would spit the juice out the window. The side of the

Peter Nielsen.

Two of Sheridan's early employees, Bob Nielsen (L) and Jim Herod Jr. (R).

truck was usually spattered with the result. But bad habits aside, Jim Sr. was one of Sheridan's hard-working pioneers. His granddaughter Doreen Rion referred to him as "an old time nurseryman; a *plantsman*."

Jim Herod Jr. started working for Sheridan as a student, budding roses in the summer. In 1938, he became manager of Sheridan's new farm at Sherway and moved his family into the house there. That farm grew to a nursery of 135 acres. It became the site of Sheridan Nurseries head office and show gardens in 1954.

Jim and his wife Elsie had four daughters: Doreen, Diane, Barb, and Joan. Doreen recalls that she could safely cross the QEW on her tricycle. She learned to bud roses and she rode the farm's two workhorses, Peggy and Pete. Her mother sometimes worked in the fields, pruning. Like most of the other children of Sheridan employees, she was "scared to death" of Howard Dunington-Grubb, though today she says she doesn't know why.

Jim never went to horticultural school. He learned everything he knew about plants from men like Herman Stensson and Constant DeGroot. His greatest interests lay in perennials and propagation. Among the plants Jim introduced were the Glenleven linden, the Sherway Perpetual viola, and the Mrs. Cornell shasta daisy. He propagated an extensive range of perennials, including many that were not in Sheridan's catalogues. In 1964, Sheridan sold all but ten acres of its Sherway property for the development of the Sherway Gardens shopping mall, which opened in 1971. Jim became manager of the new modern garden centre that opened there in 1970. Elsie worked there for many years as cashier. Over at the head office, the patch of lawn in front of the building was Jim's pride and joy. He kept it looking impeccable and would even scrape off the morning dew.

In spite of all the time and energy he devoted to his work, Jim still managed to enjoy sports. He played softball, and was a star goalie for the Sheridan Nurseries soccer team in the 1930s. He was an amateur wrestler, and a protégé of Golden Gloves boxer Bob Nielsen, who was also a Sheridan Nurseries employee who left to start a garden centre and nursery on the Lakeshore Road near Clarkson. Jim was on the Sheridan board of directors until his retirement.

Jim retired from Sheridan Nurseries in 1976. He moved to Alliston where he could be closer to two of his daughters. But Jim was a nurseryman. He couldn't stay away from the work he loved. He asked John Somerville of Somerville Nurseries near Alliston if he could work there part-time. John credited much of his company's success to Jim's knowledge and hard work. He said that Jim, who had a history of heart problems, was available to him as a consultant right up until his last trip to the hospital. The pioneering spirit was with him to the end.

Although Albert E. Brown became vice-president of Sheridan Nurseries, he wasn't a nurseryman in the manner of someone like Constant DeGroot. He was a horticulturist who began working for Sheridan in 1915, making him one of the pioneers, along with the Dunington-Grubbs, in that part of Sheridan's operations. But in a career that spanned more than fifty years, Albert served in many capacities.

Albert was born in England and as a young man he received his training at Kew Gardens. He graduated from that historic institution in 1905. He spent some time in India working on a government park project. A bout of malaria convinced him to leave India and come to Canada.

Sheridan Nurseries.

The men who guided Sheridan Nurseries through its first fifty years of growth. L–R: J.V. Stensson, Fred Stensson, Howard Dunington-Grubb, Albert E. Brown.

Albert started working as a foreman in Sheridan's landscaping department. He quickly moved up to department head. From this position, in which he was in frequent consultation with Howard Dunington-Grubb, Albert had a strong influence on the Gardeners and Florists Association of Ontario, the Canadian Rose Society, the Canadian National Exhibition, and the Royal Agricultural Winter Fair Flower Show. He retired from landscaping in 1950, and became Sheridan's publicity manager.

Albert held many directorships in the horticultural industry. He was also a life member of three prestigious organizations: the Kew Guild, the Gardeners and Florists Association, and the Ontario Landscape Contractors Association. In his later years, Albert was responsible for all of Sheridan's advertising, including the catalogue.

For many years Albert operated "Sheridan's information Centre." He was always available to people who phoned in looking for help with gardening problems. He also lectured extensively to horticultural societies and gardening groups all over Ontario. Only in the last few years of his life was he obliged to curtail some of his many activities. Albert died in March of 1967 at the age of eighty-four.

Uli Rumpf was born in East Germany and did his apprenticeship as a nurseryman there. However, he was in Switzerland when he decided to immigrate to North America. Uli contacted Sheridan Nurseries, where his friend Joe Below was already employed. He received a positive reply from J.V. Stensson and left for Canada in April 1960.

Uli was given a room in the Danish bunkhouse, which at that time was run by Thomas and Susie Frank. They were among the many Sheridan people with whom Uli would form

Sheridan Nurseries.

Ontario Landscape Contractors Association Award given to Albert Brown in 1966.

close friendships. The day after his arrival, Uli started work, digging with Joerg Leiss's gang.

In 1961, after months of working with digging crews, and while still trying to figure out some of the oddities of English, Uli was taken to Sherway to meet Jim Herod. He was being moved from field work to retail sales.

As Uli explained years later, the "old man" (Herod) said, "Here's a truck driver's wallet with some change in it, and a receipt book. All you've got to do is write the receipt and collect the money." That, said Uli, was his "training." He was relieved when his very first customer didn't speak much English. "I was afraid of falling on my face."

Uli learned the job quickly. He moved into an apartment at the Sherway head office. He got to know many of the clients well. Among the well-known customers who patronized the Sherway store were Harold Ballard, owner of Maple Leaf Gardens and the Toronto Maple Leafs, and his partner, King Clancy.

In 1976 Jim Herod retired. Uli and his wife Serita moved into the former Herod house on the Etobicoke store property, and lived there for ten years before the land was sold to Toys "R" Us. Uli then worked at the Steeles Avenue store, the Mississauga store, and finally the Etobicoke store. In 2000, Uli asked to be transferred to the farm at Glen Williams. He is still there today, after more than fifty years with Sheridan Nurseries, working as quality control manager. Serita worked seasonally in the garden centres, and is now retired.

Joe Pokluda apprenticed with nurseries in his native France. He moved to Canada in 1951 and worked for a year at a small nursery in Milton, Ontario. Then in 1952, Joe was hired by Sheridan Nurseries in Oakville.

Within a year Joe was in charge of the propagation crews under Constant DeGroot. In 1958, he became the first manager of the new Sheridan farm in Glen Williams. Under his supervision, it grew over twelve years from 300 to 941 acres, making the Glen Williams farm Canada's largest single growing area for ornamental plants.

Joe was very much involved in the mechanization of Sheridan's growing operations. He was instrumental in shifting Sheridan's tree production from seedlings to grafted and budded selections. Among Joe's most noteworthy selections and introductions were the widely acclaimed Ivory Japanese Silk tree lilac, the Sheridan silver maple, the Green Globe and Sheridan lindens, and the Kleinburg ash. Joe also selected many of the understocks used by Sheridan Nurseries. In 1965, the Ontario Nursery Trades Association recognized Joe's invaluable contributions by presenting him with the Frank Ewald Junior Nurserymen's Award.

Joe became Sheridan's first horticultural coordinator in 1988. He was responsible for the overall coordination of the growing operations at all four Sheridan farms in Southern Ontario. It meant that he was involved in the selection and evaluation of new varieties of plants selected by Sheridan Nurseries, and those brought in from other areas for possible cultivation and marketing.

For over two decades, during which Sheridan Nurseries rapidly grew as a leader in the industry, Joe Pokluda was one of the people whose extraordinary work helped to put the company on the map.

Larry Wilson (pictured in lower-right corner of collage of Stensson family and Sheridan executives, first page of second photo insert) joined Sheridan Nurseries as a member of the

board of directors in March 1993. By the following June, he had become the first president to be chosen from outside the company. Larry brought thirty years of executive experience to Sheridan. He had worked as a senior manager for both large and small companies, and had been owner and president of Cottrell Forwarding, one of the largest independent transportation companies in Canada.

Larry took the helm as Sheridan's president at a time of economic recession and guided the company through some lean years. In his own words: "We are in the business of pleasing our customers first and foremost! We must as a bare minimum offer the best products in their class at the most competitive prices, and deliver them in good condition, when they are wanted! While this statement may seem simple enough, it is quite another thing to deliver what it promises, consistently, every day and every week."

Larry's operating mottos were: "NO surprise management" and "You get what you monitor." His experience, foresight, and belief in the company made him a mentor to his fellow executives and a model for those who followed.

Larry believed in setting a good civic example, too. He served as chairman of the Community Foundation of Oakville. He was also chairman of the committee to renovate St. Jude's Anglican Church in Oakville.

When Larry's term as president of Sheridan Nurseries ended in June 1996, he became president of Fast Air Cargo. However, he remained on Sheridan's board of directors for the rest of his life. Larry died of cancer on September 4, 2000, in his sixty-fifth year.

***

It would be an understatement to describe Larry Sherk as a man of many talents. He is a horticulturist, author, company historian, and archivist. More than ten years after his "retirement" following a long and distinguished career with Sheridan Nurseries, he is still active in company affairs.

Larry was born in Sherkston, which is now part of Port Colborne. He majored in ornamental horticulture at the Ontario Agricultural College. In order to gain the required practical experience, he spent two summers as an assistant to John Weall, a lecturer at the college, and co-founder of Weall & Cullen Nurseries.

After graduation in May 1958, he enrolled in graduate studies at Cornell University in Ithaca, New York, majoring in ornamental horticulture. Upon graduation, he received the Dreer Award, which came with a scholarship that allowed him to go to Europe, visiting most of Western Europe's famous gardens.

Upon his return to Canada, Larry was employed by the Plant Research Institute of Agriculture Canada in Ottawa. He worked with native plants, and was in fact one of the first Canadian horticulturists to take an interest in Canada's native flora. Among his most significant projects was the development, with the help of agro-meteorologist C.E. Ouellet, of the Canadian Plant Hardiness Zone Map.

Larry was the senior author when he and Arthur R. Buckley collaborated on *Ornamental Shrubs for Canada*. He also wrote a bulletin called *Growing Canada's Floral Emblems*.

Larry became acquainted with Art Drysdale in 1967. Art was Sheridan Nurseries' horticulturist, and wanted to use the as-yet-unpublished Hardiness Map in a forthcoming Sheridan catalogue.

In 1969, Larry heard that Art was leaving Sheridan, and in May of that year, he became Sheridan Nurseries' chief horticulturist and advertising manager. He was in charge of the Sheridan catalogue, advertising, and public relations. In 1994 Larry became Sheridan's hardy plant product manager, responsible for buying hardy plants from outside sources for sale in Sheridan retail outlets. That job was a welcome assignment because, "I was glad to be back in touch with plants." Larry retired in 2001, but has continued to write articles and accept public-speaking engagements.

He continued with his work on the Sheridan archives well after retirement. As Larry put it, stories about Sheridan Nurseries history kept "coming out of the woodwork." Sheridan's heritage is all the richer because of his efforts.

Sheridan Nurseries.

Larry Sherk (L) and Art Drysdale (R) at the Southdown Garden Centre, live on CFRB, 1987, promoting Sheridan's new rose, Ten Ten.

Amin Datoo came to Canada from Tanzania in 1972. A church group that assisted newcomers helped him get his first "real job" in Canada. In April of 1973, Amin was hired as a field hand at Longacres, Sheridan's Unionville location.

In 1976, Amin applied for the green-goods position in Sheridan's downtown Toronto store on Yonge Street. Lou Sato was the manager. "He treated me like a son," Amin recalls fondly.

Amin was a natural salesman, and he rose to assistant manager. In the mid-1980s, he managed Sheridan's Vaughan store and then the flagship Sherway store in Etobicoke. Amin took over management of the Yonge Street store in 1990, a challenging job for any manager due to limited parking and all the problems that accompany a garden centre in a heavily urbanized location. However, in the twenty-plus years that he has been there, Amin has proven to be one of Sheridan's most successful retail managers.

Amin introduced innovations such as cut dogwood branches as an alternative to evergreen boughs for Christmas greenery. He describes his downtown Toronto store as "an island of paradise." On a busy Saturday, staff can conduct two thousand transactions, enough to keep fourteen carry-out clerks hopping. Customers in Amin's store have included former Governor General Adrienne Clarkson and hockey stars Darcy Tucker, Steve Thomas, and Eddie Shack.

Though he has been a successful retail manager for many years, Amin hasn't forgotten his early days with Sheridan. He remembers hard-slogging jobs like shovelling sawdust and loading peat moss by hand. He worked hard and earned

his success. The Yonge Street location, he says, "is the best store to be in."

Unofficially, John Reiter started working at Sheridan Nurseries at the age of four. For many years, his father, Bob, was the manager of Sheridan's Greenhedges sales station in Montreal, and later the garden centre in Dollard-des-Ormeaux. He would take John with him to water plants on Sundays when the store was closed. Bob, who'd come to Canada from Germany, retired in 1989 and passed away in 1993.

John officially became a Sheridan employee in 1974, off-loading trucks and semi-trailers manually. On his first day, the crew decided to play a joke on the "new guy" by working him extra hard. John didn't complain, but turned the tables on the jokers by out-working them all. At the end of the long day, he was the last man standing.

Over his long career with Sheridan, John has seen many changes. He recalled Sheridan Montreal's "first major entry into the modern age of material handling" in 1978, when a conveyor system was used to unload nursery stock. Even more dramatic was the leap forward into high-tech communications. At one time, John relied on three telephones with three lines that covered a 4.5-acre site. Then came fax technology, soon to be followed by email.

After moving from Montreal to Ontario, John worked at Sherway. He says he has the distinction of closing down not only three stores, but also a province. He was the last Sheridan manager in Quebec. John was assistant manager of operations at the Southdown store in Mississauga for two years, and then had the same position at Burnhamthorpe for another two years. He became the manager of the Georgetown Garden Centre in 2010.

Frank Miedzinski's father, Waclaw, went to work for Sheridan Nurseries when he immigrated to Canada from Poland after the Second World War. He spent several years in the fields digging string balls and loading trucks. Frank began working part-time for Sheridan at the age of twelve, tying roses in the budding field at Glen Williams. In 1980, he became a full-time employee as a general laborer. Over the years, Frank has held numerous positions including assistant to the foreman, foreman, and field crop supervisor. As a result, he has accumulated a vast knowledge of plants. Frank is presently distribution assistant manager.

Scott "Scooter" Baillie came to Sheridan Nurseries in 1983 with a diploma in horticulture and sales from the University of Guelph. He started at the Unionville store where he did everything from potting bare-root shrubs to sales and deliveries. In his long career at Unionville, Scott has held a variety of positions including nursery supervisor, trade supervisor, and assistant manager. Among the many customers with whom he built up a rapport were NHL stars Frank Mahovlich and Kevin Weeks. Scott has been managing the Unionville store since 2003.

Tom Whitcher started with Sheridan in 1983 at Greenhedges on Montée-de-Liesse, Montreal. He was an hourly employee for manager Bob Reiter, but was soon promoted to assistant manager. In 1986 he moved to Dollard-des-Ormeaux to help establish a major new Sheridan garden centre there.

Tom became manager of the new wholesale yard in Dorion in 1988. The site covered ten acres, but was staffed by only eight people. In spite of its great promise, this location was plagued by an on-going water-supply problem with the city of Dorion. In 1993, Tom opened and managed a second wholesale yard in Ste-Julie. Again, he ran into water-supply problems. Nonetheless, Tom was successful in forming a small but very sales-oriented staff. A major commission in 1992 was supplying trees for the prestigious Jardin de Saint-Roch in Quebec City.

SHERIDAN NURSERIES LTD.

DATE: YEAR 1973 MO. 5 DAY 31

LOCATION: Oakville or Glen Williams Glen Williams

1) Foreman in charge W. Miedzinski
2) No. of Workers in gang, including Foreman 15
3) Total No. of manhours worked 135

NO. OF PIECES DUG:

BB Conifers up to 3 ft. 495
BB Conifers over 3 ft. 80
BB Conifers over 5 ft.
BB Shrubs 70
BB Deciduous Trees 16
BB other

Total BB 661

Bare Root Shrubs 25
Bare Root Trees up to 8-10
Bare Root Trees 10-12&over

Total Bare Root Trees

String Balls, hand dug, number & Sizes
String balls, machine dug,number &Sizes

Other jobs done: (Nature & Location)
3 men loading B&B.

Comments:-
(a) Weather
(b) Problem, if any
(c) Other:

Signed --- W. Miedzinski

Sheridan Nurseries.

Example of daily records foremen kept for crews. This one is by Waclaw Miedzinski.

In 1977, Tom and Andy Weiss led the successful consolidation of all Sheridan's Quebec sales operations, both wholesale and retail, under one roof in Dollard. Tom became manager of the whole operation in 1998 when Andy moved to Ontario. Sales tripled during Tom's tenure. When it was decided to close operations in Quebec, all employees were offered employment in Ontario if they chose it. Tom is now Sheridan's sales representative for eastern Ontario, Quebec, and New England.

Sylvie Leduc joined Sheridan at Dorion in 1989, and moved to Dollard-des-Ormeaux when the trade yard transferred there in 1997. She moved on to head office in 2001. Today Sylvie is the guest service representative for Tom Whitcher's territory.

Garnet Myles joined Sheridan Nurseries in 1985 as a purchasing agent. He was the first person hired to centralize purchasing of products such as fertilizer, pesticides, tools, et cetera, for the garden centres. Garnet had previously worked for DR Garden Supply, and before that he had owned G.M. Garden supplies for eighteen years. Unfortunately, Garnet passed away in 1988 after a brief battle with cancer.

An honours graduate in agriculture from the University of Guelph, Brian Worfolk worked for Weall & Cullen before joining Sheridan Nurseries in 1985. He started as a sales representative in central Ontario and Michigan. Brian went on to become Sheridan's senior sales representative, overseeing telemarketing, in-house customer service, and U.S. sales representatives. He has been treasurer of the Toronto Chapter of Landscape Ontario, and chairman of the ANLA Committee of Wholesale Plant Sales Professionals. Brian has held national-level status as a figure-skating coach. In 2012 Brian marked his twenty-fifth year with Sheridan Nurseries.

Valerie Stensson joined Sheridan Nurseries in 1988, as the gift, patio, and Christmas buyer. She took the lead to expand the product lines for patio and outdoor accessories, as well as the gift and home decor lines. After making a proposal to the executive to bring the advertising in-house in 1993, Valerie became marketing manager, bought a new desktop computer and colour printer, and hired a graphic designer.

Valerie has been instrumental in modernizing the marketing and advertising methods at Sheridan, from the re-launch of the Sheridan catalogue to the award-winning Garden Guide, to producing customized advertisements for nursery customers, to launching Sheridan's online presence and utilizing electronic communications to reach customers.

Greg Kenny came to Sheridan Nurseries in 1989 with a degree in business administration-finance from Sheridan College. He started in order entry and invoicing, and then advanced to inventory control. Greg was soon promoted to supervisor in all these areas, and was given charge of the computer network at the Glen Williams head office. He is currently Sheridan's IT manager.

Bart Brusse earned a degree in biology at the University of Guelph. After managing a garden centre in Powassan, Ontario, he joined Sheridan Nurseries in 2000 as the assistant manager of the Norval farm. Among his many responsibilities, Bart was instrumental in initiating the new nursery training program for all of the Sheridan farms. In 2002 he became the container manager, the position he still holds today. Bart is also a certified management accountant.

Fred Paiva started with Weall & Cullen in 1968 as a carry-out boy at their Sheppard Avenue store. His hard work and determination led to positions of greater responsibility, such as delivery coordinator. Fred was entrusted with ordering annuals, general repairs, and supervising renovations. He filled the positions of nursery buyer, co-manager, and store manager. He managed the Cullen Country Barns for four years until its closing in 1993. Fred then became the assistant manager at the Sheppard Avenue store. He also successfully operated many satellite stores — temporary retail outlets Weall & Cullen opened during the Christmas season. The Weall & Cullen acquisition brought Fred to Sheridan Nurseries. He became manager of the North York store. Today Fred is the landscape design services manager, overseeing twenty freelance designers and twenty-three authorized contractors who install landscapes.

Larry Parr went to work part-time for Weall & Cullen's Scarborough store in 1972 while studying psychology at the University of Toronto. He completed his Bachelor of Science degree (he's still not sure why) and then began working full time at the Home & Design Centre in west Mississauga. Three years later he went to the North York location, and three years after that he returned to Scarborough. Larry came to Sheridan Nurseries in the acquisition, and now manages the Etobicoke store.

COMING AND GOING

A considerable number of people who came to work for Sheridan Nurseries made a life-long career with the company, some staying on for fifty years or more. Others who worked for Sheridan for a long time had their careers punctuated by periods during which they worked elsewhere, but then returned to Sheridan. Joerg Leiss, who had apprenticed as a nurseryman in Germany, began working for Sheridan in 1952. He left in 1959, and returned in 1964. He left again in 1986, having worked a total of nineteen years at the nursery. Joerg's wife Franzis also worked many years with Sheridan, at the Sherway and Southdown garden centres.

Joerg Freise first started working for Sheridan Nurseries in Oakville late in 1960. He left in the mid-sixties, but then returned to Sheridan. In 1967 he was appointed assistant manager of the new sales station in Unionville. In 1982, he became manager of Sheridan's Sheppard Avenue East location. Joerg left in 1984 to start his own garden maintenance business.

John Kesteloot moved to Canada from Belgium in 1947, and joined Sheridan in 1968 as assistant farm manager in Oakville. He left in 1973 to open his own nursery in Thedford, Ontario. In 1980, John returned to Sheridan as pesticide/herbicide control manager. He left again in 1982 to become superintendent of forestry and horticulture for the City of Etobicoke Parks Department. John came back to Sheridan in 1990 as manager of the Port Hope farm until it was closed and operations consolidated in Georgetown.

Dieter Frank, who started with Sheridan in 1960, was another experienced German nurseryman. Recalling how he was put in charge of a work crew right away, Dieter said that back then, "Anybody coming from Europe — Germans, Danes — was considered to be skilled." Dieter left in 1967 to work as a horticulturist for the town of Oakville. He returned to Sheridan in 1974 and stayed until 1990. In all, he worked for Sheridan for twenty-three years.

Andy Weiss came to Sheridan from Switzerland in 1970. He went back to Switzerland once, but then returned to Canada and spent several years doing other jobs. Andy came back to Sheridan in 1983 and served in many capacities including store manager in Montreal and Ontario before his retirement as a veteran of twenty-seven years with Sheridan.

MOVING ON

Like Ben deBoer and Bill Kegel, some enterprising employees left Sheridan to go into business for themselves. Leslie Solty Sr. and his brother Geza emigrated from Hungary to Toronto in 1949. Leslie was a landscape architect, but had to take a job driving a taxi. One day he had Howard Dunington-Grubb for a passenger, and got into a conversation with him. That chance meeting resulted in both brothers being hired by Sheridan's landscape department. Late in 1951, Leslie founded Leslie Solty & Sons. It is now the Solty Garden Centre, run by the third generation of the family.

John Putzer came to Canada from Switzerland in the 1950s and worked for Sheridan for several years. In 1960 he bought a farm and started his own business. He later started the M (Maria) Putzer Hornby Nursery near Milton. Even after leaving Sheridan, John maintained Howard Dunington-Grubb's garden on Dale Avenue in Toronto for several years.

When the price of tomatoes collapsed on the London market, Guernsey greenhouse grower D'Arcy Queripel decided to find his family a better life in Canada. Shortly after arriving in Toronto, D'Arcy and his son Sydney were hired by Sheridan's landscape department. D'Arcy was made foreman. In 1955, D'Arcy left to start his own landscape business. Sydney joined him at the end of 1956, and the two formed D. Queripel &

Son. Sydney recalls working on Howard Dunington-Grubb's garden on Dale Avenue. He also helped build the Sheridan sales station at 2827 Yonge Street in Toronto. Sydney closed his business and retired in 2004.

Herb Doernbach joined Sheridan Nurseries in Oakville in 1956. He drove trucks in his early years, and then worked in the machine shop. He eventually became assistant manager to Joe Pokluda in Glen Williams. He left Sheridan Nurseries in the 1980s.

John Van Klink and his two sons, Ted and Gerry, also joined Sheridan Nurseries in 1956. Gerry stayed for a year and Ted for three years. John left in the early sixties to join his brother who had purchased Muskoka Lakes Gardens in Gravenhurst.

Fleming Bulow came to Canada after the Second World War and went to work for Sheridan Nurseries in 1957. In 1960 he left to start F. Bulow Garden Centre and Landscaping on the South Service Road in Oakville. Later he purchased the Robert Nielsen Garden Centre on Lakeshore Road West in Mississauga.

Joe Below apprenticed with Uli Rumpf in East Germany. In 1957 he left for the West, and in 1959 came to Canada and joined Sheridan Nurseries in Oakville. During the sixties Joe left for other employment, but soon came back. In 1970 he moved to Glen Williams as assistant manager to Joe Pokluda. In 1973 he and his wife Katy established Albion Nursery and Garden Centre on Mayfield Road in Bolton. Joe left Sheridan permanently in 1974. He and Katy still have a seasonal garden centre, and their son Ernie runs the extensive landscape business.

In 1958, Otto Timm left Germany on an offer of employment from Sheridan Nurseries. He worked in the fields for three seasons. In 1962, he began a nursery-supply business in the village of Sheridan's old Sunday-school building. In 1971 he purchased land on Trafalgar Road and established his present company, Timm Enterprises.

Paul Offierski was hired by Howard Stensson in 1974 to be the first assistant for Fred Stensson, who had suffered a broken hip. Paul learned the business quickly, with Fred teaching him all the ins and outs of salesmanship, and sharing professional secrets picked up through a lifetime in the trade. Paul left Sheridan in 1976, and went on to start PAO Associates, a supplier of plants and landscape trade accessories.

THE BUNKHOUSES: HOMES FOR "THE BOYS"

Ranchers in the Old West had a saying: "A warm bunk and a good cook make a happy, hard-working cowboy." The same could very well be said of an agricultural operation like Sheridan Nurseries. In the company's first fifty years, a large percentage of the labour force was made up of single men and married men temporarily living away from their families. These workers often came to Sheridan in ethnic groups, such as the Danes and the Japanese.

The company always provided employees living on-site with comfortable accommodations. Former farmhouses on Sheridan property were renovated to suit the purpose, or new structures were built. At one point in the mid-1960s, Sheridan owned forty-seven houses that were all rented to employees of the company. Workers from specific backgrounds were generally housed with people of their own ethnic community. For people who were far from home, it was important to be living and working with friends and relatives. The "Danish" bunkhouse and the "Japanese" bunkhouse got their names from the workers who originally boarded in them. The names stuck, even though later on people of various backgrounds lived in them.

One of the great advantages to living at the workplace was the absence of daily transportation costs. Room and board wasn't free, but it was relatively cheap. In a letter J.V. Stensson wrote to a prospective cook for the Danish bunkhouse in 1953, he stated that the house in which she and her husband would live would be "handled in a way similar to our Japanese Bunk House, which is run on a cooperative basis and which has worked very well." Four cents an hour was deducted from a worker's wages to cover the cost of

Thomas Frank.

The Danish bunkhouse located on Lakeshore Road in Clarkson. Thomas Frank is on the verandah.

Nov. 16th, 1953.

Mr. & Mrs. A. Lindgaard,
Port Credit, Ont.

Dear Mr. & Mrs. Lindgaard:

We would like to confirm our conversation with both of you last Thursday concerning the house we have just purchased and in which you are going to live.

Apart ffom your own quarters we hope confortable accomodation can be provided for single men, up to a maximum of twelve. When it is in full swing we feel the house can be handled in a way similar to our Japanese Bunk House, which is run on a cooperative basis and which has worked out very well. The cook is paid per calendar month $100. of which $45. is paid by The Sheridan Nurseries Ltd. The balance of $55. plus cost of food, light & heat, and telephone if required, is split on the basis of one part for each man, including the cook's hasband and ½ part for the daughter. The cook's meals are "free". No deduction is made in a man's share for odd meals missed by him. Only when he has been away 4 consecutive days in any one month is any deduction allowed. The boys keep their own rooms clean and tidy and look after their own washing, including bedding. The cook looks after all rooms except the bedrooms and is responsible for maintaining heat.

Four cents per hour is deducted from current wage of men to cover cost of room, bedding and maintenance.

The S. N. will supply refrigator, electric stove, coal stove if desired, beds and bedding for the boys, and additional furniture. We understand that you have some furniture of your own.

The S. N. will do some remodelling, including installation of shelves and storage space in the kitchen. An attempt will be made to provide another bathroom, so that your own accomodation downstairs should be: Kitchen, Living-Room, 2 bedrooms and bath, all entirely shut off from the boys quarters. Two tons of coal and 1 load of wood will be supplied by S. N. Monday, but henceforth, wood and coal will be your responsibility.

It very likely may be the end of March before the full quota of boys arrive. The question of the cook's salary, until a reasonable number of boys arrive, we would like to discuss with Mrs. Lindgaard.

Yours very truly,

JVS/CKS

Sheridan Nurseries.

This letter from J.V. Stensson to Mr. and Mrs. A. Lindgaard provides an insight into the bunkhouse accommodations Sheridan Nurseries provided for workers. The letter concerns the Danish bunkhouse, but the conditions outlined would have applied to both of them.

room, bedding, and maintenance. The men were responsible for keeping their own rooms tidy and for their own laundry, including bedding.

The cook and her family had private quarters in the house, including a bathroom. The kitchen was the cook's domain. Her duty was to serve up hearty meals. But she wasn't anybody's servant. She expected "the boys" sitting around her table to behave respectfully.

Susie Frank, who was once the cook in the Danish bunkhouse, and her husband, Thomas, recalled how the boys used to call them Mom and Dad. Thomas was Danish and Susie was Swedish, but whether the workers in their bunkhouse were Danish, Dutch or German, Susie always thought of them as "her boys." Susie went to Park Royal to do the grocery shopping, but bread and milk were still delivered to the door. Speaking many years later, Susie and Thomas had fond memories of all the people who lived in the bunkhouse. "There wasn't much money," Thomas said, "but it was a good life."

Thomas Frank.

Hoeing crews were transported to fields in the back of Sheridan trucks.

NOTES - as discussed with C.D.G. January 18/61

1. Whenever weather is good, commencing Thursday - 8 or 10 men on hedge pruning - commencing at Orrs.
2. Rosa multiflora cuttings - make immediately. Send some to B.L. Bob Holliday would like a bundle or so for de-eyeing.
3. Chromestone - about 9 men this Thursday - Friday and Monday - Thomas to run it.
   We shall be making only 4 days a week, therefore on Fridays and Mondays about ½ crew required.
4. Burlap - 2 crews commence at once. Also send packing cases - 2 pieces plywood about 3' square and cardboard to B.L.
5. Greenhouse work:
   1. Pot centre bench Junipers
   2. Cuttings in one side bench
   3. Graft
6. Cutting wood - about February 1st-get most of rose cuttings made first. Mossing roses - commence about February 1st.
8. Cleaning up - when looking for a job Pines at Orrs; Willows in Wilson field. North west corner Dorions.
9. Oak Tubs - cut, sandpaper, and varnish (spar varnish) (Try strapping top)
10. Boxing - B. K. Buch - cutting boxes first
11. Shades - make 500 new ones
12. Odd jobs - Tees for shades to be painted
13. Carpentry jobs - note for Sam

Sheridan Nurseries.

As much as possible, Sheridan provided winter work for employees who would otherwise have been laid off during the cold months. This list from January 1961 shows some of the tasks that kept employees busy in the winter.

Sheridan Nurseries.

Hoeing crews at work in the fields at Sheridan's Glen Williams nursery. Imagine over fifty workers in one crew!

CHAPTER 5

The Plants: Making Horticultural History

INTRODUCTION

If Howard and Lorrie-Dunington-Grubb, Herman Stensson, and the other early pioneers could see a current Sheridan Nurseries catalogue, they would have good reason to be amazed at the range of plants listed in its pages. Many of the names would be unfamiliar to them, and some of the species would be plants that, in their time, were considered unsuitable for the Canadian climate. But although they would have *reason* to be amazed, perhaps they would more likely feel elated, for they would see in the modern listing a fruition of the work that they began a hundred years ago.

In 1913, the Dunington-Grubbs faced two huge obstacles. The first was the scarcity in Canada of ornamental plants. Native flora that grew wild was rarely suitable for their purposes. Lorrie imported their first perennials from Europe in the nick of time. No sooner did her order arrive in Canada in 1914 than the First World War broke out, making Europe an unreliable supply source. During the war years, Sheridan Nurseries might have found suppliers in the United States, but no records have survived to confirm this.

The second great obstacle was the level of hardiness of the plants. It was one thing to import a plant, and something else to have it survive over the winter. The plants that the Dunington-Grubbs had worked with in England didn't always adapt well to southern Ontario. In the early years, they had to make do with a rather limited selection. A statement from the 1914–15 catalogue provides an insight into the problem:

THE HADDON ESTATE COMPANY.

DIRECTORS:
THE DUKE OF RUTLAND.
MARQUESS OF ANGLESEY.

TELEPHONE Nº BAKEWELL 5.

ESTATE OFFICE,
BAKEWELL,
DERBYSHIRE.

4th August 1934.

Dear Sir,

In reply to your letter.

I mush regret to have to inform you that Haddon Hall and Grounds are entirely closed to the public, and I am sorry, therefore, that your request cannot be granted..

Yours faithfully,

Alex. Carrington

Mr J.V.Stenson,
c/o H. Farmer Esq.
High Street,
Bourton-on-the-Water,
CHELTENHAM.

Only such plants are here listed as are actually to be found growing successfully in our Nurseries. Should any variety become exhausted a substitute will be suggested, but not sent without instructions. If our suggestions are not acceptable, the cash for the missing varieties will be immediately refunded. As we are anxious to ship nothing but high class stock, true to name, and certain to give satisfaction, we are not anxious to purchase special varieties from other sources for our customers unless specifically requested to do so.

Bertha Sparre.

Left: *Howard Dunington-Grubb and J.V. Stensson often visited public and private gardens and then reported back on the plants. This letter, dated August 4, 1934, is a rare refusal of access to a property.*

Bottom: *Workers in the field take a break to pose for the camera.*

A similar explanation is found in the 1915–16 catalogue:

> Owing to the severity of our winters, we are entirely dependent upon coniferous trees and shrubs for our supply of evergreens for our gardens. The broad-leaved evergreen, such as Rhododendrons, Aucubas, Laurels and Hollies, so largely used in more temperate climates, are not hardy in Canada. We have therefore introduced an exceptionally large collection of highly ornamental hardy Conifers to take their place.

But simply "making do" would never be satisfactory for the Dunington-Grubbs, Herman Stensson, and their successors. Over the years, Sheridan Nurseries tested thousands of plants, searching for or trying to select varieties that would thrive and be commercially viable. Selections of the broad-leaved evergreens originally thought not to be hardy enough for southern Ontario were obtained from sources in the United States and Europe and proved to be suitable. Sometimes, to the surprise of all, a specimen of a plant not thought to be hardy was found growing in a place where no one expected it. One such was a cherry laurel discovered in the Toronto area. In a 1985, study on the introduction of new woody plants to the nursery industry, Howard Stensson wrote:

> I decided to browse through some of Sheridan Nurseries' old catalogues, to see what woody plants were being offered for sale in the previous 70 years. This is not to say that Sheridan "introduced" these plants to the industry. In most cases, the plants were either in the trade in some other country, or were perhaps native species that were often ignored by the early nurseries in Canada.

Howard then drew up a chart for deciduous shade trees, starting with the year 1915 and spaced them out at ten-year intervals up to 1958. He divided it into columns under the headings "Number of Tree Varieties Listed," "Number of Varieties Dropped Since Previous List," and "Number of Varieties Added Since Previous List." The chart shows thirty-three varieties of trees for 1915. In 1925, there were forty-two varieties listed, with sixteen varieties dropped and twenty-six added during the intervening decade. The entry for 1955 shows eighty-four varieties listed with eleven dropped and thirty-seven added since 1945. By 1985, there were ninety-eight listed with sixty-two dropped and twenty-two added since 1975.

The numbers on Howard's chart didn't exactly add up. That, he explained, was due in part to a lack of consistency in the listing order in the catalogues, which was sometimes alphabetical (in English) and sometimes according to botanical names. Moreover, some plants were categorically shifted from trees to shrubs, and then back again. There was also the matter of plants' names being changed.

The nomenclature of plants has sometimes been a source of confusion in the nursery industry. It's an odd tradition, in which "keeping up to date" means going back in time. A nursery can know a plant by a certain name, and list and sell it under that name. Then it is discovered that in another place and an earlier time, the same plant had been given a different name. The older name is always given preference.

In the next issue of its catalogue, the nursery has to identify the plant accordingly.

Howard also noted: "Many plants disappear from one list and reappear a few years later. This could be due to irregularities in production and procurement methods." The problem of "irregularities" was a factor, especially during the Second World War and immediately after, when everything was in short supply. In 1946, under the heading SPECIAL NOTICE TO OUR CUSTOMERS, the catalogue carried a message about horticultural rationing.

> Spring 1946 finds the supply of ornamental nursery stock throughout Canada at the lowest point for many years. Orders booked for spring shipment are so heavy that we have been forced to suspend, temporarily, listing of several varieties. Many others listed are in limited quantities, but we shall endeavour to see that they are distributed among our customers as equitably as possible.

Sheridan Nurseries.

Photo of Sheridan Nurseries trucks at the Clarkson train station. Charlie Barnard stands in front. Circa 1935.

Continuing his study, and focusing on the decade from 1975 to 1985, Howard Stensson made lists of the plants that had been added and those that had been dropped. He indicated which ones were "native." Howard then made a list of plants that had been introduced by Sheridan, or by an originator through Sheridan, that were still in the trade in 1985. Among the sixteen named were six selections of *Buxus*, a plant that would figure prominently in the story of Sheridan Nurseries.

Howard Stensson's meticulous study is a useful research document that certainly required hours of painstaking work to compile. But, like a sheet of statistics, it doesn't tell the stories behind the numbers. Sheridan Nurseries' century-long accumulation of one of the largest and most diversified inventory of hardy ornamental plants in Canada was a process of trial and error. For every success there were many disappointments. Some plants found their way into gardens; others went to bonfires. But

Sheridan Nurseries.

The original Oakville packing shed, built circa *1929.*

always the search for hardy plants continued. A tiny window into this quest is provided by a letter in the Sheridan Nurseries archives. On June 16, 1947, Howard Dunington-Grubb wrote to Henry Hohman of Kingsville Nurseries in Kingsville, Ohio: "We are looking for hardy broad-leaved evergreens. Could you give us any information on Sarcococca? Rehder gives the species Hookeriana as hardy in Zone 5."

Howard Dunington-Grubb wrote many such letters over his long career, as did his successors. It might be impossible to determine just how much searching, planning, experimentation, and hard work went into the introduction of a new hardy plant to Canadian gardens. It is nonetheless a matter of record that Sheridan Nurseries was a leader in the trade.

SHERIDAN ORIGINALS: FROM A FEW PERENNIALS TO SENSATIONAL BOXWOOD

Sheridan Nurseries' first hundred years was marked by many successes, not the least of which was the development and selection of numerous new plants. This was largely due to the knowledge and skill of Sheridan's nurserymen, and their continued efforts to build and diversify the company's list of hardy plants. Some of the most notable Sheridan originals, such as boxwood, are discussed in detail elsewhere in this book. There have been many others. A few came and went, but many are still being grown and sold today.

The 1915–16 catalogue listed one early original: the iris Sheridan Pink. It was available for only two years, and then was dropped from the catalogue.

The development or selection of new plants is a time-consuming and expensive process. It can take years. Successive generations of a plant must be tested, with the possibility of failure always looming. The work can also be sidetracked by flux in social conditions, such as an economic depression or a change in horticultural tastes.

Amazingly enough, it was during the early years of the Second World War that Sheridan Nurseries really began to make a name for developing and releasing new plants. In 1940, the spring catalogue listed new garden chrysanthemums. These plants had been under development for several years, and their introduction just happened to coincide with the darkest period of the war.

The catalogue presented the chrysanthemums as, "New EARLY flowering types of our own introduction." They were called Carl Borgstrom, H.C. Anderson, Herman Stensson, Karen Fredericksen, Mrs. Dunington-Grubb, Mrs. E. Sparre, Robin Hood, and Snow Bird. Naming some of the new plants after people associated with Sheridan Nurseries started a tradition that has been carried on up to the present. In the fall issue of the 1940 catalogue, the same plants were listed, but this time with an acknowledgement that they had been "produced at our nursery by Mr. G. Sparre."

New chrysanthemums were featured again a year later. Under "Sheridan introductions for 1941" the names of five varieties included the word *Sheridan*. A sixth was named after Lois Stensson. These were all hardy border chrysanthemums. According to the catalogue, they were, "effective border plants for fall display. Over a period of years, hybridization has been carried out at our nurseries, enabling us to now offer improved, compact, early flowering types."

Laurie Stewart was added to the list of chrysanthemums in 1955. It was followed in 1960 by H.B. Dunington-Grubb, Harry Walters, Karen Stensson, Karl Stensson, and Sheridan Bronze. The catalogue said of these hardy border chrysanthemums: "Their brilliant colours in the fall prolong the flowering period of the perennial border until frost. Very useful for cutting, hardy and easy to grow are these many varieties of proven merit."

In 1938, Gus Sparre and Sheridan Nurseries entered into an agreement to sell American patent rights to Wayside Gardens, a major U.S. mail-order nursery, for a new chrysanthemum to be called Mme Chiang-Kai-Shek. It was introduced in the 1945 edition of their catalogue. The colour was described as a blend of various shades of yellow. The entry stated, "we consider it the finest Chrysanthemum in our collection if not the finest in the country."

In 1946 the catalogue had the first listing for a new summer phlox, Sheridan Pink. Sheridan Purple was first listed in 1947. In 1958, Sherway was added to the phlox listing. The catalogue called it, "A new outstanding variety originated in our nursery. The colour is a rich, rosy-red, admired by everyone that saw it." The year 1944 had seen the introduction of the "sensational" Sheridan Red barberry. However, as detailed elsewhere, that shrub would prove to be ill-fated.

In 1949 Sheridan became the first nursery to market an American elm cultivar called Queen City. It was a selection from a tree found growing on the Lakeshore Boulevard in Toronto. It is no longer cultivated.

Sheridan Nurseries always gave high priority to the development of new hardy evergreens. The 1963 catalogue carried the first listing for Sheridan Gold yew. Another original came in 1964 with the introduction of "an extremely hardy, bushy Number Sixteen yew. Free from winterburn."

In 1973, Sheridan released Ivory Silk Japanese tree lilac. There had been an in-company contest to name this Sheridan original, won by Olga Schultz of Sheridan's head office. The catalogue announced it as "NEW! A Sheridan Nurseries selection with a sturdy, more compact oval growth habit."

On the same page, the exclamation "NEW!" marked the listing of yet another Sheridan original, DeGroot linden. "A Sheridan Nurseries selection introduced through GARDENS CANADA and named in honour of Constant DeGroot, Sheridan's long time and recently retired propagator, and one of Canada's most knowledgeable plantsmen."

One Sheridan original came from a plant that is native to eastern parts of Canada and the United States, but which had been dismissed as a high-maintenance tree, the silver maple. In 1968, Sheridan selected and planted one hundred seedling trees in a specimen block for observation. Through an ongoing trial program, the nursery finally selected the Sheridan silver maple, an excellent, fast-growing tree that became popular.

The list of Sheridan originals is a long one: Sheridan's Red barberry (1944), Mountbatten juniper (1949), Sherway phlox (1958), Glenleven linden (1962), Pincushion boxwood (1967), Park Royal Chinese elm (1968), Ivory Silk Japanese tree lilac (1973), Sheridan Spire dawn-redwood (1976), Unicorn and DeGroot Spire white cedars (1980), and Green Globe linden (1983). These are but a few.

The names of the people who were responsible for these originals would be eligible for a Canadian nurserymen's hall of fame. Constant DeGroot, Fred Stensson, Jim Herod, Joe Pokluda, Joerg Leiss, Ted McNinch, and Len Slater.

Green Velvet boxwood and Ivory Silk Japanese tree lilac were winners of prestigious horticultural awards. Howard and Lorrie Dunington-Grubb and Herman Stensson would be proud indeed if they could see a twenty-first-century garden adorned with Sheridan originals, none of which existed in 1913.

BOXWOOD: THE SENSATION

According to horticultural lore, boxwood (*Buxus*) got its name in ancient times because the very hard wood was good for making boxes and small containers. In the twentieth century, boxwood earned a place in the lore of Sheridan Nurseries. It was one of the most singular success stories in the company's history.

In order to create in Canada the kind of classical gardens they had known in England, Howard and Lorrie Dunington-Grubb needed an ornamental hedge plant that was hardy enough to thrive in the cold climate. No native plant was suitable for their landscaping purposes. They knew, though, that Korean boxwood could be a good choice.

Boxwood is a slow-growing, broad-leaved evergreen. It can survive winter temperatures as low as minus 29 Celsius (minus 20 Fahrenheit), as well as the humidity of summer. It is resistant to foraging and grazing wildlife because its leaves are unpalatable — an important point for Ontario nursery farms and rural parks and gardens, where deer and rabbits can do great damage. Boxwood grows to an average four feet high and wide. Pruning and trimming encourage denser growth. It can be sculpted to almost any shape. In spring and summer the leaves are a vivid, shiny green. In winter they have a yellow-to-purple hue. Howard and Lorrie saw Korean boxwood as an important plant for use in Ontario gardens.

In 1922, Sheridan Nurseries obtained some Korean boxwood seedlings from Harvard University's Arnold Arboretum, which had obtained seed from Korea in 1918. These were probably the first Korean boxwoods grown in Canada. The seedlings were the ancestors of the many generations of boxwood grown on Sheridan farms.

Boxwood was a prime example of the patience that was necessary to develop an imported hardy plant for the eastern Canadian market. It took ten years to get a saleable plant from seed. Additional years were required to build up stock. As one Sheridan slogan went, "We do the waiting."

Due to lack of records, it isn't known if Sheridan Nurseries sold small amounts of boxwood in the late 1920s or early 1930s. It wasn't until 1939 that boxwood first appeared in the retail catalogue. Considering the importance the plant would achieve as a Sheridan best-seller, that initial listing was brief.

From the Korean boxwood seedlings, Sheridan Nurseries made three selections: Winter Beauty was valued as a hardy cultivar, with good winter colour, purplish, not brown; Pincushion as a low-growing selection; and Tall Boy as a pyramidal selection. All three set fewer seeds and had a better winter colour than the other seedlings.

Parallel to their release was the development and evaluation of boxwood hybrids, which were a cross between hardy Korean boxwood and non-hardy English boxwood. Sheridan Nurseries had obtained English boxwood plants from the E.D. Smith nursery in Niagara. A fortunate decision was made to plant a row of English boxwood next to a row of Korean boxwood. Hybridization occurred naturally.

In 1955, seed was picked from the English boxwood. Fifty plants were obtained and evaluated. Sheridan grew over five thousand plants from each, in order to select the hardiest and best growers. The hybrids had the hardiness of Korean boxwood, and the larger, brighter green leaf of the English boxwood, as well as the latter's faster growth rate. Through testing at Sheridan, Montreal, and at the Central Experimental Farm in Ottawa, four selections were finally made from the original fifty.

Green Gem was chosen as the best for specimen planting because of its natural globe shape: dark green, dense foliage and tendency to maintain good colour through the winter. Green Mountain was the most upright selection, ideal for growing into pyramids. Green Velvet, a round, full-bodied type with a vigorous habit, proved well-suited for hedges and general broadleaf evergreen plantings. Green Mound maintained its dark green foliage throughout the year, and proved ideal for low hedges.

From its first humble appearance in the Sheridan catalogue in 1939, boxwood rose to be a featured attraction. A 1967 edition listed Pincushion, Tall Boy, and Winter Beauty, complete with photographs. In a 1971 catalogue, boxwood is described as:

> One of our most versatile, low growing, woody plants, thriving in sun or shade, and widely adapted to use in southern Ontario and other areas with as mild a winter, and where there is dependable snow cover throughout the winter. Can be used for low hedges from 6 to 18 inches high, for foundation plantings, in cemeteries and in formal parterre plantings.

This is followed by detailed entries for several *Buxus* Sheridan hybrids. Throughout the 1970s, Green Mountain Box, Green Velvet Box, Green Gem Box, and subsequently Green Mound became more than familiar names to Sheridan catalogue subscribers; they were flourishing in the gardens of Sheridan's customers. Horticulturist William Bloom of Weeping Tree Gardens in Burlington, Wisconsin, wrote in the April 1986, issue of *The Boxwood Bulletin*: "I have had 'Green Velvet' only a short time, but feel it may prove to be the best of all because it is a hybrid, having a unique colour and remaining a very pleasing dark green all year. It will become the 'standard hardy box.'"

Mr. Bloom was right. Hybrids such as Green Velvet are indeed now among the standard hardy boxwoods used in the landscaping of private and public properties in much of eastern Canada and the northern United States. Over 250,000 boxwood plants are grown at Sheridan Nurseries every year. Boxwood is grown by every major grower in the northeastern, western, and central United States and Canada. And it all started with those first seedlings obtained in 1922.

EVERGREENS: LOVING YEW

It didn't take the Dunington-Grubbs long to realize that hardy evergreens were essential to successful landscaping in southern Ontario. While the gardens would not look as attractive during the winter months as in spring and summer when everything was fresh and green, the presence of evergreens nonetheless made them more appealing to the eye than a bleak winterscape of bare branches.

The early catalogues show the importance that evergreens held for Sheridan Nurseries. The number of varieties that were offered rose steadily, even though some selections were dropped. If Tree of Heaven didn't catch on with gardeners, perhaps Bald Cypress would.

The selections were the ones most people would associate with the word "evergreen": pines and spruces. The 1925 catalogue offered, among others, Douglas spruce (now Douglas fir), Austrian pine, Jack pine, and Scots pine. However, that issue of the catalogue also listed something new; *Taxus* — the yew.

Considering the impact yew would have on ornamental gardening in southern Ontario, the first listing for Japanese yew was inauspicious: "The most satisfactory of the smaller evergreens for this climate remaining perfectly green all winter and resisting city smoke."

By 1936, the catalogue's evergreen list took up most of a page. The caption that accompanied the illustration of a hedge read:

> The Yew hedge illustrated above was planted by us with twelve-inch plants seven years ago. In spite of shade this hedge is now over four feet high. The possibility of having evergreen hedges and making the garden almost as beautiful in winter as in summer has caught the imagination of the public. The demand for Yews is increasing by leaps and bounds.

Yews were soon among the most widely used ornamental garden plants in North America, though they didn't prove hardy enough for the Canadian prairies. English yew was found to be well-suited to coastal British Columbia. Japanese yew and its hybrids grew well in much of eastern Canada.

Meanwhile, firs were also being grown commercially. The 1934 catalogue had a listing for *Abies fraseri*, a tall growing tree that was suitable as a lawn plant. It eventually became very popular as a Christmas tree.

On the same page there was a listing for *Cupressus* — the Cypress. *Lawsoniana* — Triomphe de Boskoop, the variety advertised, was described as "One of the most handsome conifers. Blue feathery foliage." It had the additional advantage of being hardy in zones six to nine.

Evergreens were vital to the growth of Sheridan Nurseries. They were also a major factor in the success of Howard and Lorrie's landscaping careers. They might even have been as significant as Lorrie's beloved perennials.

BROADLEAF EVERGREENS: BEAUTY WITH HARDINESS

In 1913, the Dunington-Grubbs had what might today be called a "want list." Broadleaf evergreens were at the top, as they were essential to the gardens Howard and Lorrie wanted to create. The need was somewhat fulfilled with the introduction of Korean boxwood. However, other hardy broadleaf evergreens would be necessary for their landscaping designs to have diversity. As well, they required plants that would be of use during the long period it took for the boxwood to develop.

One plant the Dunington-Grubbs used was *Pachysandra* then called Mountain Spurge. It was first listed in the 1915–16 catalogue, though not as a broadleaf evergreen. At the

time, Sheridan Nurseries didn't have enough selections of that type to warrant a separate heading.

Not until 1940 did the catalogue present a section devoted specifically to broadleaf evergreens. From the lonely appearance of Mountain Spurge twenty-five years earlier, the number of selections had been built up to seventeen. They were listed under the genera *Berberis* (1), *Buxus* (1), *Daphne* (1), *Euonymus* (5), *Hedera* (1), *Ilex* (2), *Pachistima* (1), *Pachysandra* (1), *Viburnum* (1), *Vinca* (1), and *Yucca* (2).

The listings provide some insight into the work that had been going on at Sheridan Nurseries. The name Mountain Spurge was gone, replaced by Japanese Spurge. According to the text: "The English Ivy [*Hedera helix*] offered by us has been propagated from a mother plant growing for more than twenty years in a very exposed situation on the north side of a brick house." That might have been Howard and Lorrie's house in Toronto.

The 1944 catalogue enthusiastically announced:

> The broad-leaved evergreens, as a group, are gaining rapidly in popularity in the States and Canada. Their toughness enables them to withstand city conditions and thrive as foundation, and other plantings, where the more familiar coniferous evergreens die. While the effect of the deciduous shrubs is limited to five months, this group stays green all year.
>
> For facing the shrub or evergreen border, we recommend the hardy Korean Box and varieties of Euonymus radicans. All of these withstand city conditions and shade.

A sidebar that focused on the virtues of Korean boxwood stated that it was "Hardy, even in Manitoba." This claim might have been stretching things a little, but it reflected the faith that Sheridan Nurseries had in this durable plant. The text of the sidebar concluded: "This importation from the Orient seems likely to become Canada's most popular dwarf shrub."

In 1954, the Sheridan Nurseries' catalogue announced, "Very exciting news" under the broad-leaved evergreens heading. Two varieties of cherry laurel, *Zabeliana* and *reynvani*, had been found growing in southern Ontario.

> These magnificent broad-leaved evergreens, so universally popular in England and Vancouver, have always been considered too tender to be given a trial in Eastern Canada. Now, however two hardier [varieties] have appeared. The former has now withstood five winters unprotected without damage of any consequence, and the latter two winters.

Sheridan had another breakthrough in 1956 with the first listing for hardy rhododendrons (broadleaf evergreens) and azaleas (deciduous). They were introduced together in the catalogue, and described as: "the most spectacular of the flowering shrubs. They are free flowering and the colours, particularly of the Azaleas, are so brilliant that the effect in spring is unequalled ... The varieties listed have proved hardy in southern Ontario if planted in a position that is sheltered from the hot noon and afternoon sun." The catalogue listed several varieties of rhododendrons and azaleas, accompanied by photographs of azaleas in full bloom.

For many years holly, a broadleaf evergreen so much associated with Christmas, was not thought to be hardy enough to be grown in southern Ontario. The wreaths and boughs of holly that decorated Canadian homes every December came from British Columbia. In 1991, the Sheridan Nurseries catalogue offered for the first time a Christmas-type holly that had been tested and proven hardy. The entry read: "These evergreen Hollies have proven to be hardy in protected gardens in areas south of the line from Toronto to Sarnia. The leaves are the typical dark green of the English Holly. Note that plants of both sexes must be planted to obtain fruit."

Today much of the cut holly found in Canadian homes at Christmas is English Holly (*Ilex aquifolium*) from British Columbia. The ones grown for use in southern Ontario gardens are two hybrids: Blue Prince and Blue Princess. Many hardier selections of broadleaf evergreens, once thought to be too "tender" for much of Canada, are now available for the milder areas of eastern Canada. It's part of a horticultural revolution that began with the Dunington-Grubb "want list."

SIGNIFICANT TREES: SUCCESS AND CREDENTIALS

Some of the trees Sheridan Nurseries introduced in the catalogues were significant because they caught on well with the public and are still popular today. The Maidenhair Tree (*Ginkgo biloba*) was first listed in the 1923–24 catalogue, in which it was described as "Formal pyramidal tree for street and park planting." The Ginkgo has been called a "living fossil." Because of fossil evidence, scientists had known long before the gingko was discovered growing in China, that it had existed during the age of the dinosaurs.

In 1928 the catalogue carried the first listing for Weeping Purple Osier Willow (*Salix purpurea pendula*), described as: "Ornamental tree of weeping habit and having red bark." Kilmarnock Willow (*Salix caprea pendula*), "A handsome weeping tree," followed in 1930. It's known today as the Weeping Pussy Willow. The Weeping Mulberry (*Morus alba "Pendula"*), with long and slender pendulous branches, first appeared in the 1931 catalogue. A listing for Pea tree, *Caragana arborescens "Pendula,"* now known as the Weeping Peashrub, was in the 1937 catalogue.

Catalpa bungei, first listed in 1950, is still popular today, but is now called Umbrella catalpa. The bigleaf wintercreeper (*Euonymus fortunei*) was first listed in 1952. It was hailed as a "magnificent evergreen with permanent glossy green foliage, grown in standard form, makes an excellent specimen for formal planting." This tree might be said to have come with impressive credentials. The Dunington-Grubbs had grown it in their own garden in Toronto in the early 1940s. These trees were all significant because they were top-grafted, a process in which a weeping or globe head is grafted on top of a short trunk.

THE LINDENS: TAKING THE LEAD IN ONTARIO

In 1963, Sheridan Nurseries introduced the Glenleven linden. This was the first of a series of lindens and other shade tree cultivars to be released by the nursery as it replaced trees grown from seedlings with uniform crops of budded or

grafted shade trees. The new trees were much better suited to mechanized cultivation. United States nurseries had been in the forefront of the development of these new cultivars due to the demand for trees to replant American streets that had been denuded by Dutch Elm Disease.

Taking the lead in Ontario, Sheridan Nurseries selected new cultivars from well-shaped specimens found in the wild, from existing street plantings of seedling trees, or from nursery fields of seedling trees. Glenleven linden was found in a nursery field. The trees were originally described as having "compact, broad, pyramidical heads." Years later, Glenleven lindens were still listed in some major catalogues as having a "pyramidical form that is a little more open and informal than Greenspire," the Littleleaf linden that became popular. In fact, forty-year-old Glenlevens that reached a height of twenty metres were only narrowly pyramidical.

The linden — or basswood, as the native Canadian species is called — isn't a showy tree. Its yellow autumn colouring isn't spectacular. But most of them produce fragrant, light-yellow flowers in June. Some linden flowers are used to make tea, and they produce excellent honey. The lindens' hardiness and stately appearance made them popular in Canada from western New Brunswick to eastern Manitoba.

SHRUBS:
THE RISE AND FALL OF SHERIDAN'S RED BARBERRY

The section on trees in the 1917–18 Sheridan Nurseries catalogue is illustrated with a photograph of a beautifully treed landscape. The caption below it reads, "A landscape constructed by us. Trees and shrubs need expert arrangement to produce results like this."

Hardy shrubs, particularly evergreens, were vital to the Dunington-Grubbs' work. They were also a mainstay of Sheridan Nurseries' trade from the beginning. As the catalogue caption inferred, garden planners would get the best results if they sought the advice of experts — like those at Sheridan.

Some of the plants originally listed in the catalogue as trees were, in fact, shrubs, and were grown from seed. One of these was the Japanese maple. It grew to a height of ten feet. The Tree of Heaven (soon to be discontinued) could be grown as a shrub, the catalogue said, if cut down to the ground every year, usually because it wasn't that hardy.

Over the years, the list of shrubs in the catalogue grew at an amazing rate. By 1936 the retail catalogue list totaled twenty-nine selections under the headings *Euonymus* (10), *Exochorda* (2), *Forsythia* (6), *Halesia* (1), *Halimodendron* (1), and *Hibiscus* (9). The *Hibiscus* listing was extensive for the time, and it is noteworthy that many of the selections are still widely grown.

More extensive listings of shrubs appeared in the Sheridan catalogue in 1946. Two boxed features drew the reader's attention. One was for dwarf Japanese maples, finally correctly recognized as shrubs. The other was for a best-seller, Sheridan's Red barberry.

> This sensational shrub, recently produced in our nurseries, has been met with enthusiasm by the gardening world. Tall growing, and with very dark foliage, it provides magnificent colour for the shrub border or makes a splendid medium

to tall dark purple hedge. U.S.A. rights sold to Jackson & Perkins and U.S.A. patent applied for. Canadian Trade Mark registered.

For more than twenty years, Sheridan's Red was very popular, and could be seen in many gardens in southern Ontario and the northern United States. Sheridan Nurseries not only listed it in the catalogues, but also ran illustrated ads in the Toronto *Daily Star*. Then in 1966, a rumour circulated that it was an alternative host for black stem rust on wheat. Canadian grain farmers feared that the infection could spread to their crops. Pressured by the farmers to take action, the Canadian government placed a ban on several varieties of barberry, including Sheridan's Red. The shrub was dropped from the catalogue listing, and eventually disappeared from Canadian gardens. No such ban was enacted in the United States. At the time of the ban, Sheridan was propagating over forty thousand barberries a year. The plant was second in numbers only to boxwood. The ban was a heavy blow to Sheridan's sales.

Many horticulturists believed that the Canadian government overreacted to the "stem rust" scare. To Sheridan, the Canada Department of Agriculture seemed to be something of a villain in the loss of Sheridan's Red. But Sheridan benefited from the work of Isabella Preston and Agriculture Canada, particularly in the development of lilies, lilacs, and crab apples. The Sheridan catalogue offered selections of Preston Lilacs: "New Hybrids with large trusses of pale pink to lilac-coloured flowers." In this way, perhaps Agriculture Canada partially compensated for the unfortunate demise of Sheridan's Red.

ROSES: SHERIDAN'S CANADIAN ORIGINALS

Roses have been used as ornamental plants since ancient times, and come in hundreds of varieties. It might seem surprising then, that the first Sheridan Nurseries catalogue, issued in 1914, listed only four roses. A year later, the catalogue listed only three roses. The problem was that even though several species of native roses grew wild in Canada, ornamental rose shrubs had to be imported.

Sheridan Nurseries started to propagate affordable roses that were hardy enough for southern Ontario. Herman Stensson conducted many tests, using different stock and different soils. The process was costly, and there were failures. But the end result was an impressive inventory of Canadian-grown roses.

The 1917–18 catalogue had the first extensive list of roses, with fifty-six listed under six different types. The booklet included a picture of a rose garden the Dunington-Grubbs had designed for Government House in Chorley Park. In the 1918–19 catalogue, the list of roses had grown to seventy-five. A year later, the number slipped to seventy-four, with Hybrid Perpetual gaining on Hybrid Teas in popularity. The base price was fifty or seventy-five cents a plant, depending on type, with eleven cultivars listed at a dollar each.

Although the first separate Sheridan Nurseries Rose Catalogue and Price List isn't dated, it was probably printed about 1925. It was well-illustrated with nursery photographs. The catalogue proudly announced that Sheridan was "now able to offer the public for this coming season, some twenty thousand rose bushes entirely Canadian grown." The listings included 104 different roses.

According to that first Sheridan Rose Catalogue, "The popularity of roses in this country is a development of very recent origin, as far as the general public is concerned." Sheridan Nurseries would be instrumental in enhancing that popularity. Roses were featured in gardens Sheridan developed for the CNE. In 1925, Sheridan entered a "Display of Roses" in an exhibit for the Ontario Rose Society. Their arrangement on a table covering twenty square feet took first prize. Sheridan won first prize for the same event in 1926.

SUMMER WITHOUT ROSES

In the winter of 1933–34, Ontario was in the grip of a deadly frost. As early as mid-November, temperatures were dropping below zero degrees Fahrenheit (-18 Celsius). Exceptionally cold weather wreaked havoc with rose bushes and hedges. On April 21, 1934, the Toronto Star *advised readers of the possibility of a summer without roses: "From all parts of the province have come reports that the long period of low temperatures during last winter killed a high percentage of rose plants, shrubs and hedges."*

J.F. Clarke of the Ontario Department of Agriculture said that approximately 90 percent of the province's climbing roses had been touched by heavy frost, and would have to be pruned almost to the ground. The plants weren't all dead, he said, but it would be a year before they could bloom. However, one place had avoided the horticultural disaster.

Howard Dunington-Grubb informed the Star that Sheridan Nurseries' well-protected roses had hardly been touched by the killer cold. He even claimed that the cold had been beneficial.

> *We needed a winter like the past one to show us the plants and hedges that we could plant as practically permanent. People were expending money unwisely in hedges that would not last through a period of severe cold. It is a good thing to find out what plants and hedges can be put in with safety.*

On May 7 a letter to the editor submitted by Howard appeared in the Star. *In a cleverly worded manner, it actually served as a bit of free advertising for Sheridan Nurseries while extolling the hardiness of Sheridan's evergreens.*

> *On the front page of the Star we see the statement that only ten percent of the evergreens in the Toronto district survived the winter. As this may possibly be a misprint, and we are the largest growers of evergreens in Canada, we feel compelled to state that our losses of evergreens, this past winter, amount to only a fraction of one percent; that none of our trees received any winter protection; and that these small losses were confined to tender varieties which we were growing for experimental purposes. A visit to our three-hundred acre nurseries near Clarkson would verify this statement.*

The message was clear: if you wanted hardy plants, you bought them at Sheridan Nurseries.

Sheridan Nurseries.

Sheridan Nurseries employees and their wives, who attended a reception held at Sheridan's head office on June 18, 1966, for Sam McGredy, the famous rose breeder. L–R: Russ Norfolk, Alice Pokluda, Franzis Leiss, Joe Pokluda, Elsie Herod, Kay Pleasants, Milt Edwards, Florence deBoer, Albert Brown, Lois Stensson, Jim Herod, Maurine Stensson, Bill Kegel, Geraldine Kegel, Ben deBoer, Barbara Edwards, Doris Laflin, Joerg Leiss, Kay Norfolk, Howard Stensson, Betty Stewart, Art Drysdale.

As Sheridan Nurseries tested new varieties of roses, their names were added to the lists in the catalogue. For example, two hardy rose standards, F.J. Grootendorst red and F.J. Grootendorst pink, were first listed in 1924. In 1939, for the first time, the Sheridan trade list offered trademarked roses. There were six varieties listed under Hybrid Teas, one under Polythana Baby Rambler, and two under Climbers. This listing came with a notice: "These varieties are being handled under agreement with the trade mark owner. It is agreed and understood that these varieties are for re-sale only at the following retail prices ..."

This was followed by a list that set a definite limit on retail prices. It was likely meant to discourage overcharging.

Both World War periods, (1914–18 and 1939–45) were marked by shortages. Like everyone else, Sheridan Nurseries and its clients and customers had to make the best of doing with less. In the 1944 catalogue, under the heading ROSES came a statement that was typical of the time:

> We regret that, owing to the very heavy demand for Roses last fall, our stock of Hybrid Tea, Hybrid Perpetual, Polyantha, and most of the Climbers has been entirely sold out. The few varieties listed are available in limited quantities. By next fall our stock will be replenished, when we will again have a large selection of varieties to offer.

The post–Second World War years — the beginning of the Baby Boom era — held great promise for everyone. People were buying houses, home owners wanted gardens, and no garden was complete without roses. Sheridan Nurseries showed that it was still in the forefront of offering the newest roses when, in 1952, it started to make available the annual winners of the All America Rose Society Award.

Sheridan Nurseries' program of looking for new cultivars of hardy roses continued through the 1950s and 1960s. In the 1970s, Sheridan started an evaluation program to test new rose cultivars from such British and European Rose breeders as Kordes, Poulsen, and McGredy. This gave Sheridan Nurseries access to many new cultivars as soon as they were released and after they had been successfully tested in Sheridan's fields. Sheridan Nurseries was allowed to name many of these cultivars, including some that were intended only for the Canadian market. The "Sheridan Family of Roses" pays homage to several iconic Canadian individuals, communities and institutions. Ten Ten (1988) was introduced in recognition of the sixtieth anniversary of the venerable Toronto radio station CFRB. City of Welland (1993) was named for the Ontario community known as The City of Roses. Parkwood Scarlet (1995) was named after the Parkwood Estate, one of the Dunington-Grubbs' most successful landscaping projects. In 1997 the Garden Club of Toronto selected the Lois Wilson rose to honour their long-time member after her passing. Lois was a great friend of Sheridan Nurseries, and author of *The Chatelaine's Gardening Book* (1970), the most comprehensive Canadian gardening book ever published. The Niagara Falls Horticultural Society chose Rainbow Niagara (2001) for the rose that honours their city. The Cape Breton recording artist Rita MacNeil, who has written songs about roses, had one named after her in 1996. Not to be overlooked in the Sheridan Family of Roses is Sunsation, the rose that was selected and introduced in 1988 to celebrate the seventy-fifth anniversary of Sheridan Nurseries. At the time of this writing, a new member of the "family" has been named Sheridan's Anniversary Blush and will be presented as the official rose for Sheridan's centennial celebration.

PERENNIALS: LORRIE'S LEGACY

It could be said without exaggeration that in the early days, perennials were the lifeblood of Sheridan Nurseries. They were first plants that Lorrie Dunington-Grubb imported from Europe. Perennials were basic to the Dunington-Grubbs' landscape projects, and they were the cash crop Sheridan Nurseries sold to local gardeners. The sudden availability of perennials that had rarely before been seen in Canada gave residents of southern Ontario the opportunity to re-create that ideal of "colonial" horticulture: the English garden. Some of the original perennial selections Sheridan Nurseries sold back then are still being sold today.

The listing of paeonies, a herbaceous perennial, was a significant first for Sheridan Nurseries. The plants evidently arrived from Europe in time to be mentioned in that landmark first catalogue. Tree paeonies were also listed in that first catalogue.

In the 1917–18 catalogue, *Eulalia Japonica gracilis univittata* and *Eulalia Japonica variegata* were listed as ornamental grasses. They were discontinued for many years, but have recently been revived and are today quite popular.

The catalogue for 1935 shows a listing that was advanced for Canada at that time: hardy cacti, a perennial more associated with the arid American Southwest than with southern Ontario. Under *Opuntia*, the catalogue listed the species *Camanchica* and *Polyacantha*. Cacti had actually been mentioned in the catalogue in 1926, but this was their first prominent appearance. The cacti plants listed were relatively compact varieties, not the giants of Hollywood Westerns. But the fact that Sheridan Nurseries had made such exotic species available in Canada at that time was remarkable. Cacti were discontinued for several years, but Sheridan brought them back in the 1990s.

In 1937, Sheridan Nurseries introduced southern Ontario gardeners to yet another interesting group of perennials, hardy water lilies. The catalogue listing included thirteen varieties. Readers were informed that: "The Water Lilies are ready for shipment from the end of May, and as they are grown in small wooden tubs, can be transported to your Lily pond any time during the summer."

Perennials are still among the most popular plants grown and sold by Canadian nurseries. Thousands of different hardy varieties can be found in gardens across the country. They are, in a sense, the legacy of Lorrie Dunington-Grubb.

Today, Sheridan Nurseries grows an extensive variety of perennials. The hundreds of varieties include a unique collection called Sheridan Garden Classics. These are distinctive "groups" of plants used for the same purpose: to make the consumer's choice easy. Collections include "plants for shade," "plants for sun," and "plants to attract butterflies." As well, Sheridan grows perennials under contract for some key mass merchants.

THE DOGWOOD: A SURVIVOR

Plants grown by Sheridan Nurseries have been purchased by customers across Canada and around the world: the Munich airport, a Japanese shipping company, and a military memorial in the American South. Every so often, head office receives a letter telling an extraordinary story about a Sheridan plant. One came in July 2011 from Christopher Clarke of Liverpool, Nova Scotia. In 1975, Mr. Clarke bought a dogwood tree from Sheridan. It was shipped by rail. Because of a strike, delivery was delayed for thirty-seven days. Amazingly, the dogwood was still alive when it reached its destination. Mr. Clarke planted it twenty yards from the seashore, where it was exposed to winter winds off the Atlantic. It first flowered in 1979 with four blossoms. "Since then," wrote Mr. Clarke, "it has gone from strength to strength." That's one tough dogwood.

CHINESE ELM: CHANGING TIMES

The first Chinese elm hedge the Dunington-Grubbs planted in Ontario was at McMaster University in Hamilton, in 1929. In 1931, Chinese elm first appeared in the Sheridan Nurseries catalogue. The 1934 catalogue hailed it as "one of the fastest growing trees known."

A speedy growth rate was a principal factor in Chinese elm's early popularity. By 1947, the Sheridan Nurseries catalogue could boast: "... the demand for this Elm has been growing by leaps and bounds. At McMaster a good six foot hedge was obtained from two-foot plants in two years. Its small leaf, dense habit, and very rapid growth make it an ideal tree for tall hedges."

In addition to being a fast grower, Chinese elm could thrive in dry sandy and gravelly soils, and needed little watering. It was hardy, and resistant to disease. Moreover, for budget-conscious homeowners and park managers, it was inexpensive.

For many years, Chinese elm hedges were a common sight throughout southern Ontario. They made excellent backdrops and windbreaks. They grew high and thick enough to make good privacy screens.

Ironically, Chinese elm's main selling point turned out to be its undoing. Its fast growth eventually produced a hedge that was bushy at the top, but had thin foliage near the bottom. Its popularity fell off as gardeners turned to hedge plants that had potential for longer-lasting results. With the passage of time and a change in horticultural tastes, most of the Chinese elm hedges disappeared, replaced by cedars and yews.

ONCE ORNAMENTAL, NOW "WEEDY"

Weeds, in the most basic definition, are plants growing where they are unwanted. They are generally considered to be the unsightly villains that interfere with more desirable plants. For dedicated gardeners, "weeding" is practically a crusade. Horticultural tastes are constantly changing. It isn't surprising that sometimes a plant that was once in great demand should fall from grace and land in the category of "weed." The Tree of Heaven is a case in point.

The 1917–18 Sheridan Nurseries catalogue had a listing *Ailanthus glandulosa*, the Tree of Heaven. It was described as, "A highly decorative tree which can also be grown as a shrub."

Evidently, the Tree of Heaven turned out to be not so heavenly after all, at least as far as Sheridan's customers were concerned. The following year, although the catalogue's list of evergreens had expanded considerably, the Tree of Heaven wasn't on it. To this day in southern Ontario it is recommended only for industrial areas.

Several other plants shared the fate of the Tree of Heaven. The Manitoba maple, once deemed worthy, is now considered a weed tree. In the 1926 catalogue there is a large, rather striking photograph of a buckthorn. The caption reads, "The black berries make this a very attractive shrub after the leaves have fallen." This plant is now classified as a weedy shrub.

CHAPTER 6

The Birth of the Canadian Society of Landscape Architects

Howard Dunington-Grubb is regarded as the father of landscape architecture in Canada. It can be fairly said that he and Lorrie, along with a few pioneering colleagues, nursed their art form through its Canadian infancy and saw it flourish. As individuals they subscribed to different, sometimes conflicting, schools of artistic thought. But as a group they nonetheless were responsible for increasing public awareness of Canadian landscape architecture, and raising it to a level that was at least the equal of what was found in England and the United States. It was no mean accomplishment that they did so in a period whose span included two catastrophic events: the First World War and the Great Depression. In the spring of 1934, amidst all the press coverage of calamity and despair, was a tiny report under the headline: LANDSCAPERS UNITE. It was about the formation of a little association that would have a far-reaching effect on Canadian landscape architecture. Humphrey Carver would recall the event years later.

> In Toronto there was a small group of landscape artists who came to know one another and enjoy one another's company very much. The Grubbs were the centre of this circle ... we used to meet in the garden of the Diet Kitchen Restaurant on Bloor Street, and together we founded the Canadian Society of Landscape Architects.

The Canadian Society of Landscape Architects and Town Planners (the "Town Planners" was eventually dropped)

was founded on March 6, 1934. It had only nine members. Sitting at the table were Howard and Lorrie, J.V. Stensson, Humphrey Carver and his mentor Carl Borgstrom, and four other pioneering colleagues: Gordon Culham, Helen Kippax, Edwin Kay, and Frances Steinhoff.

Each of these people brought something special to the group through their talents and personalities. Collectively they created the first Canadian definition of landscape architecture. To Humphrey Carver, his fellow founders were legends.

> The interesting thing about Howard Grubb is that he represents the finished work; the design that has a definition to it. It is a complete thing; it is a garden that is probably symmetrical because that expresses the idea that it doesn't occur anywhere else. It is the idea of a completely designed artifact.
>
> Mrs. Grubb, a person of flowers, is always with landscape artists in whatever they do, in the enjoyment and celebration of the beauty of the individual flower, the plant, the shape of the tree.
>
> Vilhelm Stensson, University of Toronto, Harvard School of Landscape Architecture, is the professional person. Now, the professional has the skill to record what the idea is for a particular landscape or garden. He or she has to be able to put the idea down on paper and then translate the idea into actuality on the ground, just as some person can think of a melody but doesn't have the skills of orchestrating it and putting it into a form that can be performed in the theatre and on the stage and so on. So the professional skill of Vilhelm is the monument and the legend connected with him.

Carver had equal praise for each of the other founders. He said in conclusion, "I stand and applaud the founders of the CSLA for what they have left for us in these legends."

The first president of the CSLA was Gordon Culham. Howard was its second. By 1938, the society had seventeen members. Lorrie became president in 1944. However, she had been ill since 1928, and was finally obliged to step down. After her death on January 17, 1945, at the age of sixty-eight, Howard completed her term. That year he was re-elected for another term.

Today the CSLA has over 1,600 members representing Canada's ten provinces and three territories. It is, by its own definition: "a unifying organization that develops and delivers relevant and high quality programs and services, while bringing together and representing at the national level, affiliate organizations, component associations, and professional schools across Canada."

One of the goals of the founders of the CSLA was to help ordinary Canadians become more aware of the arts of gardening and landscape architecture. Because of their collective vision and work, professional Canadian landscapers and gardeners have achieved worldwide esteem. We can only wonder if the original nine, back in 1934, ever imagined that their little society would flourish beyond even their most optimistic expectations.

CHAPTER 7

The Nursery: Through Wars, Depression, and the Tides of Change

"I should like to take a minute or two to consider the nature of the product you are going to handle, and some of the factors peculiar to its production. It is a product with endless variety, size, shape and colour and different cultural requirements. It is something alive, growing and perishable, needing a certain state of soil, temperature and moisture to keep it in healthy, viable shape. It may be subject to the elements — sun and the rain, heat and the cold, floods and drought. The product may be produced in many ways — seeds, cuttings, layers, divisions, grafting (some of which are more effective and require more skill and knowledge) — which must be planted in the soil and which must be removed. Usually it is a high density crop with a high yield per acre. There is no certainty of catch from seeds, cuttings or grafts. You may sow Taxus or Purple Barberry and have it germinate like a lawn one year, and the following year have to absorb a 100% failure ... You cannot keep your product like cans or cartons on a shelf. It requires constant husbandry and maintenance, and while shearing, pruning, root pruning may enable you to carry limited quantities of certain items beyond their normal selling point, such plants may easily become a losing proposition ... Many nurseries are forced to have a bonfire once or twice a year."

— J.V. STENSSON

As J.V. Stensson outlined in this passage from an address he made at a nursery growers' convention, they were part of a complex business with many inherent risks. The Dunington-Grubbs were certainly aware of that when they started out in 1913. If the venture didn't work out, they would lose their investment. However, should it be successful, they knew that one day they would need more land.

When business did indeed grow, the nursery had to expand. This time the Dunington-Grubbs had Herman Stensson to advise them on what land to buy. Over the first decade they bought several farms in the Sheridan area and turned them into nurseries. By 1925, Sheridan Nurseries had doubled in size to two hundred acres. By 1930 it had three hundred acres, all in the Sheridan/Clarkson/Oakville area. Then, in the midst of the Great Depression, Howard Dunington-Grubb made a bold move that would turn out to be one of the most significant in the company's history. He purchased land in Etobicoke along the new QEW for the site of a new nursery.

The first quarter-century of Sheridan Nurseries' existence was a time of dramatic change in almost every aspect of everyday life. Toronto was expanding, and suburbs mushroomed on what had been farmland and pasture. Paved highways replaced dirt roads. Agriculture, like everything else, was becoming increasingly mechanized. Horses gave way to tractors and trucks.

In the booming Roaring Twenties, money seemed plentiful. Town councils wanted their parks and other public places to reflect community pride. The barons of industry and finance tried to outdo each other in making their estates into ostentatious showpieces. Middle-class families took pride in owning a comfortable home with an attractive garden.

The old ledgers in the Sheridan Nurseries archives show that the company did well in the highly optimistic twenties. In 1927 there was a net profit of just over $12,000. In 1928 it dipped to a little under $12,000, but in 1929 the net profit jumped to more than $14,000. Those were promising figures for a small, growing company.

Then came the stock market crash of October 29, 1929; Black Tuesday! Businessmen who had been millionaires on paper were suddenly broke. Unemployment skyrocketed as factories shut down. With the Great Depression tightening its grip on Canada, there was little money available for luxuries like ornamental plants. Sheridan Nurseries' net profit for 1930 dropped to just over $3,000. In 1931, 1932, and 1933, the company operated at a loss. The net profit was $354.44 in 1934.

Thanks to projects like the Oakes Garden Theatre in Niagara Falls, Sheridan Nurseries was able to ride out the storm. Drastic reductions in prices helped to get stock moving again. It was also necessary to cut costs. Administrative expenses in 1928 had been over $32,000. By 1933, they were down by $20,000. That meant lean times for the Stensson family and other employees. But as the second half of the Dirty Thirties dragged along, the figures in the profit column slowly rose. They weren't spectacular: $2,609.05 in 1935; $6,497.48 in 1936; $7,598.93 in 1937; and then a drop to $2,396.59 in 1938.

Herman Stensson died in 1938 and his eldest son took over as manager. It was fortunate that J.V. had been groomed for the position and possessed strong executive abilities. The difficult times weren't over yet.

Sheridan's fortunes continued to rise and fall with the unstable economy. Then the Second World War put millions

of unemployed Canadians back to work. Wartime rationing limited the amount of gasoline and other commodities a person could buy, but wages earned in hundreds of factories geared to the war effort meant that after years of austerity, people had money to spend.

During the war years, with so many able-bodied men in the armed forces, female workers had to do jobs that were traditionally done by males. The image of Rosie the Riveter became iconic. Women had worked in the fields at Sheridan Nurseries previously, but during the war the company employed a large number of young women called *Farmerettes*. They planted, hoed, and pulled weeds under the supervision of First World War veterans like Constant DeGroot, Bill Pilgrim, and Charlie Barnard. Sheridan also employed Japanese-Canadians who had been uprooted from their homes in British Columbia and unfairly interned.

During the Second World War and the first few postwar years, Sheridan's net profits went up and down, just as they had during the Depression. There was a low of just under $6,000 in 1940, and a high of more than $55,000 in 1947, with fluctuations in between. Then net profits almost doubled to more than $107,000 in 1948. The terrible years of economic depression and war had at last given way to the era of the Baby Boom and prosperity. In 1949, Sheridan Nurseries' profits jumped to $142,584.50

It was again a time of rapid change. Suburbs and small urban centres became "bedroom communities" where houses were affordable for people willing to commute to jobs in the cities. Every newlywed couple dreamed of owning a home, a car, and a television set. Four was considered the ideal number of children for a middle-class family. Father drove to

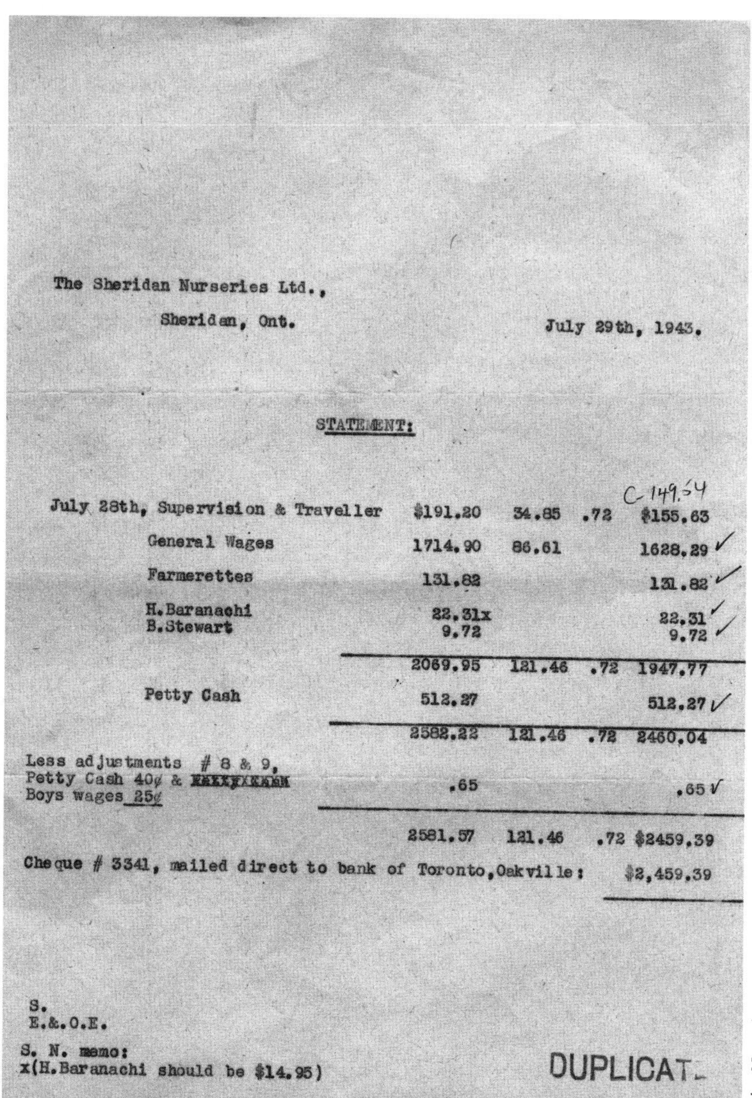

The Sheridan Nurseries Ltd.,
Sheridan, Ont.

July 29th, 1943.

STATEMENT:

July 28th, Supervision & Traveller	$191.20	34.85	.72	$155.63
General Wages	1714.90	86.61		1628.29
Farmerettes	131.82			131.82
H.Baranachi	22.31x			22.31
B.Stewart	9.72			9.72
	2069.95	121.46	.72	1947.77
Petty Cash	512.27			512.27
	2582.22	121.46	.72	2460.04
Less adjustments # 8 & 9, Petty Cash 40¢ & XXXXXXXXX Boys wages 25¢	.65			.65
	2581.57	121.46	.72	$2459.39

Cheque # 3341, mailed direct to bank of Toronto, Oakville: $2,459.39

S.
E.&.O.E.

S. N. memo:
x(H.Baranachi should be $14.95)

DUPLICAT

Sheridan Nurseries.

This monthly wage statement includes a category for Farmerettes, women who made up for the shortage of male workers due to the war.

Sheridan Nurseries.

Four farm managers. L–R: Joe Pokluda (Glen Williams), Lorne Thompson (Oro), Joerg Leiss (production manager), and Dieter Frank (Hope).

work every day while mother took on the role of homemaker. No home was complete without a garden.

Once again there was a demand for ornamental plants to beautify communities. Newly built subdivisions needed trees to line the streets. Brand-new parks had to be landscaped and planted.

The nursery business was booming, and although by this time Sheridan had many competitors, it was the leader in the trade. Over the years, Sheridan had established a solid reputation for quality, innovation, and service. To maintain that reputation, it would have to adapt to the changing times.

Starting in 1957, J.V. Stensson oversaw a major reorganization of the company. The market for ornamental nursery stock was growing by leaps and bounds, and Sheridan's farms were hard pressed to keep pace. In 1955 the company had, for the first time, recorded more than a million dollars in sales in a single year. That number was growing by over a hundred thousand annually. In 1953 the company had started a search for a new nursery location in Halton County. This led to the purchase in 1955 of three hundred acres on the banks of the Credit River just outside the picturesque village of Glen Williams, near Georgetown. Over the next twelve years, additional land purchases in the Glen Williams area more than tripled the farm's size.

The Glen Williams nursery was destined to become Sheridan's principal farm. Urban growth around Oakville was crowding the old nursery, and making the land it occupied very attractive to developers. The reconstruction of the

Sheridan Nurseries.

Field-grown Mugo Pines in Oakville.

Sheridan Nurseries.

Field of Peegee Hydrangeas in Oakville, to be dug bare root.

Sheridan Nurseries.

Aerial view of Sheridan Nurseries Ryrie farm, Oakville, surrounded by new housing developments. Circa 1960.

Uli Rumpf.

Elm trees being loaded on a Cedarvale flat bed transport at the Sherway farm in 1965 for shipment to the Expo 67 site. Standing left: Joe Vivieros and Joe Maiato, Sheridan Nurseries employees. Others: Cedarvale Tree Experts employees.

QEW into a major multilane freeway doomed the village of Sheridan. The little community that had been the birthplace of Sheridan Nurseries vanished in the name of progress in the 1960s. In 1968, when a collection of communities including Lorne Park, Clarkson, Cooksville, and Malton merged to make a single "city," Sheridan no longer existed. It had been reduced to a memorial cairn near the intersection of the QEW and Winston Churchill Boulevard. In a referendum to decide the name of the new city, "Sheridan" lost to "Mississauga," the name of the First Nations tribe that had been the area's original inhabitants.

Although the old original farm continued to be productive, as land values soared and development encircled it, the property was sold off bit by bit. The earnings made from the real-estate transactions enabled Sheridan Nurseries to invest in properties elsewhere. The company moved out of the original premises for good in 1987. In many ways it was the end of an era.

Sheridan Nurseries.

Field of Colorado spruce at the Oro farm.

While the Glen Williams farm grew in importance and became the site of the new head office in 1987, Sheridan Nurseries expanded to new locations. The Hope farm (over seven hundred acres), east of Oshawa, began production in 1974, specializing in deciduous trees and shrubs. It was managed by Dieter Franke and later Mike Forward. The Oro farm (over four hundred acres), north of Barrie, started up the following year, growing boxwood, evergreens, and euonymus. It was managed by Lorne Thompson.

Sheridan became a one-third partner in Umapine Nurseries of Milton-Freewater, Oregon, in 1977, then increased it to two-thirds in September 1980. Umapine specialized in the production of tree whips. Sheridan sold its interest in 1985. That same year, Sheridan acquired an eighty-three-acre farm at Norval, east of Georgetown. It became the main site for propagation and production of herbaceous perennials. Meanwhile, the Glen Williams farm produced conifers, trees, and roses. The original intent of buying farms so far apart was to take advantage of the climactic conditions such as snow cover in Barrie. However, as transportation became slower with congested highways, and costs of transport, overhead, and management increased, the third generation of Stenssons sold the Oro farm in 1996, and the Hope farm in 2003.

Throughout the latter part of the twentieth century, Sheridan Nurseries faced a demand for product that was not only increasing, but also evolving as customers' needs became ever more diverse. Besides the traditional gardens associated with suburban bungalows, "gardens in the sky" were gaining in popularity as apartment and condominium dwellers decorated their balconies with potted plants. The manufacture and sale of pots for both practical and aesthetic

purposes dated back to the 1950s. Now patio pots became a major Sheridan sideline.

The long period of growth and adaptation saw many changes, some of them just as profound as when Herman Stensson had to switch from horses to tractors. In 1967, Sheridan entered the computer age. It was, in fact, the first nursery in Canada to use computers.

Milt Edwards, a long-time Sheridan employee, introduced the IBM punch-card system in 1967. Milt's aunt, Elma Stong, was the office bookkeeper and treasurer. At her urging, he'd come to Sheridan in 1965 to take over her duties when she retired. Milt was involved in the upgrading of computer systems for several years.

Of course, the computers of that time weren't anything like the compact devices of today. Lynda Ferguson, currently assistant manager of the IT department, joined Sheridan in 1970. She recalls that the computer equipment she worked with filled four rooms. The computer took two or three days to do work that is now done in an hour or two. In 1972, Sheridan upgraded its computer. The new equipment required just one room. The first PC came in 1988, and cost $4,000. Sheridan remained on the cutting edge of computer technology.

Other changes were taking place at head office. At one time Lois Stensson was the only female office employee. More women filled important staff positions as the company grew. Mary Langston began working as a bookkeeper in 1944. Betty McBride was hired as a bookkeeper in 1947. She recalls the day she drove home from work through Hurricane Hazel in a car that had no brakes. She arrived safely. But when she went back to work the next day, flooding had made a watery mess of the basement at head office, and she had to help dry out records.

Lynda Ferguson recalls being one of about eight "girls" in the office. She was the first to wear a pantsuit to work. One of the older women remarked, "I don't know if I'm looking at you or Mr. Edwards."

Sheridan Nurseries.

Kay Pleasants started with Sheridan in 1955 as secretary for J.V. Stensson.

Kay Pleasants started in 1955 as secretary for J.V. Stensson who was then the Oakville farm manager. Later she worked for Howard Stensson, Fred Stensson, and other staff in the office, replacing the long-time nursery office secretary, Maureen (Barnard) Boch. Among the varied duties Kay had over the years were typing nursery orders and typing the retail catalogue manuscripts for Art Drysdale. Kay retired in the mid-1980s.

GRACEFUL SEA LION, MISSING OWL

The graceful sculpture of a sea lion that greets visitors at the entrance of Sheridan Nurseries' Georgetown head office was carved from Arkansas limestone by Canadian artist Ursula Hanes in 1957. Howard Dunington-Grubb had commissioned her to make a fountain piece for the pool at what was then the head office in Etobicoke. The sculpture went into storage when the Etobicoke office closed in 1984, and was installed in its present location in 1987. In 2007, Sheridan contacted Ursula (now living in France). She said that she was "amazed and delighted to learn that the sea lion sculpture is still alive and well."

Less fortunate was a sculpture of an owl that Sheridan first used in a garden display at the CNE. It was then installed on a concrete column at the entrance of the Etobicoke office. When the office closed, the owl was placed in storage in a barn in Oakville. Then it disappeared. The mystery of the missing owl has never been solved. There was, however, a smaller "sample" bronze owl that was to be approved before the stone sculpture was produced, which is now in Karl Stensson's possession.

Jody Thompson joined Sheridan as a receptionist in 1970. She recalls that she was what was then called a "Girl Friday." She left that stereotype behind as she rose through the office hierarchy. Today, forty-two years later, Jody is executive assistant to Bill Stensson.

Colleen Swan joined the staff at Sheridan Nurseries head office on Evans Avenue in Etobicoke in October 1974. Thirty-seven years later, she is still with Sheridan as credit manager in the head office at Georgetown.

Patricia Large came to Sheridan Nurseries in 2003 with the acquisition of Weall & Cullen (see Chapter 8: The Sales Stations) with whom she had been employed since 1983. She has worked as store supervisor, assistant manager, store merchandiser, and manager at the Etobicoke and Scarborough stores. Patricia is currently manager of the Sheppard Avenue store in North York.

Mary Beth Brown worked as a summer student in the Sheridan head office from 1989 to 1995 while earning her Bachelor of Business Administration degree at Brock University. She joined Sheridan full-time in 1995 as the senior supervisor at the Mississauga store, and then assistant manager at the Toronto store from 1999 to 2001. Honing her skills in the retail environment made her a perfect candidate for the marketing coordinator position, assisting Valerie Stensson when the position was created in 2001. When Valerie was promoted to vice-president in 2010, Mary Beth assumed the role of marketing manager for the company, and has been instrumental in developing a cutting edge website as well as the complete involvement in social media such as Twitter and Facebook.

As mentioned previously, Valerie Stensson, first hired as the buyer of giftware, patio furniture, and Christmas, became the company's first female department manager overseeing the marketing department, and now as vice-president, oversees both the marketing and purchasing departments, handles all public relations and media inquiries, as well as managing the many sponsorship and donation requests.

Inevitably, there were the changes that come with the passing of generations. J.V. Stensson had become the manager of Sheridan Nurseries upon the death of his father. He was made president in 1965 after Howard Dunington-Grubb died. When J.V. passed away suddenly in 1972, his brother Howard became president. Larry Wilson was president from 1993 to 1996. At the time there was no clear successor so Larry Wilson, who had just sold his highly successful trucking company, was hired as president on a three-year contract. As a new millennium approached, a third generation of Stenssons would fill their forebears' shoes.

CHAPTER 8

The Sales Stations and Garden Centres: "A Merchandising Problem ... Solved by Sheridan"

In the early days, most of Sheridan Nurseries' sales were done through mail order, with most large plant orders being shipped. Some customers might have gone right to the nursery, drawn there by the catalogues, the big sign Herman Stensson erected near the Clarkson train station, and by word of mouth. Sheridan plants were also taken by horse-drawn wagon to Toronto's St. Lawrence Market. But that was a day-long round trip, so it probably didn't happen on a regular basis. Eventually, most people became familiar with Sheridan's products through the sales stations.

Documented information on the early sales stations is very sketchy. Those were the days before plants were transported and sold in pots, and roots were vulnerable from the time they were dug up until they were replanted. Therefore the windows for sales were a few weeks in the spring and autumn. The first sales stations might not have been intended as permanent outlets, but rather as temporary "feelers" to see whether or not they would be successful.

From 1917 to 1918, Sheridan Nurseries had showgrounds and a sales station at 82 Bloor Street West. For reasons unrecorded, seven years would pass before another Sheridan sales station opened in downtown Toronto. Perhaps business hadn't been good enough to justify the costs involved.

Sheridan Nurseries' very first permanent sales station opened in the spring of 1923 on Highway 2 (Lakeshore Road) in Clarkson. It wasn't much to look at. The structure consisted of a small pergola that had been used for an exhibit at the Canadian National Exhibition. Attached to it was an eight-by-twelve-foot lean-to shed that served as an office. Each year, this station opened on April 1 and closed on

Victoria Day. It opened for another six weeks in the fall. The plans for the sales station and show gardens at this site were grandiose, with formal sunken gardens and the sales station resembling a "mausoleum," as Karl likes to refer to it. The gardens were started; however, the onset of the Depression and changing priorities left this as a dream preserved in a watercolour at Sheridan's head office.

In 1925, with the opening of the newly paved Dundas Highway (#5), the nursery opened a sales station near the village of Sheridan at a place called Frogmore at the intersection of the highway and the Town Line (Winston Churchill Boulevard and Dundas Highway). Herman Stensson and the Dunington-Grubbs expected that a heavy volume of traffic on the highway would result in high sales. But most of the east-west traffic still went by the old Lakeshore Road route. The Frogmore sales station was short-lived.

Meanwhile, the nursery finally made another venture into Toronto. From 1925 to 1926 there was a sales station at

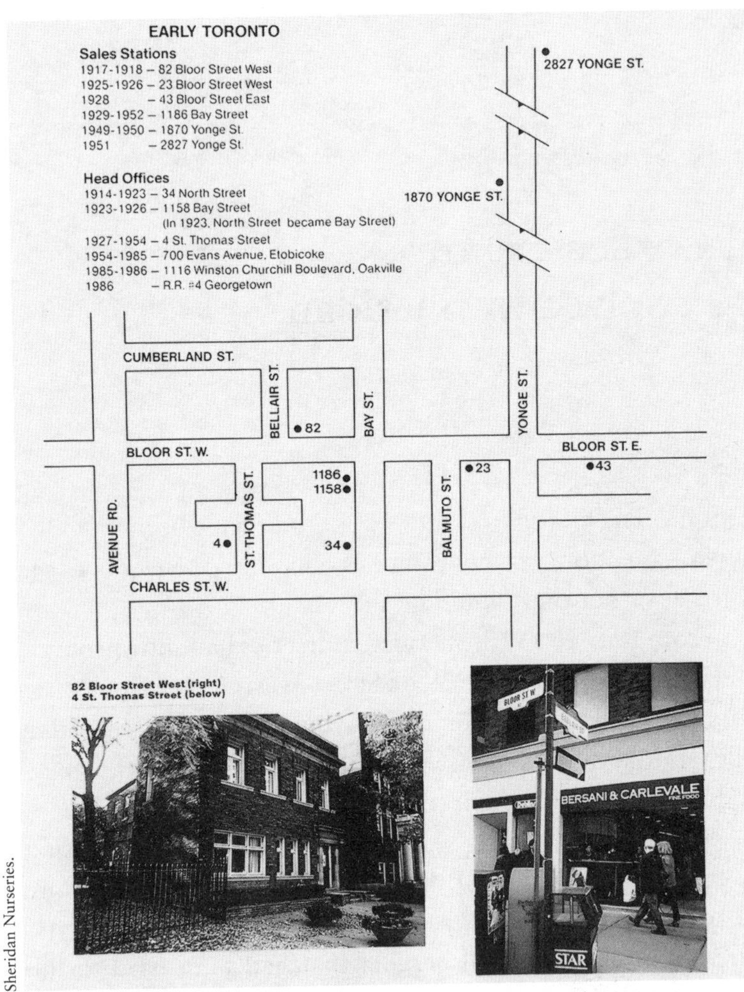

Sheridan Nurseries.

Map and recent photos of Toronto's Bay/Bloor area showing locations of early Sheridan Nurseries sales stations and the head office on St. Thomas Street from 1927 to 1954.

Sheridan Nurseries.

Highway Garden on Toronto-Hamilton Highway #2, Southdown Road, in Clarkson

23 Bloor Street West. With prospects in Toronto apparently looking better than they had a few years earlier, the company moved the sales station to 43 Bloor Street East for 1927–28. Then, in 1929, Sheridan's Toronto outlet was moved to 1186 Bay Street. It remained there throughout the years of the Great Depression and the Second World War until 1952.

Bertha Sparre.

Clarkson Highway Gardens in the 1930s. This, Sheridan's first permanent sales station, was established in 1923.

Sheridan Nurseries.

Above: *This close-up of the Frogmore sales station sign shows the prices of shrubs and perennials in the mid-1920s.*

Below: *Site of the Dundas Street "Frogmore" sales station, which operated only from 1925 to 1926. Pictured here are Howard Dunington-Grubb (L) and manager John Henky (R).*

Sheridan Nurseries.

The Dunington-Grubbs didn't limit their ambitions for Sheridan Nurseries to southern Ontario. Montreal was still Canada's largest city and main financial centre. In 1925, they opened a sales centre at the corner of Greene Avenue and Sherbrooke Street. Over the next thirty years there would be, at different times, sales stations at four Montreal locations, with the one at 5895 Côte-des-Neiges in operation from 1937 to 1956.

Toronto Transit Commission Archives.

Toronto, the intersection of Bloor and Bay streets, looking south. The Sheridan Nurseries sales station sign can be seen in the upper right part of the picture.

Sheridan Nurseries.

Sheridan Nurseries sales station on Greene Avenue in Montreal.

The Queen Elizabeth Way (QEW) was completed in 1936. Howard Dunington-Grubb believed that a site on the highway, close to Toronto, would be an excellent location for a nursery and sales station. He had his eye on a spot in Etobicoke at what was then the interchange of the QEW and Highway 27, just five miles from Toronto. On February 18, 1938, the Toronto *Daily Star* carried an article about the "NEW 19-ACRE GARDEN PLOT" that would adorn "Middle Road," the name of the old road the new highway had replaced. The article told how, in four separate cash transactions, Sheridan Nurseries had purchased "garden land fronting for 1,600 feet on the new four-lane Middle Rd. highway to Hamilton. The frontage starts just west of Brown's Line and runs to Evans Ave. ... This new botanical area will greatly beautify the approach to Toronto along the Middle Rd."

Besides establishing a new nursery and sales station in what was then "rural" Etobicoke, Sheridan also wanted to move its head office there from the old location at 4 St. Thomas Street in Toronto. All plans had to be put on hold, however, because of the Second World War and the Korean War. It wasn't until wartime restrictions were lifted that plans could move ahead. The new sales station opened in 1948, on a new street called Sherway Drive. The name "Sherway" was a combination of the first syllable from Sheridan and the second syllable from Queensway. Queensway Hospital was right across the road, on land that had been acquired by donation and purchase from Sheridan Nurseries. The new head office opened in 1954 at 700 Evans Avenue, which was actually within the boundaries of Islington.

Sheridan's Sherway property eventually grew to 135

Sheridan Nurseries.

View of QEW on the left, with exit for Highway 27 which runs to the right, with Sheridan Nurseries Sherway fields in the background.

acres. Display gardens were developed around the sales station and head office, along with an extensive hedge collection. An attractive walkway connected the office and station. During that time you could leave the garden centre and turn either left or right directly onto the QEW.

Change came, though, with urban growth and the widening of the QEW into a major expressway. Sherway Drive disappeared, and for a while the nursery had no access to any street except via a detour. In 1963, all but ten acres of the property was sold to developers for a new shopping centre.

Sheridan Nurseries.

Sheridan Nurseries new head office at Sherway. The road in the foreground is the QEW.

Sheridan Nurseries.

Howard Dunington-Grubb often used pleached hedges such as this one of lindens at the Sheridan Nurseries head office at Sherway.

Sheridan Nurseries.

Famous for saying he wanted people to walk on the grass in Toronto parks, Tommy Thompson, Toronto parks commissioner, took off his shoes and socks for the April 23, 1970, opening of the Sherway Garden Centre.

Due to delays, Sherway Gardens mall didn't open until 1971. Meanwhile, Sheridan Nurseries opened the new Sherway Garden Centre on April 23, 1970.

The head office was moved to Oakville in 1984 when that land was sold to Toys "R" Us. But the garden centre continued to evolve. A greenhouse and new covered areas were added. For the next twenty years, the Sherway Garden Centre was an Etobicoke landmark. Then, in 2004, after the purchase of Weall & Cullen, Sheridan Nurseries sold the Sherway property. A chapter in the histories of both the nursery and Etobicoke that had started seventy years earlier came to an end.

In the years during which the Sherway story unfolded, other developments were taking place elsewhere. The Montreal sales station was moved to a new address at 650 Montée-de-Liesse.

OFFICE: 4 ST. THOMAS ST., TORONTO 5, ONT.
TELEPHONE KINGSDALE 4151-2

POST OFFICE ADDRESS, SHERIDAN, ONT.
TELEPHONE CLARKSON 87-W

THE SHERIDAN NURSERIES LIMITED

GROWERS OF ORNAMENTAL EVERGREENS,
TREES,
SHRUBS, PERENNIALS
GARDENS DESIGNED AND PLANTED

Cash Order

Brown's Line, Ont., May 3 1949

M. Gerber Order No. B 2106

Address 43 Ochard Pk Drive per

When Taken Salesman J Herod

10 Yews [illegible] 18-24 @ 3.25	32.50
5 Pine [illegible] 15-18 @ 3.00	15.00
3 Juniper [illegible] 36-42 @ 5.00	15.00
25 Barberry [illegible] 15-18 @ .30	7.50
	70.00

Paid JH

Sheridan Nurseries.

Left: *A Sheridan Nurseries invoice dated May 3, 1949, signed by Jim Herod.*

Right: *Hedges at Sherway sales station.* Circa 1960. *All Sheridan sales stations had hedge collections.*

Sheridan Nurseries.

SHERIDAN NURSERIES NEW SHERWAY GARDEN CENTRE

OPENING APRIL 1970 BUTCHERD-WILSON – ARCHITECTS

"And I beseech you, forget not to inform yourself, as diligently as may be, in things that belong to gardening." John Evelyn

Sheridan Nurseries.

Original drawing of the proposed Sheridan Nurseries Garden Centre at Sherway Gardens, which opened in 1970. Note the Chris Yaneff "Stick Logo" of two stylized trees on the left.

Sheridan Nurseries.

Dave Addy.

Sheridan Nurseries.

Top Left: *J.V. Stensson and Herman Loeven (Montreal manager) at a trade show.*

Top Right: *Display of Sheridan Nurseries patio pots at Greenhedges, Montreal.*

Bottom Left: *Greenhedges, Sheridan's sales station in Montreal. Note Sheridan's first free-standing street sign, erected in the 1960s.*

Opposite: *Sheridan's sales station on Yonge Street in Toronto in the early 1950s, and site plan. Up until 1985, shrubs were "heeled" in soil on the Yonge Street property.*

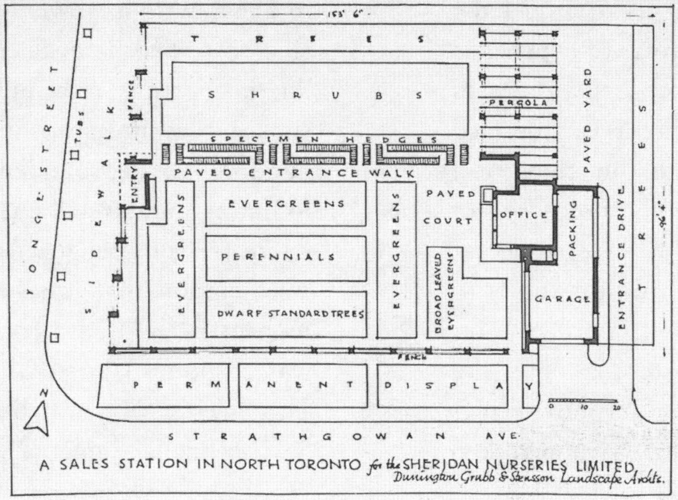

A SALES STATION IN NORTH TORONTO for the SHERIDAN NURSERIES LIMITED
Dunington Grubb & Stensson Landscape Archts.

Sheridan Nurseries.

Sheridan Nurseries established new sales stations in other important locations. In 1950, the company bought property at 2827 Yonge Street in a neighbourhood called Glenpark. The following year construction began on a new sales station there. The store officially opened in 1952, and has been in operation ever since. After sixty years the store was completely modernized and the outdoor sales area enclosed in 2012.

During this period, Sheridan also upgraded existing sales stations. Howard Dunington-Grubb and J.V. Stensson had developed some practical concepts about the make-up of a successful sales station. An article published in *American Nurseryman* in August of 1952 reported:

> A merchandising problem has been solved by the Sheridan Nurseries, Ltd., Toronto, Ont., with the opening of [an] excellently designed salesyard ... The problem had been to establish a permanent sales outlet which would possess the necessary elements to attract the retail trade ... After many years of experience with sales stations on vacant lots with leases running only a few months, it was decided in 1950 to experiment with something of a more permanent nature at the north end of Toronto. In choosing a site, ease of access, parking facilities, publicity and proximity to the best residential districts were primary considerations. After much search, a corner site 100x160 feet was chosen on Toronto's principal shopping street. Planning was undertaken with the following objectives in view ...

The article went on to discuss the importance of layout, attractiveness, display, and labelling, access to the show-grounds, and security. It concluded that the sales station successfully measured up to high standards. This was a significant acknowledgement from an expert observer that the people who ran Sheridan Nurseries knew what they were doing. The innovations praised in an American trade journal in 1952 would become standard in Sheridan sales stations.

In 1965, Sheridan completely revamped the Clarkson sales station (then referred to as the Southdown station). The old structure that had been on the site since 1923 was torn down and replaced by a beautiful, modern building. The attractiveness of the building was exceeded only by the wide variety of plants and supplies available. It drew customers from the communities that would soon make up Mississauga, as well as Oakville, Bronte, Burlington, and even Hamilton.

The Unionville sales station, known as Longacres, opened in 1967. With its towering geometric greenhouse, it was considered to be one of Sheridan's most inspiring locations. At the time, people in the industry wondered why Sheridan built such a beautiful store in the middle of farm country. The building was surrounded by an expansive lawn, pool, and fountain, and a terrace that displayed almost two dozen different types of hedges. At the time, it was the only Sheridan sales station that opened all year long. During the winter months it featured a complete line of indoor plants. There was a special Christmas display starting in late November. This sales station was built to serve Don Mills, York Mills, Scarborough, Agincourt, Markham, Unionville, Pickering, Whitby, and Oshawa. In 2007, the store was torn down and

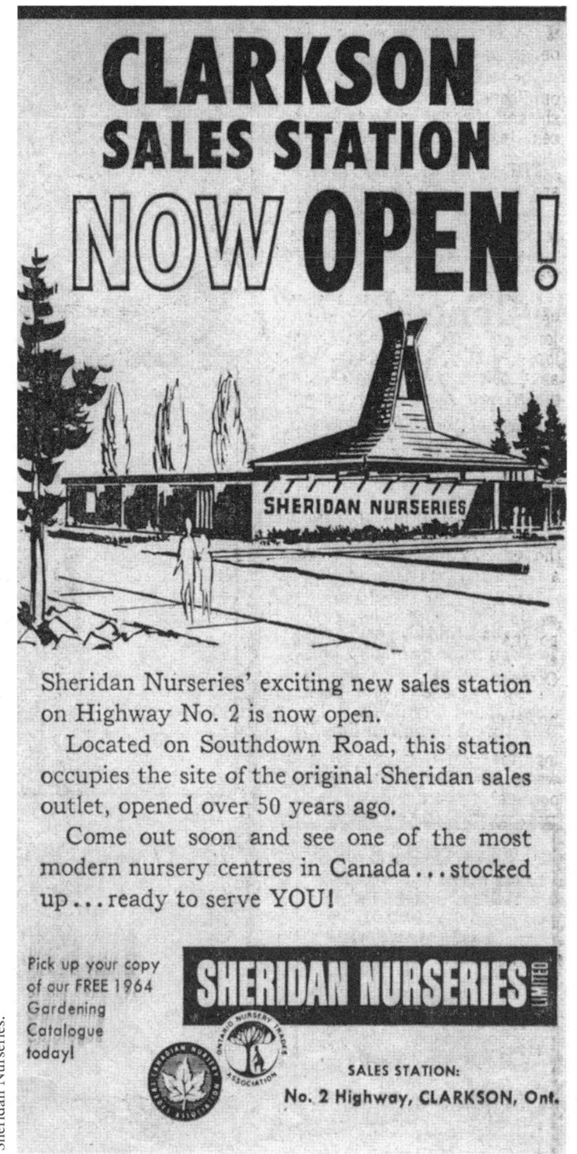

CLARKSON
SALES STATION
NOW OPEN!

Sheridan Nurseries' exciting new sales station on Highway No. 2 is now open.

Located on Southdown Road, this station occupies the site of the original Sheridan sales outlet, opened over 50 years ago.

Come out soon and see one of the most modern nursery centres in Canada... stocked up... ready to serve YOU!

Pick up your copy of our FREE 1964 Gardening Catalogue today!

SHERIDAN NURSERIES LIMITED

SALES STATION:
No. 2 Highway, CLARKSON, Ont.

Sheridan Nurseries.

Hamilton Spectator ad for the new Clarkson sales station, April 24, 1964.

Sheridan Nurseries.

Uli Rumpf was an artistic master at writing in-store signs

Sheridan Nurseries.

Aerial view of Longacres, the Unionville Hwy #7 sales station which opened in 1967.

Sheridan Nurseries.

Longacres, Sheridan Nurseries' sales station in Unionville, in the late 1960s.

replaced with a modern garden centre complete with a large tower to attract attention from the road. The garden centre is located in what is now designated the Markham town centre, and is a far cry from the middle of a farm.

In 1978, Sheridan Nurseries purchased a garden centre in the Forest Hill district of Kitchener. The big garden centre was located to serve the twin cities of Kitchener-Waterloo. The site was also chosen because it lay within easy driving distance of Guelph, Cambridge (formerly Galt, Preston, and Hespeler), and smaller communities such as Fergus and Elora.

These garden centres thrived and are still in operation. Other new stores were relatively short-lived. Of the garden centres that were purchased in Agincourt on Sheppard Avenue East (1977) and Oshawa (1978); and opened in North York (1987) and Pickering (1988); Oshawa was in operation the longest, at eleven years. The North York store closed after just two years. Vince Vaughan, from whom Sheridan purchased the Agincourt store, went on to manage the Sheridan garden centre in Kitchener.

The decision had been made in 1970 to change the name of Sheridan's retail outlets from sales stations to garden

Sheridan Nurseries.

The Weall & Cullen garden centre on Sheppard Avenue in 1948. Sheridan Nurseries eventually bought Weall & Cullen.

centres. Karl Stensson was appointed to take over the direction of all the Sheridan locations in 1985. It was his decision in 1988 to have the garden centres identified by the names of the communities in which they were located. Thus, Longacres became "Unionville," Sherway became "Etobicoke," Forest Hill became "Kitchener," and so on.

Sheridan Nurseries also took steps toward providing greater diversification in products and services. In 1993 the company became half-owner of a lawn-care business called Nutri-Lawn, located at the Sherway Garden Centre. It sold its interest to the other partner in 2004. In 2000, Sheridan at Home opened one block south of the Toronto Garden Centre. This store sold patio furniture and interior decor, but closed in 2004. Instead of opening independent gift shops, Sheridan @ Home became a boutique within each store and has gone on to become extremely successful in selling items such as giftware, patio furniture, and Christmas decor.

In 2003, Sheridan Nurseries made a significant acquisition with the purchase of Weall & Cullen Nurseries. John A. Weall, a Toronto-based garden designer, had founded the company in 1922 for the very same purpose that the Dunington-Grubbs had started Sheridan Nurseries; to provide ornamental plants for Toronto-area gardeners. In 1940, he hired his paperboy, Len Cullen, as a helper. John and Len formed a partnership in 1946. The following year, John sold his share of the company to Len, and went on to teach landscape gardening at the University of Guelph.

In 1948, Len sold the original Weall property on Avenue Road and bought five acres on Sheppard Avenue East, North York, still the site of a Sheridan garden centre today. Keeping the name Weall & Cullen, Len expanded the company into a mini-empire that included seven garden centres, a nursery, and Cullen Country Barns. He fulfilled a lifelong dream in 1980 with the opening of Cullen Gardens and Miniature Village in Whitby. Other Weall & Cullen locations were in Mississauga, North York, Scarborough, and Markham.

Len's son Mark assumed ownership of the garden centres, nursery, and supply business in 1992. After the acquisition by Sheridan Nurseries, which was a major transaction in the Canadian nursery industry, all of the former Weall & Cullen locations except the Markham store remained in operation. Several Weall & Cullen people have stayed to have successful careers with Sheridan Nurseries.

In Quebec, Sheridan closed its Montreal garden centre at Montée-de-Liesse in 1985, and reopened at 3000 Rue de Marche the next year. That garden centre was the company's main retail outlet outside Ontario until it closed in 2001. Other Quebec locations where Sheridan had established garden centres — Beaconsfield (1975), Dorion (trade only — 1988), and St. Julie (1993) — closed in the 1990s.

On April 15, 1994, Sheridan Nurseries celebrated the opening of a new garden centre adjacent to the Glen Williams head office. It was at first called a farm outlet, but later became a full-fledged garden centre. The annual fall yard sale, which is held on the weekend before Thanksgiving, attracts thousands of guests who purchase surplus plants at bargain prices.

CHAPTER 9

Landscaping: Educating the Public and Reconstructing the Land

Landscaping was the primary reason that Howard and Lorrie Dunington-Grubb founded Sheridan Nurseries. They were hampered by the absence of a local source of the ornamental plants they needed for their work, and so started one of their own. They could sell plants to gardeners and other landscapers, while at the same time producing the stock they required for big projects like Parkwood in Oshawa, and Gage Park in Hamilton.

As business grew, so did the opportunities for landscaping. Besides the Dunington-Grubb projects, there were other properties that required a landscaper's skills. Some were large estates, but even middle-class homeowners might want expert help in designing gardens perfectly suited to their modest lots.

By 1917, Sheridan Nurseries had added landscaping to its list of services. An undated Sheridan brochure on the subject was printed before 1923. Titled *The Art of Garden Design*, the booklet has cover art by J.E.H. Macdonald of the Group of Seven. The pages are well-illustrated with photographs of gardens, particularly before-and-after scenes. The pictures are accompanied by explanatory captions. Here and there, the guide offers snippets of horticultural advice, such as: "A little money judiciously spent on beautifying your property is a good investment. You will get it back with interest when you come to sell, if it has been wisely spent." It is interesting to note that ninety years later, the National and Provincial Trade Associations continue to promote the fact that landscaping increases the value of a home by between 10 and 15 percent.

Lorrie's introduction of perennials revolutionized landscaping in Canada. It was said at the time that her perennial borders were equal in aesthetic value to the works of great artists in other media. Her work at Shadowbrook in Willowdale was considered a masterpiece.

The rock garden was another feature unfamiliar to most Canadians in the early twentieth century. At one time, the only rock gardens known to exist in Canada were on the Cleveland Morgan estate near Montreal. Howard Dunington-Grubb was very fond of rock gardens, and through his plans and Sheridan Nurseries designs he helped spread their popularity.

In the early days, landscaping was labour-intensive. Land was graded by horses dragging iron scoops called slush scrapers. Workmen hand-loaded earth into horse- or mule-drawn Hoosier wagons that had a capacity of one-and-a-half cubic yards. The driver redistributed the earth by operating a lever that opened the wagon's bottom. It was a slow process, and therefore expensive, with teams of men working ten-hour days.

In 1928, the introduction of a small Caterpillar tractor modernized grading. The tractor hauled a new invention called the Fresno scraper that worked on the same principal as the old slush scraper, but moved a greater amount of earth. Conveyor belts speeded up the transfer of earth to the Hoosier wagons. In time, those wagons, too, were replaced by motorized machinery.

Of course, there is much more to landscaping than moving soil around and sticking plants in the ground. From the beginning, Sheridan Nurseries made the effort to educate property owners. The 1918–19 catalogue devoted a page to "Landscape Department":

> We want to give special prominence in this issue of our catalogue to our Landscape Department. So great have been the demands on us recently for this class of work that we believe it will prove of considerable interest to our patrons and prospective customers to be shown a few examples of gardens designed, constructed and planted by us.

In the 1928 catalogue, under the heading "A Landscape Service," Sheridan told readers:

> ... we would strongly advise application for assistance to our Landscape Service Department in all cases where difficulty, or doubt, may arise as to the right method of procedure, no matter whether the property be large or small.

The advice was essentially the same years later in the 1954 catalogue:

> Our long experience with the characteristics and arrangement of evergreens, trees, shrubs and flowers is invaluable if real value is to be obtained for money spent.

This is followed by brief descriptions of Sheridan's landscaping expertise in the laying of lawns — both sodded and seeded, tree moving, and the construction of chrome-stone terraces.

In the May 1989 issue of *The Landscape Architectural Review*, Humphrey Carver referred to Howard Dunington-Grubb as "the patriarch of landscape architecture in Ontario."

Credit: Sheridan Nurseries.

An early Sheridan Nurseries exhibit at the CNE, possibly 1916.

Sheridan Nurseries.

Sheridan Nurseries CNE exhibit, 1920

However, although Howard and Lorrie were landscape architects who were the first to use plants grown by Sheridan Nurseries, they were not technically employed by Sheridan. They owned the company, and created designs for their own projects, but they were landscape architects, not landscapers. The first landscape foreman who worked specifically for Sheridan Nurseries was Albert E. Brown.

Albert Brown began working for Sheridan in 1915. From then until 1950 he was in charge of the landscaping department. He guided it through the great change from horsepower to mechanization. Many budding young landscapers who passed through Sheridan Nurseries were fortunate to have Mr. Brown as a mentor. One was Leslie Hancock, who went on to found Woodland Nurseries in Mississauga.

In 1950, Mr. Brown moved from landscaping to manager of publicity and photography to lessen his workload. His position was taken over by Walter Menne who had come to Canada from the Netherlands in 1949, and joined Sheridan Nurseries in Clarkson shortly after.

Harry Van Dyk, who was married to Walter's sister Anya, joined Sheridan as a foreman. He became landscape manager when Walter moved to California in the late 1950s. Anya worked as secretary for the department until her retirement in 1990. Harry was still manager when he died in 1978.

Sheridan Nurseries.

Sheridan Nurseries exhibit at the CNE National Plant & Garden Show, 1938.

Sheridan Nurseries

Part of the Sheridan Nurseries exhibit at the 1951 CNE

Tom Van Ryn took over after Harry. He, too, was from the Netherlands, and was a long-time employee in the department. Tom was followed by John Midlane, who had been employed in sales for the landscape department. John's successor was Len Vermaas, who joined the department in 1955, working first on the landscaping of the Ford Motor Plant in Oakville. Len remembers working with Howard Dunington-Grubb on many of the flower shows that Sheridan Nurseries participated in during the 1950s and 1960s. Len was manager in the 1990s when Sheridan decided to close the department.

The rest of the operations had become so much bigger that landscaping was a small percentage of Sheridan's overall business and was taking too much time to manage in relation to retail stores and wholesale orders. A landscaping service was reinstated in 2003 when Sheridan acquired Weall & Cullen, which had a thriving landscaping design service. However, the actual landscaping has been done by authorized contractors.

Most of the landscaping work done by the Dunington-Grubbs no longer exists. Residential, commercial, and industrial developments now occupy the sites of their splendid gardens. The same is true for the work of Albert Brown and his successors. Nonetheless, some remnants of their creations have survived the passage of time and changing tastes, and still grace private estates and public parks. Landscaping designed by the Dunington-Grubbs can still be seen at Gage Park in Hamilton, and Ormscliffe, the Mimico estate of Albert B. Ormsby. The grounds surrounding the Oakville Ford plant were also originally landscaped by Sheridan Nurseries.

One site in particular that was installed (though not designed) by Sheridan is seen by millions of people travelling to and from Toronto on the Gardiner Expressway. In 1988, a private businessman named Gerry Mahoney got the idea to have plant advertising logos installed along a section of the Gardiner. He chose a grassy slope on the north side of the expressway, between Roncesvalles Avenue and Wilson Park Avenue. The property was owned by Canadian National Railway, but lay vacant and unmaintained. Sheridan Nurseries was contracted to do the landscaping. First, twenty-six tons of garbage had to be removed. Then yews were installed to form the logos. The result was a unique bit of scenery along one of the busiest thoroughfares in Canada. Though Sheridan did the original landscaping, the logos have changed over the years.

CHAPTER 10

The Catalogues: Advertising with Style

The Sheridan Nurseries catalogue was a groundbreaking venture. It was the first comprehensive ornamental plant catalogue published in Canada. However, it also owes part of its fame to the involvement of J.E.H. Macdonald of the Group of Seven.

Though Howard certainly contributed, Lorrie was principally responsible for the early catalogues. It was she who recognized the need not only to advertise, but also to educate potential customers. Most Canadians knew very little about English-style gardening. They had to be informed not only of the plants that Sheridan Nurseries had available, but also on how to select, plant, and maintain the flowers and shrubs in order to have a successful garden. Novice gardeners who were disappointed with their first efforts were liable to give up on it.

Of course, for the catalogues to work, they had to find their way into people's homes. The first catalogues were mailed out to anyone who ordered them by post or phone. They would also have been handed out at the CNE and to visitors at the nursery. Catalogues were probably available at the early sales stations, though no records confirm this.

The catalogue was the mass-marketing tool of the early twentieth century. Dozens of them were in circulation, from big department stores like Eaton's, to small companies like Sheridan Nurseries. If a retailer wanted his catalogue to be perused from cover to cover, and not dispatched to the seat of the outhouse, it had to be worth keeping; it had to be interesting. This was an area in which Lorrie shone.

THE FIRST EDITION

The very first Sheridan catalogue was dated Autumn 1914/ Spring 1915, and was printed by Brigden's Limited of Toronto, a company that did western Canada catalogues for Eaton's. A copy of this original catalogue is one of an almost complete collection in the Sheridan Nurseries archives. It measures four-by-six inches and has thirty-two pages. The cover illustration by an unknown artist shows a formal garden scene above one of Lorrie's favourite words, *herbaceous*. This image would be reused often.

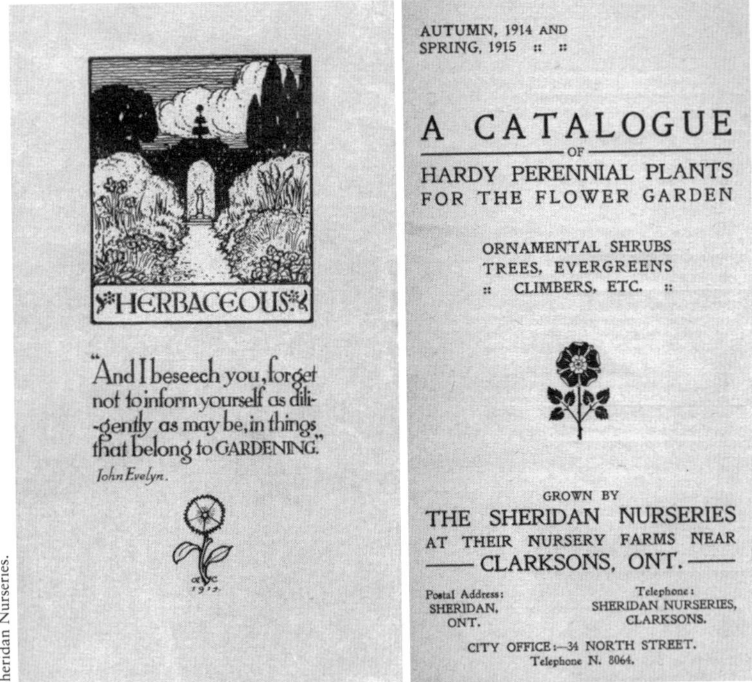

HERBACEOUS

"And I beseech you, forget not to inform yourself as diligently as may be, in things that belong to GARDENING."
John Evelyn.

AUTUMN, 1914 AND
SPRING, 1915

A CATALOGUE
OF
HARDY PERENNIAL PLANTS
FOR THE FLOWER GARDEN

ORNAMENTAL SHRUBS
TREES, EVERGREENS
CLIMBERS, ETC.

GROWN BY
THE SHERIDAN NURSERIES
AT THEIR NURSERY FARMS NEAR
CLARKSONS, ONT.

Postal Address:
SHERIDAN,
ONT.

Telephone:
SHERIDAN NURSERIES,
CLARKSONS.

CITY OFFICE:—34 NORTH STREET.
Telephone N. 8064.

Sheridan Nurseries.

The cover and first page of the first Sheridan Nurseries catalogue, published for 1914–15.

On the cover is a quote from the seventeenth-century English diarist and gardener John Evelyn (1620–1706): "And I beseech you, forget not to inform yourself as diligently as may be, in things that belong to gardening." It was a company favourite that would grace catalogues, exhibits, and garden centres for almost seventy-five years.

There are no illustrations inside the catalogue except for a stylized ink drawing of a flower on the title page. Because Sheridan Nurseries was new, there were no attractive photographs available of the nursery itself. However, Lorrie could have illustrated the catalogue with pictures of Canadian gardens they'd had a hand in creating. Such photographs appeared in later editions. But for this one there was probably a problem of time and money. Lorrie had to get it out in a hurry and likely wanted to keep costs down.

Nonetheless, the title page flower adds a touch of elegance. So, too, does a very small stylized plant figure that appears at the bottom of a few pages. The little figure doesn't appear in any of the other catalogues.

The title page informs the reader that the little book is "A Catalogue of Hardy Perennial Plants for the Flower Garden." At that early time, hardy perennials were Sheridan's most successful product, because they were new to Canada. The following selection from an instructional article in the catalogue shows that Lorrie was aware of Canadians' general unfamiliarity with these plants.

> For the assistance of customers who experience difficulty in making a suitable choice of perennials for their gardens, we take pleasure in making the following special offers:

TERMS AND REMARKS

The following prices are net and include carriage to Toronto. Special quotations will be made on orders exceeding $25.00. Cash should accompany all orders under $25.00. Customers are requested to address all orders to the city office.

Every reasonable care will be taken to ensure the safe delivery of the plants at their destination, after which our responsibility ceases. Orders will be sent out in the order received.

Only such plants are here listed as are actually to be found growing successfully in our Nurseries. Should any variety become exhausted a substitute will be suggested, but not sent without instructions. If our suggestions are not acceptable, the cash for the missing varieties will be immediately refunded. As we are anxious to ship nothing but high class stock, true to name, and certain to give satisfaction, we are not anxious to purchase special varieties from other sources for our customers unless specially requested to do so.

Although we do not anticipate any errors in nomenclature, mistakes are occasionally bound to occur in the best managed Nursery. In such cases we expect to be immediately notified as soon as the error becomes apparent, when it will be either rectified at the earliest possible date or the money refunded.

Our Nursery farms are situated on tne West side of the town line between the Counties of Halton and Peel. They front on to the middle road between Toronto and Hamilton about one and a half miles west of Clarkson's Station, being intersected by the right of way of the G.T.R., C.P.R. and C.N.R. The distance from Lake Ontario is about one mile.

THE HARDY HERBACEOUS FLOWER GARDEN

"Who loves a garden, still keeps his Eden."

The very considerable interest shown recently in gardening in this country is producing a more general love for flowers, and a desire for a wider, as well as a more intimate, knowledge of their culture and arrangement. No longer will the bed of exotic looking Cannas, Coleus, and Scarlet Salvias satisfy the appreciative gardening public. People are wearying of the endless ribbon borders of Blue Lobelias, Scarlet and variegated Geraniums, of the early Victorian carpet bedding, and of the heterogeneous masses of summer annuals planted hotch-potch regardless of color and good taste. All this is rapidly being replaced by a modern revival of the old-fashioned flower border of hardy herbaceous perennials. By herbaceous perennials we mean all such flowering plants as may be allowed to remain permanently out of doors, the roots being sufficiently hardy to withstand the winter frosts. The foliage and stems die down to the ground level each autumn, but shoot up again with renewed vigor in the spring. It is this characteristic which makes autumn planting of perennials so satisfactory.

Although these hardy plants are becoming increasingly popular, yet comparatively few people realize how easy they are of culture and what a great variety of color and form they offer throughout the entire season from early summer to late fall.

The initial cost of the plants and the proper preparation of the ground to receive them is the only expense worth considering. The after maintenance will be found insignificant when compared with the very considerable annual expense of buying or raising tender summer bedding plants.

It will be readily seen that where space is limited great care should be taken to select plants that have a long period of blooming in order to avoid, as much as possible, ugly gaps in the beds and borders. For example, the perennial Blue Flax and the Viola Cornuta in its white and purple forms will be found to flower almost the entire season, and there are many others equally good.

It is not generally known that a number of our early summer hardy plants will bloom again later in the season if the first crop of flowering stalks be cut off close to the ground immediately they show signs of deterioration. In this connection we may mention the Canterbury Bell (Campanula Media) and the perennial Larkspurs or Delphinium.

Failure to grow successfully these truly beautiful garden subjects is traceable to several causes. In the first place, it is most important to see that, previous to planting, all beds be deeply trenched or dug, poor soils should be amply enriched by the addition of well rotted manure, and that the drainage be good. Clay soils especially should

3

be well drained. The necessity for this is borne out by the fact that many plants which are apparently quite hardy on a dry sandy soil will winter-kill on a water-logged clay. On the other hand, where clay soils have been drained the same plants will prove equally hardy on either sand or clay. It is not so much the severity of our winters that injures our gardens as the treacherous alternate thawing and freezing during the early spring. A top dressing in the autumn of dry litter or straw will do much to ameliorate this condition. Want of moisture at the roots is another common cause of mortality in the flower garden. It is better, during dry weather, to give the borders a good soaking once or twice a week, than a mere sprinkling every day. A frequent use of the hoe to break up the surface of the soil will do more to conserve moisture and keep the plants healthy than dozens of light and inefficient sprinklings of water.

The artistic success of the herbaceous border depends entirely on the color grouping and bold massing of the plants. Their time of flowering and their heights also should be borne well in mind. Indiscriminate dotting of single plants and haphazard mixtures of colors result in failure and disappointment. To obtain complete satisfaction, we strongly recommend a carefully thought out plan specially prepared by an expert to suit the needs of each individual client. This work we are prepared to undertake from the preparation of the beds to the supplying and planting of the stock.

We are well aware that in many instances the accompanying catalogue of plants will be no more than a mere list of unfamiliar names, and that intending purchasers would be unable to make suitable selections in order to obtain any specially desired result. In cases such as these we are most willing to give all the assistance in our power free of charge either by phone from our city office or by mail.

For the assistance of customers who experience difficulty in making a suitable choice of perennials for their gardens, we take pleasure in making the following special offers:—

(1) We are prepared to plan, supply stock, and plant herbaceous borders of any size, exceeding 10 square yards, in Toronto or its immediate vicinity for the sum of $1.90 per square yard.

(2) For the sum of $10.00 cash in advance, we will supply, carriage paid, 66 perennial plants of our own selection of varieties most likely to give satisfaction, including in the order not more than five plants of any one variety.

(3) For the sum of $25.00 cash in advance, we are prepared to supply, carriage paid, 200 perennial plants of varieties most likely to give satisfaction, including in the order not more than five plants of any one variety.

"Not wholly in the busy world, nor quite
Beyond it, blooms the garden that I love."

4

Sheridan Nurseries.

First pages of the original Sheridan catalogue. Lorrie Dunington-Grubb was likely the author of the article on the right.

1. We are prepared to plan, supply stock, and plant herbaceous borders of any size, exceeding 10 square yards, in Toronto or its immediate vicinity for the sum of $1.90 per square yard [as little as $19.00!].

2. For the sum of $10.00 cash in advance, we will supply, carriage paid, 66 perennial plants of our own selection of varieties most likely to give satisfaction, including in the order not more than five plants of any one variety.

3. For the sum of $25.00 cash in advance, we are prepared to supply, carriage paid, 200 perennial plants of varieties most likely to give satisfaction, including in the order not more than five plants of any one variety.

A "Terms and Remarks" page outlines Sheridan's basic business policies and promise of quality. However, there is a *caveat*.

> Although we do not anticipate any errors in nomenclature, mistakes are occasionally

PLANTS

ACHILLEA. Yarrow.

Hardy herbaceous border and Alpine plants. Easy of culture. Dwarf forms excellent for bedding.

Cerise Queen. Bright cherry red. 2 feet. June-August.
Eupatorium. Golden yellow. 3 feet. June-August.
Eupatorium filipendula (noble yarrow). Golden yellow. 2-3 feet. June-August.
holoserica. Rare, yellow. 20 cents.
millefolium rubrum. A fine red form, good for cutting. 2-3 feet. June-August.
Ptarmica (The Pearl). Pure white, double, good for cutting. 2 feet. June-August.
tomentosa (Woolly Yarrow). Yellow dwarf creeping. Suitable for dry spots in rock garden. 1 foot. June-August.

All Achilleas, except as otherwise stated, 15 cents each.

ACONITUM. Monkshood. Wolfbane.

Autumnale. Large violet blue flowers, late bloomer. 4-5 feet. Roots very poisonous, should not be planted near vegetables, etc. 25 cents each.

AGROSTEMMA. Rose Campion.

Hardy perennial, easy of culture. Well adapted for borders.

Alba. Flowers white, silvery leaves. 1-2 feet. July 15 cents each.

ALYSSUM. Rock Mad Wort.

Dwarf shrubby perennials. Excellent plants for rockeries or fronts of borders. Blooms in early spring.

Saxitile (Gold Dust). Golden yellow. 12-18 inches.
Saxitile compactum. A compact form of the above. 1 foot.
Saxitile luteum. Pale yellow. 1 foot.

All at 20 cents each.

ANCHUSA. Alkanet.

Handsome hardy perennials with gentian blue flowers. Very suitable for large borders.

Italica, Dropmore variety. About 4 feet. Blooms mid-summer. 25 cents each.

ANEMONE. Windflower.

One of the best hardy perennials, as they bloom from August until the frost kills them back, and are splendid for cutting.

Japonica (Honorine Joubert). Snowy white. Single. 2-3 feet. 15 cents each.
Japonica (Whirlwind). Snowy white. Double. 2-3 feet. 15 cents each.

1 Dozen of Any One Variety for Price of 10. 5

The plant listing on the right was the very beginning of a catalogue that would become the "Bible" of southern Ontario gardeners.

bound to occur in the best managed Nursery. In such cases we expect to be immediately notified as soon as the error becomes apparent, when it will be either rectified at the earliest possible date or the money refunded.

The title of the lead article, "The Hardy Herbaceous Flower Garden," is underlined by a quote from American philosopher Amos Bronson Alcott: "Who loves a garden, still keeps his Eden." The article's author isn't named, but it can almost certainly be attributed to Lorrie. The topic was close to her heart. Aware that most of her readers would be amateur gardeners, she took care to explain things carefully and informally.

> By herbaceous perennials we mean all such flowering plants as may be allowed to remain permanently out of doors, the roots being sufficiently hardy to withstand the winter frosts. The foliage and stems die down to the ground level each autumn, but shoot up again with renewed vigor in the spring. It is this characteristic which makes autumn planting of perennials so satisfactory.

The catalogue has entries for eighty genera of herbaceous perennials, twenty-nine of shrubs, twelve of trees, and four of climbing plants. Many of these are accompanied by information on numerous species and varieties. Lorrie packed a lot into thirty-two pages, and had clearly dedicated many hours to the catalogue's preparation.

ART AND INNOVATIONS

Lorrie used much the same formula for the second catalogue (Autumn 1915/Spring 1916). The title this time was: A GARDEN MANUAL AND CATALOGUE OF HARDY PERENNIAL PLANTS FOR THE FLOWER GARDEN, indicating that the book held more practical information on gardening than the previous one had. The catalogue had grown to forty-one pages. More plants had been added to the list. Most notably, the catalogue was illustrated with photographs, including one of the Sheridan Nurseries rock garden exhibit at the CNE in August 1915.

In the years that followed, Lorrie changed printers numerous times, and used a variety of innovations to improve on the look of the catalogue and make the contents more interesting and informative. The Autumn 1917/Spring 1918 edition was enlarged to a seven-by-eight-and-a-half-inch format; the physical shape the book would have until 1951. A variety of artistic logos incorporating the *S* and *N* for Sheridan Nurseries were used. The catalogue first used glossy paper in 1918. It was also the first time the landscape department was featured. That issue carried a disclaimer that provides an insight into the times. "Owing to abnormal trade conditions due to the war, the prices in this catalogue are subject to change without notice."

In 1920, the "Terms and Remarks" entry was replaced with a less formal introductory foreword. An index of common plant names was added in 1923, and would become a standard feature. Over the years, more and more photographs were added to liven up the pages. These included pictures of the nursery, and of Dunington-Grubb landscaping projects such as the Rand Estate in Niagara-on-the-Lake, Ormscliffe in Mimico, and the Oakes Garden Theatre in Niagara Falls.

Sheridan Nurseries.

Sheridan Nurseries.

A.S. Carter's design for the 1917–18 catalogue.

Sheridan Nurseries.

Artwork for plant category headings, used in Sheridan catalogues from 1938 to 1941.

The first issue with a full-colour cover came out in 1932. Unfortunately, the name of the artist isn't known. That issue also included a list of books on "horticultural and kindred subjects" that could be ordered through Sheridan Nurseries. In 1937, a notice in the catalogue invited patriotic Canadians to "plant a Coronation Tree" to commemorate the crowning of King George VI. Each tree came with an official Coronation Planting Committee label; 75 cents for the small one, and $1.25 for the large. This was in the midst of the Great Depression, when many people could barely afford bread and milk, let alone a tree for the new king. Accordingly, Sheridan's Depression-era catalogues offered plants at reduced prices.

In 1940, the catalogue introduced a new separate section. This was a list of Sheridan's newest plants. It came under a bold heading: SPECTACULAR VARIETIES OF RECENT INTRODUCTION. Among the treasures awaiting adventurous gardeners were new Forsythia and Lilacs.

The cover art is one of the most important — and priceless — features of the early Sheridan Nurseries catalogues. Since the latter part of the nineteenth century, developments in lithography had transformed catalogues from simple price lists into thick, bound, and beautifully illustrated books. The technology to mass-produce catalogues and posters ushered in a golden age in commercial art. Companies wanted logos and iconic images that would be instantly recognizable. This trend would eventually lead to the creation of such artistic "mascots" as the Cracker Jack characters Sailor Jack and his dog Bingo, and Borden Milk's Elsie the Cow. Many young artists who would one day become famous served apprenticeships creating commercial art. Among them were Canada's Tom Thomson and future members of the Group of Seven.

Executives and the Stensson family over the years at Sheridan Nurseries. Note Larry Wilson in the lower-right corner.

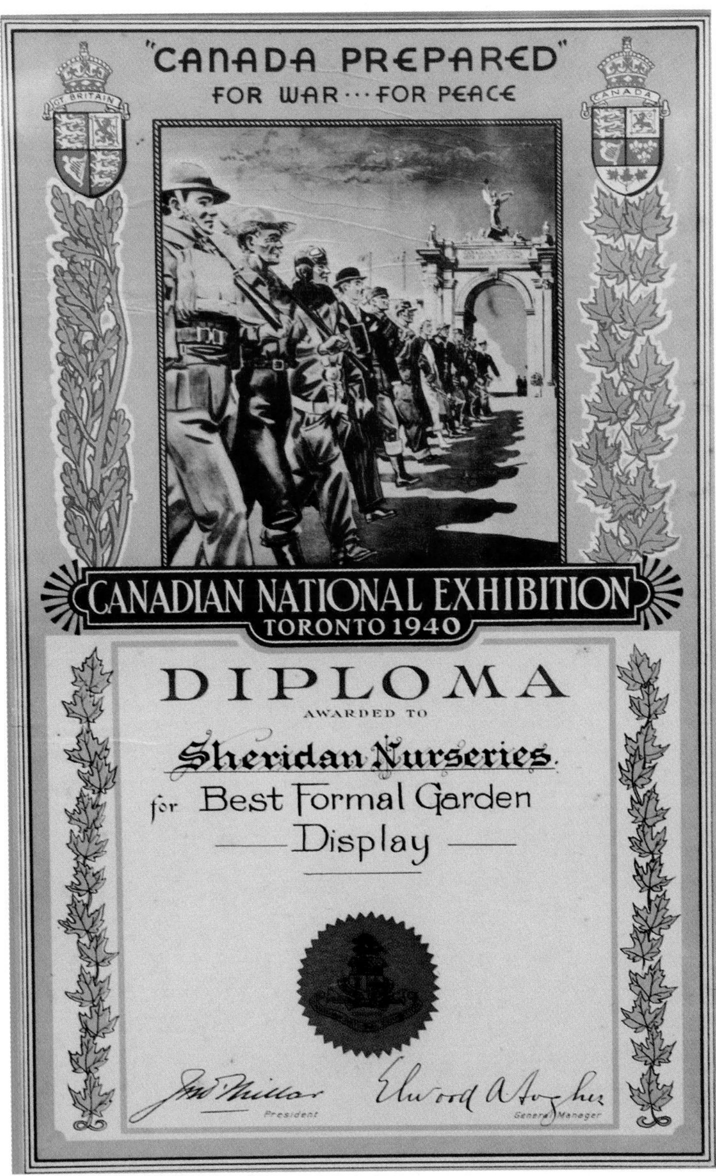

Diploma awarded to Sheridan Nurseries for Best Formal Garden Dislay at the 1940 Canadian National Exhibition (CNE), Toronto, one of several won over the years.

The Sheridan Nurseries garden at the 1956 CNE featured a colourful coastal scene as a backdrop.

The Sheridan Nurseries garden at the 1973 CNE.

Sheridan Nurseries first exhibited in the 1915 CNE and won medals as early as 1919, and for many more years. Shown here are medals from 1936 and 1950.

This colourful Sheridan Nurseries garden graced the foyer of the O'Keefe Centre (now the Sony Centre), Toronto for the 1968 Garden Club of Toronto Annual Flower Show.

This large photograph of a design by Howard and Lorrie was the focal point of the Sheridan Nurseries garden at the 1970 Garden Club of Toronto Flower Show at the O'Keefe Centre, Toronto.

SHERIDAN ORIGINALS

Left: *Mountbatten juniper was first introduced in 1948 after many years of extensive testing.*

Centre: *DeGroot Spire is a popular narrow white cedar, widely used in today's gardens, large and small.*

Right: *Unicorn cedar continues to be popular for cedar hedging and for specimen plantings.*

Green Gem boxwood is a compact, slow-growing boxwood.

Sheridan Gold euonymus adds colour and contrast to today's gardens.

Ivory Silk Japanese tree lilac, a Sheridan Original, is one of the most popular smaller flowering trees and is widely planted today.

Glenleven linden, also a Sheridan Original, is a popular street tree and today is ideally suited for use on smaller front yards.

Sheridan Nurseries' current head office is located in the centre of the Sheridan farms near the village of Glen Williams, Georgetown, Ontario. Note the popular sea lion sculpture by Ursula Hanes which adorns the pool in front of the office.

Sheridan Nurseries executive 2012. L–R: Pieter Joubert, vice-president, nursery operations; Valerie Stensson, vice-president, marketing and purchasing; Karl E. Stensson, president; W.S. (Bill) Stensson, chief executive officer; Rick K. Friesen, senior vice-president, finance and administration; Manuel Sobrinho, vice-president, nursery sales; Art Vanden Enden, vice-president, garden centre operations.

Sheridan Nurseries operating committee. L–R: Gwen Ferris, payroll and benefits manager; Rob Naraj, wholesale business manager; Shelley Elgar, seasonal plant product manager; Bart Brusse, Glen Williams container farm manager; Mary Beth Brown, garden centre marketing manager; Amin Datoo, store manager, Toronto Garden Centre; Liz Kavanagh, manager of financial accounting.

The Spring 2012 head office staff surround the pool in front of Sheridan's head office, Glen Williams, Ontario.

Sheridan Nurseries garden centres all have their trucks covered with these colourful wraps.

An aerial view of Sheridan Nurseries extensive nursery fields near Georgetown, Ontario. Note the bio-irrigation pond in the lower left quadrant, which is the largest of its kind in Canada.

Sheridan Nurseries Farm management team, Spring 2012. L–R: Mary Jane Ash, propagation manager, Norval farm; Frank Miedzinski, assistant manager of distribution, Glen Williams; Yvonne Devogel-Anderson, assistant manager of operations, Glen Williams; Bart Brusse, manager, Glen Williams container farm; Jigar Joshi, manager, Norval farm perennials; Wilson Moncada, distribution manager, Glen Williams; Mike Forward, assistant manager, Glen Williams; Uli Rumpf, quality control manager, Glen Williams; Stephen Johnson, assistant manager of distribution, Glen Williams.

Sheridan Nurseries Georgetown distribution facility at the height of the Spring 2012 season.

Sheridan Nurseries Glen Williams farm in the fall.

Pot-in-pot production of trees has now replaced in-the-field growing at Sheridan.

Perennial production at Sheridan Nurseries Norval Farm, Ontario, now produces over six hundred varieties of hardy perennials.

Over 250,000 boxwood are produced each year in the Sheridan Nurseries container fields in Georgetown, Ontario.

The original thirty acres of container in Georgetown, Ontario, is still in use today.

This automated potting machine has a capacity of filling twelve thousand pots daily with a crew of ten.

The Professional Supply Centre located within the Sheridan Nurseries Garden Centre in Unionville, Ontario.

Sheridan Nurseries Unionville Garden Centre was completely rebuilt in 2008.

Sheridan Nurseries garden centre managers. Back row, L–R: Larry Parr, Etobicoke; John Reiter, Georgetown; Steven Cline, Whitby; Michael Davis, Kitchener; Andrew Jinkinson, Scarborough; Pat Large, North York; Front row, L–R: Scott Baillie; Unionville; Erica Lowartz-Corrarin; Mississauga; Amin Datoo, Toronto.

A display of Sheridan Nurseries private label "Garden Classic" perennials.

Sheridan Nurseries downtown Toronto Garden Centre was completely renovated in 2012.

Sheridan Nurseries garden centres sell literally millions of colourful annuals each spring into summer.

Unique planters sourced all over the world each year help to differentiate Sheridan Nurseries from other retailers.

A unique gift section features scarves, jewellery, and handbags sourced in North America.

Merchandising is a big part of selling products at all Sheridan Nurseries garden centres.

Sheridan Nurseries has been selling a wide range of patio furniture for over forty years, now including IPE wood furniture from Ecuador.

Betty (Stensson) Stewart was a great hostess and gardener. She is shown here in her backyard garden in Clarkson, Ontario, with a plant of Nova Zembla rhododendron and her husband Ross Stewart, June 1991.

Howard Stensson was involved in the selection of new roses at Sheridan Nurseries for many years and is shown here in front of a field of the rose named after his wife, Maurine, in July 1990.

The Sheridan-sponsored Artists' Garden "Changing Channels" installed in 2000 at Harbourfront, Toronto, by Janet Morton (now removed).

The Sheridan-sponsored Artists' Garden "Swamped" installed in 2000 at Harbourfront, Toronto, by Brad Copping and Sue Rankin (now removed).

The formal Boxwood garden of Sheridan Green Gem, Green Mountain, and Green Velvet, given to the Royal Botanical Gardens, Hamilton, Ontario, in 1987 and installed that year in the Laking Gardens in honour of Sheridan Nurseries seventy-fifth anniversary.

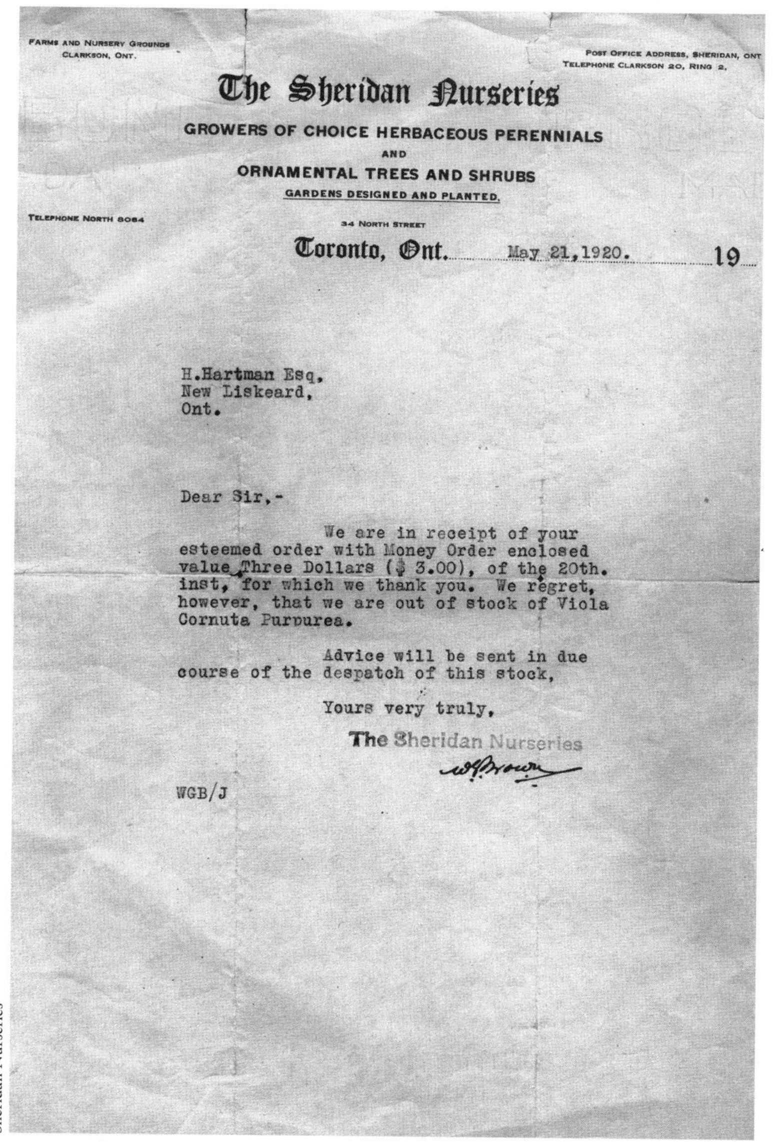

FARMS AND NURSERY GROUNDS
CLARKSON, ONT.

POST OFFICE ADDRESS, SHERIDAN, ONT
TELEPHONE CLARKSON 20, RING 2.

The Sheridan Nurseries

GROWERS OF CHOICE HERBACEOUS PERENNIALS
AND
ORNAMENTAL TREES AND SHRUBS
GARDENS DESIGNED AND PLANTED.

TELEPHONE NORTH 8064

34 NORTH STREET

Toronto, Ont. May 21,1920. 19

H.Hartman Esq,
New Liskeard,
Ont.

Dear Sir,-

We are in receipt of your esteemed order with Money Order enclosed value Three Dollars ($ 3.00), of the 20th. inst, for which we thank you. We regret, however, that we are out of stock of Viola Cornuta Purpurea.

Advice will be sent in due course of the despatch of this stock,

Yours very truly,

The Sheridan Nurseries

W.G.Brown

WGB/J

Sheridan Nurseries

This letter written in 1920 shows the attention that was paid to every little detail.

Lorrie knew that her catalogue covers would have to impress not only amateur gardeners, but also owners of grand estates. The illustrations had to tell those people at first glance how beautiful Sheridan Nurseries could make their homes.

J.V. Stensson's name isn't in the *Dictionary of Canadian Artists*, but he was nonetheless a skilled illustrator. In 1935, J.V. produced the catalogue cover art. His stunning view of the interior of a walled garden is meticulous in its detail, perhaps showing the influence of Howard Dunington-Grubb. J.V. followed it with a somewhat similar theme in 1936, this time with an archway as the visual portal into the garden.

Not all of the artists who did catalogue work for the Dunington-Grubbs are known. Some artists didn't want their names associated with mercenary commercial work. But other artists Lorrie commissioned had no qualms about signing their names to catalogue cover illustrations. Today those names are in rather illustrious company. Their Sheridan works stand out both collectively and individually as splendid examples of the commercial art of the day.

Howard Dunington-Grubb knew Alexander Scott Carter through the Arts & Letters Club. He was an architect who had come to Canada from England about 1912. He was also an excellent graphic artist who would become best known for his work in heraldry. Among other things, he designed coats-of-arms for universities all over the world. Carter drew cover illustrations for the catalogues in 1917, 1918, 1925, 1926, and 1934. The 1925 illustration had actually been used on the 1912 Christmas card sent out by the landscape architects Dunington-Grubb & Harries.

In 1928, the Sheridan catalogue entered the realm of Canadian artistic legend. J.E.H. MacDonald agreed to do

Sheridan Nurseries.

This cover for the 1928 catalogue was designed by Group of Seven artist J.E.H. MacDonald.

Sheridan Nurseries

J.E.H. MacDonald, a personal friend of the Dunington-Grubbs, also designed the cover for the 1929 catalogue.

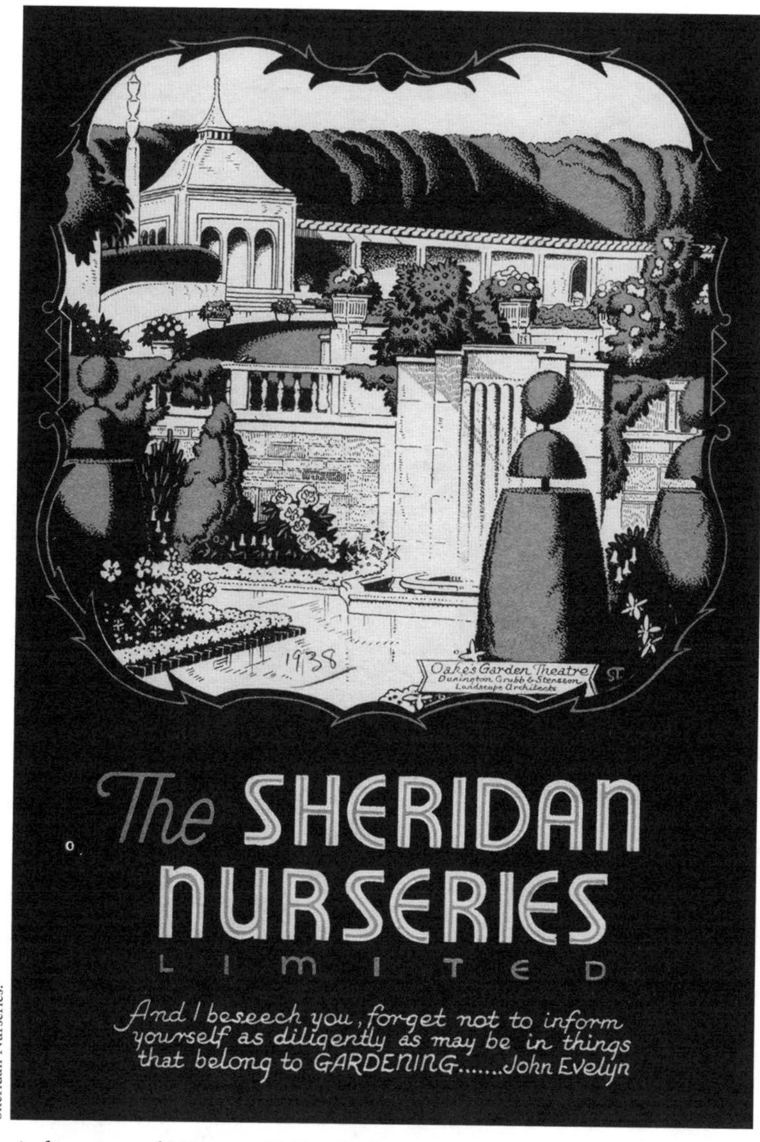

Sheridan Nurseries.

A drawing of Niagara Falls' Oakes Garden Theatre, designed by Dunington-Grubb & Stensson, was used on the cover of the 1936 catalogue.

Sheridan Nurseries.

J.V. Stensson created this cover for the 1936 catalogue. The view is of the Stensson home.

This cartoon illustration created by Bryant Wilkins Fryer for the 1937 catalogue was one of Sheridan's most unusual catalogue covers.

Sheridan Nurseries.

a cover illustration. Lorrie could well have considered this a major accomplishment that brought considerable prestige to both the catalogue and the company. MacDonald's work appeared on the covers again in 1929, 1930, and 1933. The last illustration appeared after MacDonald's death in 1932.

In 1937, the catalogue cover took a dramatic change. Instead of a classical or rustic image, this one was a cartoon. The artist was Bryant Fryer, a Canadian pioneer in film animation, who also did a famous oil portrait of Howard Dunington-Grubb that now hangs in the company's boardroom. The light-hearted, busy-looking overview that Bryant created for the catalogue was one of Sheridan's most whimsical illustrations.

Another noteworthy artist created a catalogue cover in 1938. Stanley F. Turner had won first prize in 1913 for his *Eaton Jubilee Cover*, and was famous for his illustrations in Canadian historical novels and magazines. During the Second World War, he illustrated war maps for the *Globe & Mail*. Turner would create cover illustrations for Sheridan again in 1951 and 1952.

THE CATALOGUE'S NEW LOOK

It isn't certain just how long Lorrie remained in charge of the catalogues. Poor health forced her to withdraw from active participation in most aspects of the business several years before her death in 1945. The catalogue had become the responsibility of Albert Brown by 1950 when he took charge of all publicity and photography. He had probably already been working on the catalogue in Lorrie's absence. It was around that time that the catalogue took on a whole new look.

The first "modern" Sheridan catalogue appeared in 1951. It was eight-and-a-half-by-eleven inches, and had the slick visual appeal that had become standard for popular catalogues. Readers were treated to more photographs of flowering plants and gorgeous landscaping — at least, as gorgeous as black-and-white photography could suggest. Colour photographs appeared as early as 1941, but it wasn't until 1956 that they became a regular feature. Production costs meant that they still had to share the pages with black-and-white images. The first full-colour Sheridan Nurseries catalogue wouldn't come out until 1965.

In 1960, the catalogue provided readers with a rare summary of the number of plant varieties grown by Sheridan Nurseries:

> Every name appearing in this catalogue represents living plants in quantity actually growing in the field. No plant reaches the catalogue until we have sufficient specimens of that variety to satisfy anticipated demand. Number of species and varieties growing at Sheridan Nurseries is as follows:
>
> Perennials lead the list at 620. Roses are a distant second at 227. They are followed by shrubs (216), trees (102), evergreens (90), Broad-leaved evergreens (43), vines (29), and Rhododendrons and Azaleas (18). The total of 1,345 plants "propagated from seed, cuttings, grafts, or division" did not include "a large

> number of species and varieties not yet sufficiently tested or not yet in sufficient quantities to offer for the market."

Art Drysdale joined Sheridan Nurseries as Albert Brown's assistant. Years later, Art recalled the occasion:

> I started in August 1962, but was only in the office for a little more than a week, as I had already booked a two-week vacation to Vancouver/Victoria. During the time I was away, as I recall, Sammy [Kayama] built a duplicate of Mr. Brown's wooden desk for me.
>
> When I returned, I immediately began work on the 1963 catalogue, which was to be the first to be printed using the Offset method (Web), and the printer we chose was London Printing and Lithographing (LPL). There was a great deal of work to do, using the original copper plates for each picture. Each set had to go to LPL and they in turn had films made which were used in that first offset catalogue.
>
> So, while I worked in great detail on that 1963 catalogue, so did Mr. Brown. But for the 1964 version, I was on my own. And the same applied up to that for 1970.

After Mr. Brown's death, Art took over Sheridan's advertising, including responsibility for the catalogue. As part of Sheridan's contribution to Canada's 1967 centennial celebrations, the spring catalogue presented the first official Canadian Plant Hardiness Map, which had been produced by Agriculture Canada. An accompanying article written by Art explained the map's importance.

Following Art Drysdale's departure, Larry Sherk stepped in to handle advertising and the catalogue. He kept the position from 1969 until 1994, when he assumed the position of hardy plant product manager. Under Larry's tenure, the catalogue continued to evolve. In 1971, for the first time, the listings included fruit trees, small fruits such as strawberries, and hardy ferns. In 1972, after more than half a century of being given out *gratis*, the catalogue had a selling price of one dollar. But inside each copy was a $1 Sheridan Nurseries coupon.

The catalogue's first French edition was published in 1985. In 1987, the price went up to $2, with a corresponding coupon. Meanwhile, the cover illustration continued to be a compelling feature.

Sheridan Nurseries.

1987 billboard for Mississauga Garden Centre on Southdown Road

From time to time, one of the classic images from the early days graced the catalogue cover. But more often, on the front of the book was an eye-catching gem of the photographic art, always focused on the beauty of plants. The 1987 cover photo of a tulip called Pink Impression was a Sheridan exclusive. In 1988, Sheridan Nurseries seventy-fifth anniversary year, the cover featured a photograph of the prize-winning Sunsation Rose, a Sheridan introduction.

Even though the little publication that Lorrie started in 1914 had blossomed into a reference book that for many years was considered the "Bible" of gardeners and horticulturists, the recession of 1991 almost rendered it expendable. Fortunately, it was reborn when Valerie Stensson, Sheridan's marketing manager at that time, brought all of Sheridan's catalogues and advertising in-house. The Sheridan Nurseries *Garden Guide* has admirably taken up where the old catalogue left off. In 2008, the *Garden Guide* was made available in CD format, and in 2009 it became available for purchase on the Sheridan Nurseries website.

Recent editions of the *Garden Guide* have received several industry awards, and now include extensive information on plant care, plants for specific uses, inspirational plant combinations, and more. As Lorrie knew when writing for those first-edition catalogues, many of the readers are amateur gardeners and the importance of informing the reader, in an informal way, continues to be an important consideration.

In 2000, the first Outdoor Living catalogue was produced to reflect the growing diversity of products available at Sheridan garden centres. In 2004, the first Flowering Annual catalogue was printed and distributed door-to-door throughout the Toronto area. Both publications have received many industry awards, and have introduced consumers to an ever-expanding product selection at Sheridan Nurseries.

THE TRADE LISTS

In addition to the catalogues, Sheridan Nurseries published trade lists. These were wholesale catalogues that went out to members of the trade: landscapers, garden centres, municipalities, and other bulk buyers. The year in which the oldest surviving trade list was published is uncertain because it isn't dated. It may have been 1924, because the first dated edition was printed for the spring of 1925. All succeeding editions are dated. They also offered wholesale yard lists and specimen tree lists.

Browsing through these old documents, one can actually follow Sheridan Nurseries' growth. To impress potential customers, the company's acreage was always included. It starts at 150 acres, and over the years increases to 250 acres, 260 acres, and so on. The trade lists sometimes reflect the times in which they were made. During the Great Depression, for example, wholesale prices were reduced. As a primary source, even something as mundane as a commercial trade list can be a valuable historical document.

Trade lists were issued for both spring and fall until they were combined into one issue for Fall/Spring 1969–70. The format was designed to increase the price and sizes of plants after they grew in the summer months if needed. Some nurseries still follow this method today. Sheridan followed this format until 1979 when a trade list was issued for the calendar year as they are today. Between 1985 and 1997,

WHOLESALE
PRICE LIST
of
TREES, SHRUBS
EVERGREENS
PERENNIALS,
ROSES, VINES
Spring, 1925
THE
SHERIDAN
NURSERIES
150 Acres of Ornamental Nursery Stock
CLARKSON, TORONTO, MONTREAL.

Sheridan Nurseries.

French-only issues were also produced. Since then they have been bilingual. An edition with prices in U.S. dollars was produced for American guests in 1997. As of 2012, only one version for Canada and the United States is produced in the fall, as the exchange rate is no longer a wide variance. Of course, the option exists to revert to two trade lists if the currency difference were to once again increase.

A separate price list is also produced for the five professional supply centres attached to the garden centres in Georgetown, Kitchener-Waterloo, Mississauga-Oakville, Whitby, and Unionville.

Left: *The cover of the wholesale price list for Spring 1925. This was a separate publication from the retail catalogue, and intended primarily for trade buyers such as municipalities and garden centres.*

Right: *Logo of the Eastern Canada Nurserymen's Association in 1922.*

Sheridan Nurseries.

EVERGREENS—Continued.

	Less than 5	Per 10	Per 100
Pseudotsuga douglassi. Douglas Spruce.			
2 to 3 feet, B. & B.	1 50	12 50	100 00
3 to 4 feet, B. & B.	1 75	15 00	125 00
4 to 5 feet, B. & B.	3 00	25 00	200 00
douglassi. Colorado Blue.			
2 to 3 feet	1 75	15 00	125 00
3 to 4 feet	2 50	20 00	150 00
Retinospora filifera. Thread-leaved Cypress.			
2 to 3 feet	2 50	22 50	200 00
3 to 4 feet	4 00	35 00	
Taxus cuspidata. Japanese Yew.			
18 to 24 inches	3 00	25 00	200 00
2 to 3 feet	4 50	40 00	350 00
Thuya occidentalis. White Cedar (Specimens bushy).			
2 to 3 feet	80	7 50	60 00
occidentalis compacta.			
2 to 3 feet	3 50	30 00	
occidentalis froebeli.			
18 to 24 inches	3 00	25 00	
Thuya occidentalis pyramidalis.			
3 to 4 feet	3 50	30 00	250 00
4 to 5 feet	4 50	40 00	350 00
5 to 6 feet	7 00	60 00	
occidentalis vervaeneana.			
2 to 3 feet	3 00	25 00	
occidentalis wareana.			
2 to 3 feet	2 50	20 00	
3 to 4 feet	3 00	25 00	
Tsuga canadensis. The Hemlock.			
2 to 3 feet	3 00	26 00	
3 to 4 feet	4 00	35 00	
4 to 5 feet	6 00	55 00	

TREES

	Less than 5	Per 10	Per 100
Acer saccharinum. Soft Maple.			
6 to 8 feet	$ 0 70	$ 6 00	$ 50 00
Aesculus hippocastanum. Horse Chestnut.			
4 to 5 feet	1 25	10 00	
Alnus glutinosa. Black Alder.			
8 to 10 feet	1 50	12 50	
Betula alba. White Birch.			
5 to 6 feet	1 00	9 00	75 00
papyrifera. Paper Birch.			
4 to 5 feet	90	8 00	70 00
Catalpa speciosa. Western Catalpa.			
6 to 8 feet	1 50	12 50	
Fagus sylvatica pendula. Weeping Beech.			
4 to 5 feet	6 00	50 00	
5 to 6 feet	8 00	75 00	

	Less than 5	Per 10	Per 100
Fraxinus excelsior. Common Ash.			
6 to 8 feet	80	7 50	70 00
8 to 10 feet	1 25	10 00	90 00
Populus bolleana. Silver Poplar.			
5 to 6 feet	80	7 50	
6 to 8 feet	1 50	12 50	
caroliniana. Carolina Poplar.			
6 to 8 feet	60	5 00	40 00
8 to 10 feet	85	7 50	60 00
10 to 12 feet	1 00	9 00	75 00
fastigiata. Lombardy Poplar.			
6 to 8 feet	70	6 00	50 00
8 to 10 feet	90	8 00	70 00
10 to 12 feet	1 25	10 00	90 00
Salix babylonica pendula. Weeping Willow.			
6 to 8 feet	1 75	15 00	
Sorbus aucuparia. Mountain Ash.			
6 to 8 feet	1 50	12 50	100 00
8 to 10 feet	1 75	15 00	
Ulmus americana. American Elm.			
5 to 6 feet	60	5 00	35 00
6 to 8 feet	70	6 00	50 00
8 to 10 feet	90	8 00	70 00

SHRUBS

	Less than 5	Per 10	Per 100
Amelanchier botryapium. Juneberry.			
18 to 24 inches	$ 0 40	$ 3 50	$ 30 00
Amorpha fruticosa. False Indigo.			
2 to 3 feet	27	2 20	20 00
Aralia spinosa. Hercules Club.			
3 to 4 feet	60	5 00	
4 to 5 feet	85	7 50	
6 to 8 feet	1 25	10 00	
Berberis ilicifolia. Holly-leaved Barberry.			
2 to 3 feet	70	6 00	
thunbergii. Japanese Barberry.			
15 to 18 inches	22	2 00	18 00
18 to 24 inches	27	2 50	20 00
2 to 3 feet	35	3 00	25 00
Caragana pygmea. Siberian Pea (Dwarf).			
2 to 3 feet	70	6 00	
Cephalanthus occidentalis. Buttonbush.			
2 to 3 feet	27	2 20	20 00
Cornus stolonifera flaveramea. Yellow-barked Dogwood.			
2 to 3 feet	27	2 20	20 00
3 to 4 feet	35	3 00	25 00
elegantissima. Silver-leaved Dogwood.			
12 to 18 inches	70	6 00	50 00
Cydonia japonica. Japanese Quince.			
18 to 24 inches	60	5 00	40 00
Deutzia pride of Rochester. Snow Flower.			
2 to 3 feet	27	2 20	20 00
3 to 4 feet	35	3 00	25 00
Eleagnus angustifolia. Oleaster.			
4 to 5 feet	37	3 30	30 00
Euonymus europeus. Spindle Tree.			
2 to 3 feet	27	2 30	21 00
3 to 4 feet	32	2 80	24 00

Sheridan Nurseries.

Inside pages listing trade prices in the first dated Wholesale Price List, 1925.

Sheridan Nurseries.

Cover of 1958 Wholesale Price List show an aerial view of the Oakville nursery headquarters.

Sheridan Nurseries.

Spring 1963 Wholesale Price List shows drawings of Sheridan patio pots and evergreens.

Sheridan Offers Nursery Plants

A to Z (almost)

Try as we might, we couldn't find a plant on our list starting with 'Z'. But in all, Sheridan offers 900 varieties of evergreens, trees and shrubs to its customers across Canada. And you get more than variety from Sheridan Nurseries — you get traditional Sheridan quality. Sheridan Nurseries ensures quality by offering only hardy varieties selected for excellent growth habits. And the skilled staff on Sheridan's three farms make sure that you receive superior nursery stock. Have a look through your Sheridan Trade List, and then give Sheridan Nurseries a call. Get Sheridan's variety and quality working for you.

"Drop in and see us at one of our farms. Maps and directions are in your Sheridan Trade List"

LANDSCAPE ONTARIO

SHERIDAN NURSERIES LIMITED
RR #4 — 10TH LINE
Georgetown, Ontario L7G 4S7
Tel: (416) 873-0522, 840-0111
Fax: (416) 873-2478

Sheridan trade ad used in the late 1980s.

Sheridan Nurseries.

In 1974, Sheridan Nurseries hosted a dinner in Glen Williams for one thousand members of the American Association of Nurserymen during their annual convention in Toronto.

OTHER ADVERTISING

The catalogues were just one method of advertising used by Sheridan Nurseries. Word-of-mouth, generated by satisfied customers, has always been important. The company also used other forms of media. From 1915 on, visitors to the CNE saw impressive Sheridan Nurseries displays and were handed brochures. The company participated in numerous horticultural shows that received newspaper coverage. In the late 1920s, Sheridan's ads began appearing in *Canadian Homes and Gardens* magazine.

In the mid-1930s, Sheridan started placing small ads in newspapers. The one that appeared in the Toronto *Daily Star* on May 3, 1934, provides a typical example:

> Inspect our stock of evergreen trees, shrubs, perennials, at our sales stations at 1186 Bay, and Toronto–Hamilton highway at Clarkson.
> Sheridan Nurseries.

This was economy advertising, tucked away amongst dozens of other ads on a gardening page offering such items as "rich black loam," "velvet-like sod," and "old cow manure." However, by the mid-1940s, Sheridan was purchasing newspaper space for substantial, illustrated ads. Newspaper advertising would continue to be vital to Sheridan's marketing.

Radio audiences first heard Sheridan Nurseries commercials in the 1960s. For the last thirty years, Karl Stensson has been Sheridan's radio "personality." The company experimented with bus boards and billboards in the 1970s, but only briefly. Sheridan's venture into television advertising in 1976 was also short-lived.

Most of Sheridan's advertising today is done through flyers, newspapers, and radio. Email, commercial, and social media also play a big part in current marketing methods. Visitors can go to the Sheridan Nurseries website at *www.sheridannurseries.com*, where they will find one of the most extensive horticultural websites in North America. The Plant Finder feature has over 2,400 varieties with full-colour photos.

Sheridan is now interfacing with and inspiring guests on Facebook and Twitter. Improving guests' experience with a presence on these social media platforms builds a quality shared community to anticipate guests' needs and improve their experience with the Sheridan brand. On Facebook, Sheridan can generate horticultural conversations, provide gardening tips, and increase awareness of long-term commitment to responsibility and sustainability. Twitter enables Sheridan to promptly share horticultural information, tips, and news with guests who follow company updates. Through Facebook and Twitter, guests have a place where they can feel welcome and engage with the growing Sheridan Nurseries online community.

Reminiscent of the old English "Pleasaunce" this rose arched walk invites the visitor to stroll under bowers of climbing roses. A view of the new rose garden executed by us at Gage Park, Hamilton, Ontario, for the Hamilton Parks Board. (H.B. & L.A. Dunington-Grubb, Landscape Architects.)

Formal gardening is essential as a setting for public monuments. The approach to the monument at the Stoney Creek Battlefields Park, Ontario. Executed by our Landscape Department. (H. B. & L. A. Dunington-Grubb, Landscape Architects.)

Garden Design

"As ages grow to civility and elegancy, men come to build stately sooner than to garden finely, as if gardening were the greater perfection." —*Francis Bacon.*

Fine gardens are of even greater importance as a national asset than fine houses, since they are indicative of a higher development in civilization.

Leaders of fashion and connoisseurs of beauty dare no longer neglect the art of garden design, for to do so will be to find themselves left in a backwater by the flood of modern intellectual progress.

The greater artists and sculptors known to history, such as Raphael, Vignola and Michael Angelo were the designers of the famous gardens of the Italian Renaissance.

If you desire a beautiful garden you must call in highly trained experts to plan and to plant.

The Sheridan Nurseries Limited are fully equipped to give you complete satisfaction in this direction.

The SHERIDAN NURSERIES *Limited*

Head Office, 4 St. Thomas Street
Toronto 5

Nursery Farms, Clarkson, Ontario

Montreal Sales Station
1240 Greene Ave., Westmount, P. Que.

Sheridan Nurseries.

Gage Park and Stoney Creek Battlefield Park landscaping ad in Canadian Homes and Gardens, *August 1928.*

Delivery of evergreens in ball and burlap by truck to the job eliminates delay and ensures safety in planting

EVERGREENS

FORTY FIVE ACRES of our extensive nurseries at Clarkson, Ontario, are devoted exclusively to the propagation and culture of evergreens.

Raised from seed, grafts, cuttings, and layers, our evergreens are born to withstand the Canadian climate.

Frequently transplanted, and root pruned, they form a compact mass of fibrous root, ensuring their success when properly planted in suitable soil.

In ball or burlap they can be shipped by truck or rail at almost any time of year while the ground is not actually frozen.

We offer for sale almost every variety of evergreen suited to this climate.

The astonishing increase in the demand for Sheridan Evergreens during the last few years proves their superiority over imported stock.

A block of Junipers growing in our Nurseries, giving an idea of the extent of our evergreen planting.

Head Office:
4 St. Thomas Street, Toronto 5

Phone KIngsdale 4151

Nursery Farms: Clarkson, Ont.

Montreal Sales Station:
1240 Greene Ave., Westmount, P. Que.

Sheridan Nurseries.

Ad for Canadian grown evergreens in Canadian Homes and Gardens, *June 1928.*

CHAPTER 11

Recognition and Reputation

It's important for any company to attract the public's attention and make people aware that it stands for quality. Centuries ago, tradesmen and merchants hung signs with eye-catching images in front of their shops. Passersby could see at a glance what product or service was available there. As businesses grew from small shops to large companies and advertising became more sophisticated, the image on the shop sign evolved into the concept of the company logo.

Howard and Lorrie Dunington-Grubb knew that Sheridan Nurseries needed a trademark image that was at once simple, dynamic, and unique. However, they couldn't afford the services of such prestigious graphic design companies as Toronto's Grip Ltd., which employed artists like Tom Thomson and C.W. Jefferys. The fact that the names of the designers of the first Sheridan Nurseries logos were not recorded indicates that either Howard or Lorrie drew the images themselves, or they informally hired artists they knew personally.

Starting with the 1917–18 catalogue, the Dunington-Grubbs experimented with various designs that appeared sporadically until 1933. They all incorporated the initials *SN* with stylish figures of plants, and were placed conspicuously in the catalogues. There was also a logo designed especially for the Sheridan Nurseries letterhead that was used at least as early as 1923 (see example in letter on page 47). No Sheridan Nurseries logo appeared in the catalogues from 1934 through 1950. The reason why remains a mystery, because the artwork had been compelling. The catalogues were very much Lorrie's responsibility, and it's possible that as her health failed, she was unable to give much attention to such details. After 1950, the logos began to appear again.

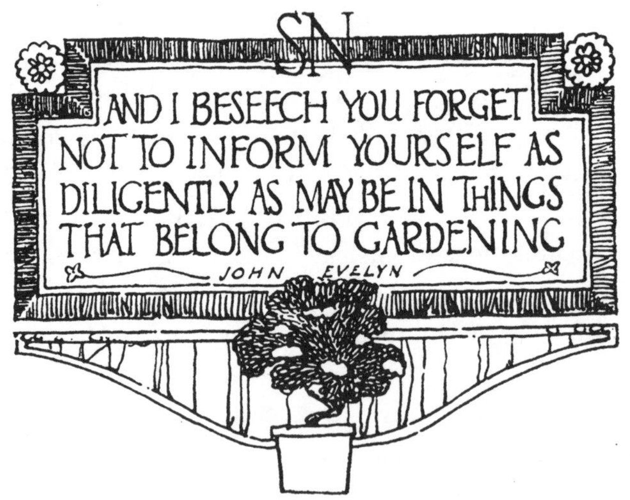

Sheridan Nurseries.

Selection of logos used by Sheridan Nurseries in the early years

In 1967, two years after Howard Dunington-Grubb died, Sheridan Nurseries decided that the company needed a modern, standout logo that could be used in visual advertising, signage, and on company business cards and stationery. The old images, however elegant, were too dated. Sheridan hired Chris Yaneff to create the design.

Yaneff was an artist who, with his partner Fred Gotthams, had created some of the most recognizable trademarks and package designs in Canada. Among their clients were Conklin Shows and Windsor Salt. He went on to design the CN Railway logo that is still in use today. Yaneff's design for Sheridan Nurseries was described in a memo from his office:

> The new trademark for Sheridan Nurseries Ltd. features the two most typical shapes of trees: triangular and globular. It represents in a symbolic way the most important field of a nursery's activity, the growing of evergreens, ornamental trees and shrubs. The stylized treatment of heavy lines follows nature's play of interlocking branches and overlapping shapes. Printed in a warm yellow-green, its gay and airy appearance conveys the feeling of springtime and growth. Because of its simplicity, the trademark will always keep its striking effect whether it is 8 feet high or a ½ inch on a calling card.

Sheridan used the "stick" logo until 1988, when it became the basis for a more solid-looking design that placed the two trees inside a greenhouse structure. Later a banner proclaiming "Since 1913" was added. In 2000, Sheridan contracted Watt Design to examine the corporate look in the company's garden centres. Everything, including the logo, was scrutinized. Using the original catalogue logos for guidance, Watt redesigned the Sheridan Nurseries logo that is familiar to gardeners and the company's guests today; a stylized image of a leafy tree flanked by two flowering shrubs and set on a grassy base. It is reminiscent of the old logos, but without the initials. Like the nursery itself, the Sheridan logo evolves and adapts.

As already mentioned, recognition goes hand in hand with a reputation for quality and excellence. In 1919, when Herman Stensson was still struggling to make a real nursery out of the Dunington-Grubbs' patch of ground in Sheridan, the Canadian National Exhibition in Toronto was Canada's premiere showplace for all things agricultural. Winning an award at the CNE was a major coup. That year, Sheridan Nurseries won first prize for the best rock garden.

Sheridan Nurseries would go on to win fifteen more medals at the CNE, as well as several CNE diplomas. But the company was never content to sit on its laurels. Sheridan's horticulturists were constantly seeking to improve plants and introduce new ones. Awards also came from such prestigious bodies as the Ontario Rose Society, the National Flower and Garden Show, the International Lilac Society, and Canada Blooms. The prestigious Pennsylvania Horticultural Society twice honoured Sheridan with gold medals: for Ivory Silk Japanese tree lilac in 1996, and Green Velvet boxwood in 1997. And even though some plants were not introduced by Sheridan, the nursery won awards for growing plants like gingko, Spreading Blue Chip juniper, Weeping Jade crab apple, and Deborah Norway maple.

Growing prize-winning plants is only part of the story. The plants have to be sold. Over the years, Sheridan Nurseries has been a leader in the marketing and retail sectors of the industry, winning over sixty Landscape Ontario Association awards for display, promotional events, merchandising, and garden guide. Most recently, the Unionville store was named Canada's best garden centre in 2011. Unique among Sheridan's collection of awards is a gold medal presented for the catalogue in April 1960, by the *Mostra Del Fiore* (Flower Show) of Trieste, Italy.

A hundred years ago, Herman Stensson did most of the manual work with the help of a few hired men, including his children as soon as they were old enough. Over the decades, as the company grew, so did the number of staff. Sheridan's management has always been aware of the importance and wisdom in maintaining good employee relations in a pleasant and efficient workplace. In 1998, 1999, and 2000, Sheridan was selected as one of Canada's 50 Best Managed Private Companies. Sheridan's Apprenticeship Program earned the company the Employer of the Year Award of Excellence in 2002.

Sheridan Nurseries has always worked closely with communities in order to be a responsible citizen and good neighbour. That's a tradition that goes back to the days of the Dunington-Grubbs and Herman Stensson. Since moving to Glen Williams from Oakville, Sheridan Nurseries has maintained an excellent relationship with the various administrative departments in Halton Hills, and that has resulted in several civic awards.

In 1995, Sheridan received the Halton Chamber of Commerce Civic Pride Award. The community of Glen Williams selected Sheridan for its Citizen of the Year Award in 2007. In 2010 and 2011 respectively, Sheridan's new bio-pond initiative was recognized with the Halton Hills Business Achievement Award and the Landscape Ontario Environmental Award. Sheridan's commitment as a community-minded business has also earned awards from the Halton Hills Fire Department, the Halton Hills District School Board, and the Georgetown Jaycees.

Most of Sheridan's large collection of awards — plaques, ribbons, gold medals, and certificates — can be seen on what might be called the Wall of Fame in the main conference room in Sheridan's head office, or here and there in other parts of the building. In addition to awards bestowed on the company itself, are those earned by individuals in the Sheridan family of employees. Perhaps the most notable honour at the time of this writing is the selection of Sheridan Nurseries as Grower of the Year in Canada for 2012.

Of course, the ultimate goal for Sheridan Nurseries is not to win prizes, but to win guests with quality products and first-rate service. However, the fact that Sheridan keeps winning awards in all of the important categories of the business lets management, staff, and the public know that the company continues to strive for excellence. The promise behind the logo is being fulfilled.

CHAPTER 12

A Century of Milestones

Throughout the first hundred years, Sheridan Nurseries has endured many hardships and regrouped to become stronger each time. In the early years, there was the First World War and then the Great Depression. As things were looking up after the Depression, the Second World War came along. And there have been three recessions to cope with in the last forty years.

It is a well-known fact that in many family-run businesses, the first generation establishes the business, the second generation grows the business, and the third generation destroys the business. This has not been the case with Sheridan. Many key decisions or "milestones" over the last thirty years have been made to set Sheridan on a path of strength and stability.

WARRANTY

In the mid 1980s, the guarantee policies at nearly all Canadian garden centres were cumbersome and certainly favoured the companies and not the customer. Sheridan took the lead in changing this. When Karl Stensson assumed the responsibility of managing the stores in 1985, the warranty on a plant was for one year and a one-time replacement only with the exact same plant. The first thing to be changed was that a dead plant could be exchanged for any plant with equal or less value. It seemed irrational that when a plant died in a certain location in a garden, the exact same plant needed to be purchased to comply with the warranty.

The next change was to allow more than a one-time replacement. Karl always stated that a customer did not buy a plant to "kill it on purpose." Therefore, if the second plant died then there was something wrong with the location or the plant. It was then that the policy was changed to guarantee success. It was the garden centre staff's responsibility to determine what killed the plant and then what to do to ensure that the replacement plant survived.

Perennials were then added to the warranty. To this day, many garden centre operators argue that perennials should not be covered under warranty over the winter. In all the years that Sheridan has been tracking replacements, perennials have been found to be the lowest number of replacements for any category.

The next change put in place was the "No Hassle Warranty." This basically stated that no replacement would be refused provided proof of purchase was presented. In essence, if a customer backed over the plant with their car, they could bring it back for a new one. Again, the rationale was that people do not intentionally want to kill a plant that they have purchased and laboured over.

The last major change was to increase the warranty period to two full years. When box stores came into the Canadian market, they immediately copied Sheridan by offering a two-year warranty. However at the time of this writing, all have reverted to a one-year warranty. Sheridan continues to be an industry leader in plant warranties. To reinforce the point, Sheridan tracks all replacements, as well as all scrap on the garden centre property. To this day, there are more losses on the store property than there are replacements.

COMMON NAMES

Sheridan garden centres were also the first to display plants by the names most familiar to the general public. In nearly all cases, this would be the common name as opposed to the Latin name. This was tantamount to committing heresy in the horticultural industry. Sheridan staff at the time objected to this change, so a survey of retail guests was conducted at the Unionville store. Seven hundred customers were asked a simple question: "If you had a choice, would you rather see plants listed alphabetically by their common or botanical name"?

The response was overwhelming. Six hundred and ninety-five customers wanted common, two wanted botanical, and three didn't care. The decision to list by common name still stands today and many in the industry have followed. What Sheridan did find out was that the staff did not like the change because suppliers, including their own nursery, listed order forms and trade lists in botanical format so it was difficult to cross-reference in the ordering process. Sheridan then made it optional for the wholesale customers to receive invoices in either common or botanical and gradually received compliance from outside suppliers in doing the same.

SHERIDAN PREFERRED PARTNERS

In the early 1990–91 recession, sales were sluggish at the nursery farm. More and more of the nursery wholesale customers were joining buying groups. Some of these groups would not buy from Sheridan as the company did not want to

give large discounts to customers who bought small amounts simply because they belonged to a buying group.

After a number of brainstorming sessions Bill Stensson, who was at the time nursery operations manager; and the wholesale manager, Manuel Sobrinho, determined that the only way to counter this reduction in orders was to develop our their own buying group. With Sheridan having substantial buying power with their own garden centres, it was thought that these discounts could be extended to other non-Sheridan garden centres.

The Sheridan Preferred Partner Program was formed in 1992. This was the first time that a nursery had actually formed a buying group, and to our knowledge continues to be the only buying group run by a nursery. There is no fee for joining, but a garden centre must commit to purchasing a substantial portion of their hardy nursery stock from the Sheridan farm. Over the years the program has evolved and grown. There are over 140 members from Ontario to Newfoundland. Members have access to hard goods deals that are negotiated by the Sheridan retail division product managers. The Sheridan marketing department also offers a full service marketing initiative (for reasonable fees) such as a customized flyer program and signage.

The Sheridan Parkwood brand of fertilizers and other hard goods is also offered to partners. The marketing initiatives, product pricing, and private label products are all items that would not be accessible to smaller independent stores. The program has built a solid base of sales for the farm, assisted in getting even better pricing for the retail stores and, above all, assisted many small independents in growing their business and their bottom line.

EXPANSION

In the 1980s and 1990s there were three major garden centre chains in the Toronto market: Sheridan, White Rose, and Weall & Cullen. It's a common belief that there's not room for three major players in any market segment in a geographic area. Because White Rose was expanding rapidly, and Weall & Cullen was represented in the media by owner Mark Cullen, it was speculated that Sheridan was the weak one of the group and would lose the race. Over the late 1990s, White Rose expanded at a great rate, but by the turn of the millennium they had gone out of business, leaving Sheridan and Weall & Cullen as the two main garden centre chains.

Every few years, Sheridan conducts strategy sessions with its key managers. In 1998, the strategic meeting set a goal of doubling sales in five years. This was to be accomplished through increasing sales or through acquisition. While the management teams went about setting goals and finding new products and services to enhance sales, Larry Wilson contacted Mark Cullen to see if Weall & Cullen was for sale. At the time, he declined. A chance meeting between Mark and Bill Stensson at a Landscape Ontario trade show rekindled the idea, and after a few months of negotiations the deal was signed in late April 2003.

The fit was almost perfect. Sheridan and Weall & Cullen went after the same customer base, with Sheridan concentrated mostly in the west, and Weall & Cullen in the east. The target audience and approximately 80 percent of the products sold were the same. Almost five years to the date of setting the target of doubling in size, the combined companies' sales efforts reached the goal of 100 percent growth.

CONTAINER GROWING

Another milestone was the change from field growing to container growing. At first, Sheridan slowly evolved its container production. By the company's seventy-fifth anniversary in 1988, there were over one thousand acres of field growing and only thirty acres of container production. After that, the process was speeded up until there were 165 acres of containers. The original container-growing facility was in Oakville. When the land was sold, the new container field was built on a thirty-acre flat piece of land next to the Credit River in Glen Williams. Soon more space was needed and the expansion started "up the hill" next to the head office and shipping facility. There are many advantages to growing in containers, but the main ones are the ability to harvest and ship on demand, winter protection, shorter crop cycles, and the condensing of growing area.

Field-grown plants can only be harvested when they are dormant, mainly from late March until mid-May, and then again from October to early December. Other times, the plants are either frozen into the soil or are too tender during the growth spurt of summer. Therefore, shipping was limited to spring or fall, or plants had to be held above ground over the summer months, an expensive and tricky process to keep them in excellent condition. Container plants are literally accessible to ship twelve months of the year, as their roots are totally intact in the growing container. This allows for "just in time" shipping, lower inventory carrying costs at garden centres, and easier access for landscaping jobs throughout the summer.

Over the years Sheridan has suffered some serious plant losses due to harsh winter conditions. One year over $500,000 worth of euonymus were lost after the temperature

Sheridan Nurseries.

"Root ball" being dug by hand.

Sheridan Nurseries.

Left: *Burlap is placed around the soil ball after it is lifted out of the hole.*

Top Right: *Burlap is tightly tied around the ball to secure it for moving.*

Bottom Right: *Balled and burlap evergreens placed on pallets on a wagon going to the shipping dock*

Sheridan Nurseries.

Sheridan Nurseries.

remained at minus 25 Celsius for ten consecutive days. Plants suffer from "winter burn" when there is no protection such as snow cover to shield them from harsh winds. Plants with winter burn are unsalable until new growth appears in four months. This can even result in the loss of the entire plant. The solution was polyhouses. These aren't hot, humid greenhouses, but long plastic tents that protect the plants from the wind and the cold. Gas heaters in some of the polyhouses emit just enough warmth to keep the temperature from dipping below minus 5 degrees Celsius for more sensitive plants such as euonymus and hydrangeas. You wouldn't sleep comfortably in a polyhouse on a cold winter night, but plants do.

Predicting what plants will actually sell six, seven, or even ten years down the road is tricky and errors can be costly. Container growing is usually only a two- to three-year cycle, so the time between predicting sales and getting the actual sales is considerably shortened. And finally, under most circumstances, four to five container plants can be grown in the space that is taken up by one field-grown plant.

Factoring in all of the above, in 2005 the executive group at the recommendation of Bill Stensson, decided to suspend all field-growing operations and concentrate solely on container growing. This was a bold move and one that would ultimately strengthen the nursery unit. Even large caliper trees switched from field growing to pot-in-pot style of growing.

Sheridan Nurseries

Sheridan's "poly" houses; covered with polyethylene plastic, ready for winter.

Sheridan Nurseries

Tree spade blades cut into the ground to form a ball for this specimen spruce

Sheridan Nurseries

Tree spade lifts the ball out of the ground

Sheridan Nurseries

Crew places burlap around the soil wire basket and ties it securely.

PLANT SOURCING

Another change in the nursery in the eighties was the development of a sourcing department. At the urging of Manuel Sobrinho, who had wanted to do this for years, a separate department was formed to provide a one-stop shopping experience for large landscape jobs. There are no nurseries that grow every plant, so in order to supply a complete list of plant material to landscapers, "sourcing" was set up to find the best growers at the most competitive prices so the landscaper would have to make only one call when looking for plants. This department has grown every year since its creation and now accounts for 20 percent of nursery sales revenue.

STANDARDS OF EXCELLENCE

In the 1980s, a Standards of Excellence protocol was established to ensure that all facilities were neat, clean, and organized. This listed mundane tasks such as washing windows and floors and dusting shelves. The tasks were divided up, ensuring that everyone in the store had a task and that no job was overlooked. The Standards of Excellence has evolved over the years, but the same principles apply. It is known within the industry that Sheridan stores are among the cleanest and most well-organized in the business.

GUESTS

With a reputation for clean stores, in the early 2000s, the Sheridan stores placed a major emphasis on providing service that exceeded customer expectations. Management seemed to understand the concept, but a way was needed to ensure that staff could clearly understand the objective. In a brainstorming session, the idea of declaring "The Year of Hospitality" at Sheridan was born. Sheridan wanted staff to compare the Sheridan stores to their homes. The first change was to refer to customers as "guests." The objective was to clean stores for guests, greet guests at the door, and entertain guests, ensuring that they would want to return. This analogy resonated with staff and the Year of Hospitality has become a permanent training tool.

When Karl Stensson took over as president in 2009, the Standards of Excellence and Hospitality training was extended to all nursery departments. All corners of the nursery were cleaned and reviewed to ensure that guests saw only excellent plants, and there were no unsightly distractions along the sides of roads or buildings. The entire company now uses the same "terminology," making for a unified team approach to the business. This was one of the factors contributing to Sheridan Nurseries farms being awarded Grower of the Year for 2012.

CHAPTER 13

Sheridan Today: Growing in the Twenty-First Century

By the time of Howard Dunington-Grubb's death in 1965, the nursery he and Lorrie had founded fifty-two years earlier had grown into a prosperous major company.

He left 25 percent of his estate to the Meadowvale Botanical Garden, which subsequently became the Dunington-Grubb Foundation, 25 percent to senior employees, 25 percent to the Stensson family, and the remaining 25 percent to members of the Dunington and Grubb families. In the 1970s, Sheridan Nurseries purchased the shares from the Dunington-Grubb Foundation.

This allowed the foundation to fulfill the Dunington-Grubb mandate. As has been outlined in previous chapters, Herman and Annie Stensson's children assumed the roles of leadership and then passed it on to their own children, all of whom grew up with the nursery in their blood.

THE STENSSON FAMILY

The third generation of the Stensson family who make up part of the Sheridan Nurseries executive didn't just step into their current positions. They had to earn them. Just as their parents; Howard, Fred, and Betty did in Herman's day; Bill, Karen, Karl, and Laurie began working for Sheridan at part-time and summer jobs in the fields, office, or garden centres. They neither expected nor received preferential treatment. Nonetheless, sometimes being closely related to the brass could result in an awkward incident. One such occurrence took place when young Bill was sent to work with a hoeing crew supervised by Thomas Frank, who hadn't met him before and didn't realize that he was Howard Stensson's son and J.V. Stensson's nephew and namesake. When the new kid

identified himself as Bill Stensson, Thomas thought he was a smart-aleck playing a joke.

The younger Stenssons didn't all follow the same route into careers at Sheridan. Laurie was an arts student at Alma College in St. Thomas, graduating in 1962. She pursued a career as a musician and music teacher, but Sheridan was always a large part of her life. As a teenager she'd joined in the crucial springtime chore of writing labels for plant orders. Later she assisted her mother and Uncle Chris with employee time cards. By the time Laurie became a member of the Sheridan Nurseries board of directors in 1994, she had accumulated an impressive list of credentials: Mississauga Junior Citizen of the Year, executive director of the Mississauga Arts Council, member of the board of governors for Sheridan College, and director of the University of Toronto's Erindale College Art Gallery Advisory Board, to name a few. Laurie resigned from the Sheridan board in 2000 when she became a Justice of the Peace. At the encouragement of Bill Stensson, she returned to Sheridan in 2010 to take her current position as a member of the board.

Karen attended the University of Western Ontario in London and graduated at the age of nineteen with a degree in English in 1964. She worked for the Ontario Department of Education in Oakville, and then the Department of Recreation in Oakville. But as with the other Stensson grandchildren, her life revolved around the nursery. She had weeded in the fields and had made cuttings, nicking her fingers so often that the head propogator Constant DeGroot took her off that job. In 1979, Karen went to work in Sheridan's sales department. The responsibilities of marriage and parenthood kept Karen out of the office for a while, but she was never far from the nursery. From 1979 to 1986 her home was the old cottage that her grandparents had moved into in 1914.

Karen returned to work full-time in 1986 as the office supervisor for the Southdown Garden Centre in Mississauga. In 1987, she became a customer sales representative. Karen was made Sales Representative for the Atlantic Provinces in 2000. She and her husband, Lee Gazley, bought a house in Heart's Content, Newfoundland. During the summer, Karen works out of her Newfoundland office, but lives in Burlington, Ontario, the rest of the year.

Bill earned a degree in computer science at the University of Waterloo before going to work full-time in Sheridan's shipping department in 1974. In 1978 he was appointed assistant manager of nursery operations. Over the next few years Bill was promoted to manager of operations and vice-president of nursery operations. He was appointed president in 1986, and built one of the finest teams of dedicated managers and staff in the industry. In 2009, he was appointed chairman and CEO. Bill has been active in the industry, serving on many boards and associations. He was president of the Canadian Nursery and Landscape Association (CNLA) for 2011–12.

After Karl graduated from the University of Guelph in 1973 with a degree in landscape architecture, he worked for the City of Toronto as a parks planner, and then as the coordinator of planning and design for the City of North York. These were to "prove he could get a job somewhere other than Sheridan." Karl returned to Sheridan in 1976 to manage the wholesale sales division. In 1984, he took over management of all Sheridan garden centres and landscape supply yards, as well as the landscape design department. Then in 1997, Karl became senior vice-president of retail operations. He was appointed

president in 2009, and in 2011 Karl appointed himself director of brand integrity, ensuring that all members of the Sheridan team knew that their involvement with the guest could either help or hurt the Sheridan brand. He wanted to ensure they all knew that only helping the brand was acceptable.

Karl is past president of Landscape Ontario and the Canadian Nursery and Landscape Association Garden Centre of the Year Awards Program. He has received many prestigious awards, including the Frank Ewald Junior Nursery Award, the Honorary Life Member award from Landscape Ontario, and the Trillium Award for Outstanding Contribution to the Horticultural Industry. In 2010, Karl became one of only four people to receive the Canadian Nursery and Landscape Association's President's Award. He is a highly recognized and popular industry speaker, as well as a member or chair of several committees and associations. Karl and his wife Valerie also served as international judges for the Australian Garden Centre Association for their Garden Centre Awards Program in 1995.

As third-generation members of a large family business, all of Herman Stensson's grandchildren have their own stories. For example, when Karen worked in the sales department, her brother Karl was sales manager and it seemed at times that they were the only two people in that department. Karen wrote out the orders, and found that thanks to Latin she had picked up in school, the official names of plants just seemed to come naturally to her. Karen has also seen the family influence in the company extend to the next generation; her daughter Heather is currently the home decor supervisor for Sheridan's Etobicoke store.

In Laurie's years at Sheridan, she learned that the prevailing mandate was that you finished the day's work, because if you didn't, you'd never catch up. Laurie was often her mother's reliable right hand when Betty was planning and presiding over her famous Sheridan parties. However, even though all four Stensson grandchildren have made their own vital contributions to Sheridan, there are two incidents involving Bill and Karl respectively that particularly stand out due to their impact on the company.

One of Bill's earliest contributions to Sheridan Nurseries was revolutionizing the labelling system. For years, all of the labels attached to plants being shipped out had to be handwritten. This was a major springtime chore that kept employees busy for a collective seven hundred to nine hundred hours a week. Family members were called upon to help. The information on the stringed labels, which were colour-coded to destination, had to be written in clearly legible script.

Bill modernized the operation. The information was fed into a computer, which printed it out on address stickers. These were easily peeled off and stuck on stringed cardboard labels. The computer system did more than eliminate the need to write out thousands of labels; it allowed more information to be put on a label. Postal codes, barcodes, and customized customer names did away with the old colour-code system. A further innovation was the digging tag, which covered many labels and was invaluable to foremen handling bulk orders. The new labelling program probably saved Sheridan Nurseries more money in office costs than any other program change.

One of Karl's most memorable experiences in management began in the 1970s when he was approached by representatives of a German company called Lappen. Due to a shortage in Europe, they were interested in purchasing linden, locust, and ash trees.

The trees had to be perfectly straight, with no branches below three metres. Because of the international economic situation, it was to Lappen's advantage to buy from Sheridan, whose Hope farm had just what they were looking for.

The trees were to be shipped by container. But before they could even be packed, inspectors from Agriculture Canada had to make sure they were "bare root." Power hoses were used to blast away every speck of soil. Then Sheridan's own Herman Maiato oversaw the loading, which was a science in itself; four hundred trees to a container, loaded frontwards and backwards to cross them over and ensure survival and minimum damage during the voyage.

That first sale to Lappen led to a steady stream of Sheridan trees across the Atlantic; sometimes as many as ten thousand a year. Other European companies, such as Arbor in Belgium and Raven in Denmark, purchased trees from Sheridan. They bought caliper trees, and then grew them in their own fields for a few years before selling them.

The recession of the 1990s ended this remarkable export of Canadian trees to Europe. But by that time Sheridan had shipped up to one hundred thousand trees overseas. Karl eventually learned that a legacy of his meeting with the Lappen representatives can be seen today around the huge international airport at Munich. The linden trees that line the roads in and out of the airport, as many as three thousand of them, are from Sheridan Nurseries.

Valerie Stensson has been involved in the wholesale and retail business at Sheridan Nurseries since 1988. She was originally hired as a buyer, then championed the movement of bringing marketing in-house, eliminating outside agency support and building a team of experts, who now produce all marketing and packaging materials for the entire company.

Valerie became marketing manager in 1994 and was promoted to vice-president of marketing and purchasing in 2010. With her combined purchasing and marketing experience, she has been instrumental in developing the private label brand for Sheridan retail locations, overseeing new store design, directing product development, and managing the corporate brand for both the wholesale and retail divisions. The combining of the two disciplines under one leader ensured that the right products were purchased for the right marketing campaign and brand image.

Valerie has been active in the industry serving as a judge for the Canadian Hardware show, as a member of the marketing committee for Landscape Ontario, on the marketing committee for the launch of the Canada Blooms inaugural show, and marketing consultant for nursery sales customers. She is on the Deans Advisory Council for the Wilfrid Laurier School of Business and Economics. In 1995, Sebastio Silva, an employee of Sheridan, asked Valerie and Karl separately to attend the wedding of his son and the rest as they say, "is history." In 1998, Valerie and Karl married in Hawaii.

THE MANAGEMENT TEAM

Sheridan Nurseries is a privately held business with shareholders consisting of family members from the Dunington-Grubbs, as well as long-term employees. The Stensson family holds a majority in terms of number of shares. There is a board

of directors, which provides overall governance and direction of the company. This consists of eight people, including Bill and Karl Stensson, and Laurie Pallett mentioned above. There are currently three outside directors. They are Basile Papaevangelou, who was chairman of Allied Signal and director of the Aerospace Industries Association of Canada; Howard Kitchen, who was formerly an owner and director of marketing of Lansing Build Supply; and Albert Plant, who was a retail specialist most notably as president of Beaver Lumber and later CEO of United Co-operatives of Ontario. The other two board members are long-term Sheridan employees and shareholders.

Rick Friesen, who is senior vice-president of finance and administration, joined Sheridan in 1985 as the result of an extensive search by Sheridan's auditors to find the right fit for the Sheridan management team. He graduated in 1977 with a Bachelor of Commerce in Finance and Accounting, and Transportation from the University of British Columbia. In 1980, he became a chartered accountant in Vancouver. That year, Rick was the plant controller for a manufacturer of transport trucks, Western Star Trucks, followed by the distribution parts operations manager for the same company in 1983. He has been on various committees and groups during his time at Sheridan Nurseries, representing a range of activities for Landscape Ontario and the CNLA, steering committee items for Ontario Chartered Accountants Institute and the Region of Halton. He is a past president of the National Horticultural Credit Association.

Rick has been instrumental in bringing accountability to each department manager, as well as assisting the drive for advanced technology in all divisions of the company, including implementing the Point of Sale system at all stores. He also handles all legal and property issues for Sheridan, including the re-zoning of land for the Sherway property as well as ninety acres of land in Georgetown to become a progressive residential district. Rick is a member of the Sheridan board of directors, and the corporate secretary thereof.

Manuel Sobrinho joined Sheridan in 1956. He was among the first wave of Portuguese immigrants who came from the Azores islands. Manuel was a quick study and wanted to advance. He put extra effort into learning English and as a result became the unofficial "translator" for some of the other workers, as well as being able to quickly move up the ranks.

Over the years, Manuel was assistant shipping manager, co-ordinated the perennial mail-order department, made cement planters, and served as the Farm Foreman. Manuel then moved to the retail division as assistant manager at the Mississauga store, followed by manager from 1969 to 1987. Karl Stensson worked a few summers for Manuel and learned many valuable lessons from him.

With all his experience and knowledge, Manuel was promoted to wholesale sales manager in 1987, overseeing house accounts, sourcing, and landscape supply sales — he really enjoys the wheeling and dealing of the job. From the very beginning, Manuel was convinced that sourcing product to provide a complete package for landscapers was needed and would be a "winner." Manuel was placed in charge of setting up a sourcing department and today it is a major part of the Sheridan wholesale business with five people working in that department. Manuel has been the vice-president of nursery sales since 1997 and is a member of the board of directors of Sheridan.

For many years the executive consisted of Karl, Bill, Manuel, and Rick. Succession planning was discussed at the board and executive level and it was agreed that in order to have an organized transition of management, two major initiatives were undertaken. One was to expand the executive. In 2010, three new vice-presidents were added to the executive team. Valerie Stensson became vice-president of marketing and purchasing.

Art Vanden Enden was appointed vice-president of garden centre operations in 2010, with direct responsibility of the nine retail stores, five professional supply centres serving pick-up landscape trade, and the landscape design service. Art joined Weall & Cullen in 1978 at the original Whitby location located at 1625 Dundas Street West and attended Durham College for environmental horticulture. In 1998, Art received his certified horticultural technician certificate. He has actively volunteered with Landscape Ontario in promoting certification, as well as serving on the Garden Centre Sector Group in Landscape Ontario.

As a high school student, Art worked at the garden centre on weekends, in the evening, and some days in the morning before school. Art has held many positions in retail, from sales, guest services, landscape designer, product coordinator, assistant manager to store manager. When Weall & Cullen was purchased by Sheridan in 2003, Art was kept on as the operations manager for the Weall & Cullen stores and then eventually for the east stores, culminating in his promotion to garden centre operations manager in 2007. Before joining Weall & Cullen, Art worked at his parents family-owned greenhouse business in Ajax where they grew hothouse tomatoes.

Pieter Joubert joined Sheridan in May 2002 as nursery operations manager. Sheridan had been on the lookout for a nursery operations manager for a couple of years in anticipation of relieving Bill Stensson of some of the day-to-day responsibilities to concentrate on more corporate duties. Pieter had emigrated from South Africa and had applied for the position of distribution manager at the farm. Bill quickly realized that Pieter had the capabilities and qualities Sheridan was looking for in an operations manager and Pieter was subsequently hired for the operations role instead.

Pieter holds an MBA from Edinburgh Business School in Scotland and has held several key management positions with firms in South Africa. His background in industrial engineering, manufacturing, supply-chain management, and logistics/operations has proven to be beneficial in nursery operations. While horticulture is a specific profession, the business of growing plants is similar to any other manufacturing business. Applying manufacturing principals while perfecting the art of growing, Pieter has managed to significantly reduce costs while raising the bar in quality standards. Pieter was appointed vice-president of nursery operations in 2010.

The Sheridan executive meets formally once a week to review key corporate operations and strategies going forward.

In spring 2010, the second step taken in the succession planning process was to form the operating committee (OC). This is a group of dedicated management who form a "second tier," dealing with many day-to-day issues such as health and safety, the Sheridan environmental initiatives, employee events, as well as preparing for the Sheridan one-hundredth anniversary. This group meets once a month on its own and once a

month with the executive team. Members of the OC include Amin Datoo, who has been with Sheridan for forty years and is currently manager of the Toronto Yonge Street garden centre; Mary Beth Brown, marketing manager, who has been employed by Sheridan for twenty-four years; and Liz Kavanaugh, manager of financial accounting, who has been with the company for twenty years. Bart Brusse, the container farm manager, and Shelley Elgar, the seasonal plant product manager, have both been with Sheridan for thirteen years. Rounding out the OC are Rob Naraj, wholesale business manager at eleven years for Sheridan and previously six years at Weall & Cullen; and Gwen Ferris, payroll and benefits manager at six years.

ENVIRONMENTAL STANDARDS

"Where green is more than a colour, it's a lifestyle" isn't just a catchphrase at Sheridan Nurseries — it's company policy. Sheridan has developed an environmental plan that details a firm commitment to decreasing the company's environmental impact. The mission statement reads: "We are committed to promoting and working in an environmentally sustainable way. We will continue to improve all processes that affect the environment in all areas of our business." Sheridan's determination to stand by this commitment has brought about a series of innovations, the largest of which was the design and installation of one of the first bio-ponds in Canada.

It takes a lot of water to grow millions of plants and keep them healthy. For Sheridan's nursery at Georgetown, that means over 2 million gallons a day. Rainfall provides only a fraction of that need. The rest must come through irrigation.

The technology for collecting water and distributing it to acres of plants has come a long way since the days when Herman Stensson had to haul it in horse-drawn wagons. Herman would be awed to see how the modern Sheridan Nurseries not only moves water, but also conserves it.

The Georgetown nursery draws water from the Credit River, and has pumped over 2.3 million gallons in one twenty-four-hour period. Initially, sprinklers were used for overhead irrigation in all areas of the farm, but that method wastes water through evaporation and run-off. That posed a problem, especially during dry times when conservation regulations limited the amount of water Sheridan could take from the Credit River. The solution was to use less water more efficiently. Sheridan devised a new state-of-the-art irrigation system. It incorporates computer-operated pumps, artificial wells, and miles of pipes and feeder tapes (called spaghetti lines) that deliver water directly to the plants' roots. This method is used for many plants in the farm, reducing evaporation and saving up to 80 percent of the water needed in an overhead irrigation system.

A new million-dollar water-capture system has practically eliminated run-off waste. Almost all water from rainfall and seepage is directed through a series of swales (ditches) and ponds. Three ponds and swales filled with water plants hold and naturally purify the water. The main pond, with a capacity for 31 million gallons of crystal-clear water, irrigates the nursery during dry spells, greatly reducing dependence on the river. The Georgetown nursery, practically self-sufficient in water, has become an industry model. At the writing of this book in the summer of 2012, Ontario was experiencing one of the most severe droughts in its history and Sheridan was required to stop pumping water from the Credit River as a condition of the water permit it held with the Ministry of the Environment. Fortunately, the new pond saved the day and after two weeks the Ministry gave special permission to again draw water on an emergency basis.

Another innovation involves a substance so plain in appearance it seems remarkable that it could have so profound an impact on environmentally friendly nursery operations. *Coir* is the natural fibre extracted from coconut husks. It has long been used in the manufacture of floor mats, rope, string, fishing nets, brushes, sacking, and upholstery stuffing. But this humble product also has some special natural properties that make it a little miracle for nurseries. Coir is free of bacterial and fungal spores. It deters weeds and snails without causing environmental damage, and it is an excellent insulator that helps preserve moisture. It also prevents weed growth. For these reasons, coir is used to make the "coco rings" that lay on top of the soil in Sheridan's potted plants. A coco-ring doesn't look very impressive, but it does a lot of jobs.

Efforts are currently underway to find a biodegradable material to replace plastic in the manufacture of nursery pots. In the United States, a substance made from chicken feathers is being tested, while other materials such as compressed grass clippings are also in use. Sheridan is conducting its own experiments with containers made from coir. Other initiatives include Plant 'N Grow coir pots. Plants are grown in plastic nursery pots and then flipped to coir pots prior to shipping so the plastic can be recycled or reused.

Plastics blended with various other biodegradable products are under investigation as alternatives to traditional plastic pots. Sheridan has also taken the lead with plug trays and pots, and is experimenting with biodegradable tree bags. Sheridan retail stores have a complete recycling program in which pots, whether purchased from Sheridan Nurseries or not, are collected and then sent to be reused in the farm or ground up to become some other product in their next life.

In order to be proactive in its environmental responsibilities, Sheridan has a registered Canada-Ontario Environmental Farm Plan, which identifies potential environmental risks and the strategies to reduce them. Community involvement has included the Earth Day 22-Minute Makeover, participation in the annual Green for Life Day as part of National Tree Day, and the Maple Leaves Forever program, which grows native maple trees for conservation groups and schools. The Sheridan Marketing team created the Growing Up Green program to encourage children to learn about and care for the world we live in. With the co-operation of parents and teachers, future gardeners learn to develop their green thumbs and become active participants in the nurturing of their environment while experiencing the satisfaction of watching a garden grow. Receipts from items purchased at Sheridan Nurseries can be used for credits. These credits are redeemed in the form of plants for school grounds, or gardening supplies for school projects such as seed-starting kits and raffle prizes.

Sheridan's Little Diggers Club is for kids aged four to ten. Fun classes held at colourful garden centres allow children to explore the world of plants and insects, and create crafts they can take home with them. In more ways than one, Sheridan is planting the seeds for a green future.

In another initiative, Sheridan has gone one step further with all plastic bags and trunk liners used in the Sheridan

retail operation being made from degradable plastic, which is a step better than bio-degradable. While bio-degradable plastic must be activated by burying it in the ground, degradable plastic disintegrates whether it's in the ground or not, ensuring stray bags are not a blight on the landscape.

Sheridan has also taken on responsibility for all the rural roads that pass by their farms. The grass is maintained, and hundreds of new trees have been planted to enhance the environment and replace rural trees that have died or been cut down and not replaced by the municipality. More than an environmental responsibility, this is a continuation of civic duty that dates back to the time of the Dunington-Grubbs.

Internally, Sheridan has designated "Green Stewards" who lead specific initiatives within the company. Sheridan's leadership in meeting environmental concerns has been recognized both locally and provincially. In 2011 Sheridan was the recipient of the Halton Hills Chamber of Commerce Green Business Award and the Landscape of Ontario Award of Excellence — Water Conservation Award. At Sheridan, excellence in environmental stewardship is the standard.

A PLANT'S JOURNEY, FROM POT TO POT

Any plant purchased at a Sheridan Nurseries garden centre has an interesting biography. It is the product of a combination of nature and human care. Some of the plants begin their lives at one of Sheridan's own farms. Many are brought in from nurseries across North America and Europe, depending on the type of plant. Some of Sheridan's best suppliers are on the west coast of Canada and the United States. The moderate climate there allows plants to grow faster in their younger stages.

The small "starter" plants are called "liners." These plants are about two or more years away from being ready for retail sale. *Pot* liners grow in pots to spare them from transplant shock. *Plug* liners are smaller than pot liners. They aren't in pots, but still have soil on the roots. Almost all of these plants will pass through the potting barn, in what might be called a plant's junior matriculation.

In the potting barn, the plants go through a process called "bumping up," in which they are transplanted from small containers to larger ones. The potting machine is fed soil that's brought in by the truckload, and can fill up to twelve thousand pots a day, with Sheridan potting over 1 million plants a year.

The soil that goes into the pots is part of Sheridan Nurseries' commitment to environmentally friendly policies, with much of it derived from composting. Sheridan uses approximately 40 percent of the green waste collected in the entire Region of Halton. Separating your garbage really does make a difference!

From the potting barn, the plants are moved to the farms where they will grow and be groomed until they are ready for market. They are trimmed by hand to maintain consistency in size. The constant process of growing and grooming requires a lot of care. Sheridan's staff has no shortage of tactics that help plants to thrive. For example, larger junipers need more space apart to maximize their sun intake, so smaller, low-growing junipers are placed in between them to fully utilize the growing area.

Of course, weeds are banished from the nursery grounds. That is not only because the weeds themselves are a threat to young plants, but also because they can provide homes for an even greater danger: Japanese beetles. These ravenous bugs feast on some two hundred different species of plants, and have no natural predators in North America. Sheridan uses non-toxic beetle traps to ensure that any pests are caught if they happen to show up in the area.

There are always threats to any business; however, some threats are worse than others. In the mid-2000s, the Emerald ash borer was moving north from the United States. This insect destroyed ash trees, and there was no known remedy. By 2010, Sheridan had discontinued selling ash, and almost ten thousand trees that were in production had to be destroyed.

In 2012, a little-known disease called Boxwood Blight was confirmed in both the United States and Canada. As Sheridan grows hundreds of thousands of these plants, this could be a serious blow to sales and profits. Sheridan took the lead in developing protocols to prevent the disease from spreading. Unlike the Emerald ash borer, this disease cannot "fly." It must be transferred by contact with an infected plant. The instant reaction of installing biosecurity protocols, foot baths, and tire baths have, at the time of this writing, effectively prevented the disease from attacking the valuable boxwood crops.

Plants that are sensitive to too much sunlight are kept under shade cloth, which is like a plant's version of sunblock. This material resembles dark mosquito netting, and comes in varying degrees of thickness and density. A 60-percent shade cloth, for example, allows in 40 percent of the sunlight.

In late fall, the plants go undercover. Their space can be condensed because it doesn't matter now if one plant touches another because they don't grow during the cold winter months. Anyone driving past Sheridan Nurseries' farms in the dead of winter, when the deciduous trees are bare and the evergreen boughs are heavy with snow, will see long white rows of polyhouses. There are over thirty-seven kilometres of these winter protection "houses" on Sheridan property. Inside them, hundreds of thousands of slumbering plants await spring.

With the arrival of spring, the nursery becomes a beehive of activity. This is the busiest time of the year. Orders are waiting to be filled for mass merchants, landscapers, municipalities, and commercial garden centres — including Sheridan's own. Plants that are mature enough for sale are ready for shipping. But first they have to be tagged.

About 1 million labels (over $250,000 worth) are kept in the label room, which resembles a post office mail-sorting room. Each label has a picture of the plant to which it will be attached. On the reverse side is such useful information as the plant's characteristics and a planting guide. Sheridan's most recent labels are colour-coded to denote either sun, shade, or partial shade light requirement. Tagging is the last step a plant goes through before shipping.

The shipping area is divided into numbered "parking spaces" where orders on shipping racks and skids wait to be loaded into trucks. Sheridan uses thousands of skids and shipping racks. Manufacturing them is part of the winter works program in which personnel are employed at constructing a variety of necessary items. Once the racks and skids are shipped about 50 percent are not returned, due to the long distances they are shipped without an economical means of retrieval. Research into different types of material such as recycled cardboard have so far not provided the answer to using less wood for the skids.

During the peak spring shipping season, thirty-five forklifts keep fifteen loading docks operating at capacity. The shipping yard is lit up at night to keep the potted plants moving. Trucks leave the yard at the rate of more than thirty a day. Approximately 65 percent of the annual sales are shipped out within a ten-week period.

Within a few days — perhaps even a matter of hours — many of the plants will be in their new homes, beautifying private residences, public parks, and institutional landscapes. Most of each plant's journey, from the time it was just a little liner, will have been made in a pot.

PHILANTHROPIC WORKS

Howard and Lorrie Dunington-Grubb believed that success went hand in hand with recognition of social responsibility. They supported many benevolent causes. Over the years, Sheridan Nurseries has remained faithful to that tradition. Even during the difficult days when money was scarce, Herman Stensson would still donate flowers to the local church.

Today, philanthropy is an important part of Sheridan's corporate culture. Staff across all departments work together to achieve a common goal. One of Sheridan's most compelling success stories has been the "Stand Up for Michael" campaign. While on vacation in Jamaica in 2004, Bill Stensson visited the home of Ron Campbell, who has been an offshore worker with Sheridan for forty years. He found that Ron's son Michael, twelve, had severe scoliosis, and his condition had deteriorated to the extent that he could no longer walk. Doctors in Jamaica told Ron and his wife Margaret that the spinal surgery necessary to correct Michael's crippling condition was too complicated for them to attempt.

When Bill brought this information back to head office, the Sheridan Nurseries family banded together to help Michael. A huge fundraising campaign, led by Karl Stensson, got underway. Cash checkout "round-ups," a lottery, and every form of bake sale imaginable raised a total of $140,000 to provide Michael with four major operations and therapy. Valerie Stensson was instrumental in fighting through the frustrating layers of bureaucracy and red tape that stood between Michael and treatment in a Canadian hospital. The search for a hospital that would take on the procedure took several months. Once Shriner's Children's Hospital in Montreal agreed, then more months of government holdups finally led Valerie to MP Michael Chong, who quickly and efficiently cleared the path. Sheridan Nurseries had to guarantee that Michael or his parents would not be a "burden" to Canadian taxpayers before Michael was finally allowed to travel here. Michael has now been able to re-attend school, and has a chance at living as near normal a life as possible. His treatment has been ongoing up to the present, and Sheridan's campaign raised an additional $10,000 for his future education.

Other philanthropic causes Sheridan has supported haven't been quite as "close to home" as Stand Up for Michael, but have nonetheless been important and reflective of the ideals of the Dunington-Grubbs and Herman Stensson. In 2010 alone, Sheridan Nurseries raised over $50,000 for the Children's Wish Foundation, the Jesse Gaudreau Scholarship, the Canadian Cancer Society, and Upopolis, a private social utility that connects young hospital patients to family, friends, and school. Through a scholarship at the University of Guelph, the Dunington-Grubb Foundation has given out scholarships for the last forty years and Sheridan Nurseries has donated approximately $100,000 to the Landscape Ontario Horticultural Trades Foundation. Sheridan provided $25,000 (U.S.) to set up the Sheridan Research Fund with the Horticultural Research Institute in the United States.

Sheridan has also been a participant in Pink Days. These are events in which garden centres across Canada and the United States raise funds for the Breast Cancer Research Foundation through the sale of specially selected pink flowers. Such a cause would certainly have the support of Lorrie Dunington-Grubb, the socially conscious "Lady of Flowers."

Janice Johnston (now Janice Nikkel) was a fifteen-year-old student at Oakville Trafalgar High School when a tragic plane crash near Gander, Newfoundland, took the lives of 256 American soldiers and air crew. They were on their way home from a peacekeeping mission in the Middle East. Janice thought Canada should do something to honour the victims and their families, so she started a campaign to have 256 trees planted at the deceased Americans' home base of Fort Campbell, Kentucky. Sheridan Nurseries learned of the project and donated 256 Canadian sugar maples. They were planted with the assistance of Re-Tree International and the 101st Airborn Division. A plaque was provided for each tree. Twenty-five years later, Janice visited Fort Campbell with her husband and children to see the living memorial she had helped to bring into being. The little saplings Sheridan Nurseries had provided had all matured into stately maples.

Sheridan Nurseries has been the horticultural sponsor of the Artists' Gardens at the Harbourfront Centre in Toronto since their inception in 1990. Artists have been commissioned to use their imagination in designing gardens "that do not look like parks department flower beds." Sheridan has supplied all of the plants and horticultural direction for the various gardens, some lasting only one year, and others more than twenty years. Because of construction at Harbourfront, no new gardens have been installed for the last few years, but ten are still being maintained.

Every year for the past forty years, Sheridan has donated plants to a local church for a "shrub" sale that earns money to keep the Glen Williams Town Hall in good repair. In addition to all of these ongoing donations to charities and worthwhile causes, every year Sheridan receives over a thousand requests for sponsorships and donations, all from worthwhile causes. Unfortunately not all can be accommodated. However, they are all carefully scrutinized and responded to with hundreds actually receiving some sort of support in the way of advertising or "in kind" in plants.

PRODUCT SELECTION, QUALITY, AND CONSISTENCY

In the hundred years since the Sheridan catalogue listed the nursery's first big seller — imported perennials — product selection has grown beyond anything the Dunington-Grubbs and Herman Stensson could have imagined. Top-quality ornamental garden plants still make up the largest percentage of Sheridan's inventory, but diversification has made each Sheridan garden centre into a plant lover's dream come true. Years of careful consumer studies and anticipation of guests' needs, as well as a tradition of being on the leading edge of horticultural fashion and trends has ensured that Sheridan can fill every order.

Sheridan still offers many of the plants that made the nursery famous: perennials and annuals, boxwood, roses, and chrysanthemums, to name just a few. But in addition there are lush tropical house plants, unusual evergreens and topiaries, patio plants, and plants for water gardens. Gardeners who like to produce their own edibles will find everything they need to grow fruits, vegetables, and herbs.

A century ago, Herman Stensson did most of his work with a shovel and a wheelbarrow. What he wouldn't have given for a modern Sheridan Nurseries garden centre! He'd have had access to one-stop shopping for all the supplies and equipment available to Sheridan's guests today; everything from sprinklers and hoses to products that combat weeds, insects, and disease. He'd have been able to purchase scientifically improved fertilizers that surpass the "barnyard shavings" of his day. If Herman ever got the urge to be decorative, he could even have picked up a few garden accessories such as statuary, fountains, and birdbaths. Herman could even have bought books on gardening. But all things considered, perhaps that's one item available in a modern garden centre he might not have needed.

Named after one of the grand estates whose grounds were partially designed by Howard Dunington-Grubb, and entirely developed by Sheridan Nurseries, Sheridan's Parkwood line of products is known for unsurpassed quality. From nutrients for lawn and flowers, to seed for wild birds, Parkwood products are all specially formulated for Sheridan Nurseries. This is one more example of the numerous ways in which Sheridan has branched out in the twenty-first-century retail world.

Over the years, Sheridan has increased its offerings of plants and related horticultural products. However, the big "revolution" has come in the offering of other products that enhance the garden and home decor experience. Patio furniture and Christmas items were added about forty years ago and have been enhanced continuously. With respect to patio, Sheridan has become one of the largest dealers of quality patio furniture in Canada. Only the finest furniture that can live up to Sheridan's quality and serviceability is selected. And while the Christmas line started out as cut Christmas trees, it quickly grew to include decorations and everlasting trees in all shapes and sizes. In 2000, Sheridan's Toronto store manager, Amin Datoo, started another innovation in the industry by selling decorative urns with cut branches for outdoor winter decorations. The category is referred to as Custom Design, and has grown each year, becoming a major category in the business and in the industry. Sheridan sells over eighty varieties of branches and uses a wide assortment of items in these arrangements including shatterproof balls, and such exotic items as pomegranates, Osage oranges, and pineapples.

The gift areas developed over time, but flourished when Sheridan decided to take a different approach in 2010 with offerings of hand-selected, stylish, unique products that are designed for the home, and which go beyond the traditional gardening accents. In addition to garden furniture, garden giftware, and patio accessories, you'll find jewellery, dinnerware, handbags, stationery and cards, hostess gifts, gourmet foods, soaps and lotions, and even pet products. It's an excellent place to shop for that perfect gift.

One of Howard Stensson's favourite anecdotes concerning Howard Dunington-Grubb was the story about "Grubby" pointing out certain plants to Gus Sparre and telling him,

"Looks like hell. Burn it!" Neither Dunington-Grubb nor Herman Stensson would deal in sub-standard merchandise. That policy holds true with Sheridan Nurseries today. It is ensured by Sheridan's in-house marketing department, as well as a director of brand integrity and a quality control team.

For over sixteen years, Sheridan has fostered an innovative partnership with more than 140 independent garden centres known as Sheridan Preferred Partners. It is promoted as a program to "Grow Your Business." The partnership is a buying group but instead of a monetary fee, the partners simply need to purchase nursery stock from the Sheridan wholesale division and in return receive many benefits of the retail division that would not normally be available to an independent store. Partners have access to such value-added services as the Ready to Retail® perennial rack program, Simply the Best free plant tags and customized pre-priced labels, custom marketing flyers, discounts on a broad range of hardgoods, access to the Parkwood private label products, as well as a buying show and seminar program run by Sheridan.

Sheridan Nurseries' growing operation is constantly looking for new and unique plant varieties and is one of only five Diamond Level Growers of Proven Winners® Colour Choice Shrubs in North America. Through this program, Sheridan has access to new plants that will not be released to the general network of growers until after they have been introduced over a couple of years through the Diamond Growers. They are also Network Growers for the Endless Summer Collection™ and First Editions®. Sheridan is one of only two exclusive growers for the United Kingdom–based Raymond Evison Clematis Collection in Canada.

True to the memory of the Dunington-Grubbs, pioneers in Canadian landscape design, Sheridan Nurseries still offers a landscape-design service. Trained landscape-design professionals can assist clients in creating anything from a garden to a home addition. These experts can provide consulting services for do-it-yourselfers, or complete the whole project from planning to installation. Sheridan's design service will create inspiring arrangements that complement the home, indoors or out, no matter what the season or occasion.

"Potscaping," as container gardening is now called, has become a popular form of gardening that requires little space and maintenance. Yet, it affords colour, form, fragrance, and texture. Sheridan's talented design staff is trained to transform a balcony or any other small space into a beautiful and relaxing environment. Sheridan also has a floral-design service whose team of expert designers can create memorable and lasting floral tributes, bouquets, arrangements, sprays, baskets, and wreaths. Each one is customized according to taste and occasion. There are flowering plants in decorative containers for home or office, and seasonal flowers such as Easter lilies, gerberas and poinsettas; personalized, wrapped, and ready to go, are ideal for corporate gifts.

SHOPPING SHERIDAN TODAY

Sheridan Nurseries retail operations have certainly come a long way in one hundred years. The earliest customers had to send for plants through the mail-order catalogue, or travel to the first little sales station in Clarkson. Today, Sheridan's guests can shop in nine modern garden centres in Georgetown, Kitchener,

Mississauga, Etobicoke, North York, Scarborough, Toronto, Unionville, and Whitby. These attractive stores offer a selection of plants and other products unheard of a century ago.

SHERIDAN'S SLOGANS

Catchy slogans are a marketing device that help a company get the public's attention. Over the years, Sheridan Nurseries has used a variety of memorable slogans:

Slogan	Year
Green Thumbs Up	*1972*
Let's Start a Growing Friendship	*1974*
Love Bucks ($1 coupons)	
For the love of lawns	
For the love of flowers	
For the love of plants	
For the love of birds	
For the love of Christmas	
Green Survival … It Depends on You	*(industry) 1975–76*
Great Selection, Fair Prices and Friendly Service	*1977–81*
Direct from the Grower	*1980*
Where Great Gardens Begin	*1982–87*
For the Love of Gardens, and More	*1988*
For the Love of Gardens	*1989–90*
85 Years and Still Growing	*1998*
Growing Memorable Gardens	*2005–06*
Where Green Is More Than a Colour — It's a Lifestyle	*2011*

For guests who prefer to do their shopping online, the Sheridan Nurseries website is widely seen as one of the best websites in the gardening industry. Simply type in *www.sheridannurseries.com* and you can access:

- **Plant Search,** which provides easy-to-find detailed information, along with images, for gardens and landscaping, as well as plant-care instructions.

- **Outdoor Living** presents a great selection of furniture pieces and settings that help create backyard living space.

- **Sheridan Garden Classics** presents garden themes for annuals and perennials.

- **Water Gardening** de-mystifies the outdoor pond with detailed water plant images, informative videos, and a Q&A section.

- **My Garden** allows guests to create a virtual garden by browsing the Plant Finder database or adding their own plant photos.

WORKING FOR SHERIDAN NURSERIES

Sheridan Nurseries offers a complete human resources package for its employees, including training, development, career advancement, succession planning, benefits, and social programs. Sheridan's corporate vision emphasizes a goal that is a destination for all, including employees.

Many factors have contributed to Sheridan's reputation as a first-class employer: opportunities for students such as those in the horticultural apprenticeship program and the specialist high skills major program, health and safety instruction, in-depth training for new employees in their native language (currently English, Spanish, and Punjabi), and task-specific horticultural training. An important part of Sheridan's team comes through the seasonal agricultural workers program. The nursery currently has over ninety workers from Jamaica and Mexico, some of whom have been returning for almost forty seasons.

Sheridan offers a tuition-reimbursement program that enables staff to take external training courses. There are a number of initiatives for employees to advance, including a job shadowing program, employee development meetings, and participation in management and strategic planning sessions. The operating committee trains middle management to take upper-management roles.

Since 1997, Sheridan has offered the Good Suggestion Program, which rewards staff financially for innovative ideas. The Employee Satisfaction Survey, which all full-time and part-time employees complete every two years, encourages staff to make suggestions concerning health and safety, benefits, compensation, training, morale, and general working conditions. Sheridan Nurseries values the good people who make up its diverse team. There is an employee of the month program in which outstanding individual efforts are recognized. The Sheridan newsletter, *What's Growing On,* highlights employees and their contributions to the company. For twenty-six years, Sheridan has hosted an annual baseball tournament for all employees and their families, and has recently started hosting an annual Years of Service dinner. This dinner recognizes employees who reach a minimum of ten years of service, as well as every five-year increment. Sheridan has also sponsored a nursery-wide tractor rodeo to promote safety awareness.

The Sheridan management team is always looking for ways to enhance the staff experience. Without good, reliable employees, Sheridan would not be able to enhance the guest experience by providing service that is more than the guest expects.

LOOKING BACK

It has been an extraordinary first century. Over the past one hundred years, Sheridan Nurseries has done more than survive — it has adapted and grown. The original plans that began with Howard and Lorrie Dunington-Grubb blossomed into something much larger than even they conceived of, and which reaches beyond Canada's borders. The small selection of perennials that Lorrie imported and Herman Stensson so skillfully cultivated has grown into one of the most comprehensive selections of plants in North America, with Sheridan being at the forefront of introducing new varieties. Sheridan's plans and plants have been recognized with awards and accolades. But above all, there have been the people of Sheridan Nurseries. From the first pioneers, down to the Sheridan family of today, the people who have worked in the fields, the offices, the retail outlets, and all the various departments have built on the foundation established by the Dunington-Grubbs and the first generation of Stenssons. It has been because of the people that a dream, which took root in the village of Sheridan in 1913, is today the Sheridan brand, a leader in the retail marketplace in Toronto and in the North American horticultural market. Thanks to people like them, Sheridan Nurseries continues to grow.

PLEASE SHARE YOUR SHERIDAN NURSERIES MEMORIES

What we have presented here is only the first hundred years of Sheridan Nurseries as we know them. As we are continuously updating our archives, we'd appreciate hearing from you about your Sheridan Nurseries experiences and memories. If you have photos, anecdotes, documents, or artifacts pertinent to Sheridan Nurseries, please contact us at *info@sheridannurseries.com.*

CHAPTER 14

Postscript: Nursery Tales

Any company that has been in business for a century and has touched the lives of generations of people is bound to have a rich lore full of humour, irony, and anecdotes about hard-learned lessons. The Sheridan Nurseries story, with its historically dynamic background and frequently exotic cast of personalities, certainly has its share; far too many for all of them to be related in the previous chapters. The following are just a few of the "Nursery Tales" that are factual accounts of the people of Sheridan Nurseries.

THOU SHALT NOT ...

In 1928 the Sheridan Nurseries catalogue offered the following tips to gardeners:

> Don't try to put every variety you ever heard of into a border 50 feet by 6 feet.
>
> Don't mix up Shrubs, Perennials, and Evergreens. One or the other of them is sure to get the worst of the fight.
>
> Don't blame the Sheridan Nurseries when you forget to stamp soil firmly round the roots of the nursery stock you were planting.

ART CRITIC

Howard Dunington-Grubb bought a painting called *Interior with Garden Window* by British abstract artist Patrick Heron for the new head office. When Annie Stensson first saw the painting, she remarked, "The man who painted that, and the man who bought it, are insane." The painting is now part of the David Thompson Collection.

THE CUSTOMER IS ALWAYS RIGHT, *RIGHT?*

Amin Datoo recalls his very first plant sale. A customer pointed to a shoot in a perennial bed that was tagged in front as "iris," and said to him, "I want that perennial." Not yet familiar with iris leaves, Amin sold it to her. She came back several weeks later to complain. The "perennial" was a dandelion.

BARBEQUED GIRAFFE

Howard "Doc" Savage of the University of Toronto presented his friend Howard Stensson with an unusual problem: he had the cadaver of a giraffe that had died at the Toronto Zoo, and wanted to boil away the flesh so he'd have a skeleton. Howard offered the use of the nursery, where the smell wouldn't offend anyone. Workers carved up the animal and boiled the pieces in an old bathtub that had a fire under it. "Giraffe soup" was the joke of the day.

THE LADIES ROOM

When Lois (the future Mrs. Fred Stensson) first started working in the Sheridan Nurseries office, the only "necessary" was an outhouse. Lois was the company's first female office worker. If she didn't want to use the same privy as the men, she had to walk up the hill to use the bathroom in the house. That was something of an inconvenience, especially in bad weather. One day Constant DeGroot stopped her on her way up the hill and asked if she wanted a "crapper." Constant built Lois her own outhouse. He must have given it a pretty secure latch, because one day Lois accidentally locked herself in. She had to call for help through the half-moon in the door.

AND IN THIS CORNER

Robert Nielsen, an experienced nurseryman who came from New Brunswick to join Sheridan in 1925, went on to start Nielsen's Garden Centre in Mississauga after the Second World War. Bob was also a Golden Gloves boxer. He would sometimes visit Sheridan Nurseries for lunchtime sparring matches with the men. The staff always looked forward to these bouts, to see if anyone could beat Bob Nielsen.

TEN CENTS FOR A TRIM: PRACTICAL JOKES FREE

Jim Herod Jr. was Sheridan Nurseries' official barber for many years. At lunchtime he earned extra money by cutting hair for 10 cents a head. He eventually raised the rate

to 25 cents. It was a good deal for the employees because they didn't have to go to town for a more expensive haircut in a barbershop. Jim's fellow employees admired his entrepreneurship, but they also knew that he had a revulsion for rodents. As a practical joke, they would hide a dead mouse in his barber's apron. When Jim picked up the apron and unfolded it, the dead rodent would come rolling out, to Jim's distress and everyone else's amusement. Of course, no one would ever admit to being the perpetrator of the dirty deed. An irate barber might decide to get even, and you wouldn't know until you looked in a mirror.

NOW YOU'RE COOKING

The house in which Jim Herod's family lived at Sherway had an old-fashioned coal- and wood-burning iron stove. The stove made the kitchen a cozy place in the winter, but in summer it was like a sauna. Whoever did the cooking just had to endure it. Jim's daughter Diane recalled that one summer Sunday, either Howard Dunington-Grubb or J.V. Stensson — she couldn't remember which — had been out to see her father, and just before getting into the car to leave, remembered that he had to make a phone call. He went back into the house to use the phone in the kitchen. Elsie Herod (also known as Rhoda) was cooking, and the heat was oppressive. By the time the visitor finished talking on the phone, his handkerchief was soaked from wiping sweat off his face. Within days, to Elsie's delight, a brand-new electric stove was delivered to the house.

A TOUCH OF IRONY

When Larry Sherk took up the task of organizing the Sheridan Nurseries archives, he came across a surprising document. It was an old letter from his mentor, John Weall, to Howard Dunington-Grubb. The letter suggested that a young Canadian graduate from the Ontario Agricultural College named Larry Sherk should be considered for employment in Sheridan Nurseries. Howard evidently didn't respond to the letter. Larry eventually became Sheridan's chief horticulturist. He never had the opportunity to meet Dunington-Grubb personally, and the letter didn't come to light until after Larry had retired.

A CLOSE CALL WITH DANGER

After Lorrie Dunington-Grubb's death, Howard lived alone in their house on Dale Avenue in Toronto. The only other occupant was a housekeeper named Beatrice. One day Howard came home from work, opened the front door, and immediately noticed that something was wrong. Rather than step inside, he closed the door, turned around, and left. He went to a neighbour's house to call the police. The investigating officers found that Howard's house had indeed been broken into. Moreover, evidence showed that when Howard had been standing at the threshold, wondering if he should go in, the intruder had been behind the door with a fireplace poker.

ON THE LAM

Howard Stensson told of an incident that occurred after Sheridan Nurseries had asked an employment agency for some temporary workers. The nursery wanted to use offshore workers, but the agency insisted that Sheridan use "local" help. They sent fifteen young men and told Sheridan only that they were from North Bay. Within two days, said Howard, half of the workers were gone, and by the end of the week only two of the fifteen were still there. It turned out that the young men were from a Department of Corrections work farm near North Bay. Most of them had taken advantage of the excursion to Sheridan to run away.

A WALK ON THE WILD SIDE

Bernard Schultz had a long, distinguished career with Sheridan Nurseries in Glen Williams, but one of his most memorable days came on May 30, 1963, one day after he first set foot in Canada. His first day on the job, Bernard became acquainted with some of Canada's native flora and fauna. First, he had an encounter with a skunk. Next, he found himself in poison ivy. Then he was face to face with a garter snake. It caused him to jump, because he thought it was a rattlesnake.

TOO MUCH SODIUM

Tom Whitcher recalls the time when Sheridan's wholesale yard in Dorion was having difficulty getting connected to the municipal water system. Advised that there was plenty of groundwater, they sank a well. Soon they had their own source of clear water for irrigation. Things went well for about eighteen months. Then the quality of the ground water began to deteriorate. Tests showed a high sodium content. The land had once been the bed of the prehistoric Champlain Sea. The long-gone body of water had left high concentrations of sea salt in the ground. Sheridan sued the municipality, and owing to the fact that Tom kept extensive notes on everything that occurred on every day, Sheridan won the case.

SHERIDAN NURSERY STORE LOCATIONS

ETOBICOKE/EAST MISSISSAUGA GARDEN CENTRE
2069 Burnhamthorpe Road East
Mississauga, ON
L4X 2S7

GEORGETOWN GARDEN CENTRE
RR# 4, 12266 Tenth Line
Georgetown, ON
L7G 4S7

KITCHENER/WATERLOO GARDEN CENTRE
100 Elmsdale Drive
Kitchener, ON
N2E 1H6

MARKHAM/UNIONVILLE GARDEN CENTRE
4077 Highway #7
Unionville, ON
L3R 1L5

MISSISSAUGA/OAKVILLE GARDEN CENTRE
606 Southdown Road
Mississauga, ON
L5J 2Y4

NORTH YORK GARDEN CENTRE
784 Sheppard Avenue East
North York, ON
M2K 1C3

SCARBOROUGH GARDEN CENTRE
1774 Ellesmere Road
Scarborough, ON
M1H 2V5

TORONTO GARDEN CENTRE
2827 Yonge Street
Toronto, ON
M4N 2J4

WHITBY GARDEN CENTRE
410 Taunton Road West
Whitby, ON
L1P 2A9

ACKNOWLEDGEMENTS

The authors are indebted to Larry Sherk for the tremendous amount of research he conducted for this book. Larry organized a century's accumulation of documents in the Sheridan Nurseries' archives into an accessible collection. He spent months travelling around southern Ontario, taping interviews with former Sheridan employees and members of their families. He interviewed many long-time employees who are still with the company. This book would not have been possible without Larry's work and dedication to the project.

The authors would also like to thank the many other people and the numerous institutions who were of assistance: University of Guelph McLaughlin Library, Archives and Special Collections; Mississauga Public Library, Canadiana Reading Room; Guelph Public Library; University of Calgary, Archives and Special Collections; McMaster Divinity College, Canadian Baptist Archives; Brantford Public Library; Hamilton Public Library, Local History & Archives; City of Toronto Archives; Metro Toronto Reference Library; Toronto Urban Affairs Library; Thomas Fisher Rare Books Library; University of Toronto; Government of Ontario Art Collection; Archives of Ontario, Women's Art Association of Canada; the Arts & Letters Club of Toronto (R. Scott James, archivist); Heritage Mississauga (Matthew Wilkinson, historian); Royal Botanical Gardens of Burlington; the Garden Club of Toronto; Niagara Parks School of Horticulture.

Norm Abbott, Maureen (Barnard) Bock, Richard Brightling, Evelyn (Savage) Bullied, Ronnie Campbell, Amin Datoo, John DeGroot, Art Drysdale, Milt and Barb Edwards, Ejnar Faerge, Lynda Ferguson, Thomas and Susie Frank,

Dieter and Margaret Frank, Mary Iwasaki, Harry Kayama, Mary Kayama, Bill and Geraldine Kegel, David Langstone, Mary Langstone, Joerg and Franzis Leiss, Bill Mason, Betty (Lambert) McBride, Paul Offierski, Sheila Orr, Evan Oxland, Laurie (Stewart) Pallett, Sarah Pallett, Alice Pokluda, John Reiter, Doreen (Herod) Rion, Rene Robinson, Uli Rumpf, Bernard and Theresa Schultz, Monica (Barnard) Slessor, Manuel Sobrinho, Bertha Sparre, Bill Stensson, Howard Stensson, Karen Stensson, Valerie Stensson, Jon Stewart, Ruth Stoner, Jesse Tadeo, Jody Thompson, Ken Thornton, Anya Van Dyk, Len Vermaas, Andy Weiss, Tom Whitcher.

Special thanks to Michael Carroll of Dundurn.

BIBLIOGRAPHY

BOOKS

Allsopp Hillier, Du Toit. *The Art of the Avenue: A University Avenue Public Art Study*. Toronto: Planning Urban Design Landscape Architecture, 1989.

Barnsley, Roland. *Thomas B. McQuesten*. Toronto: Fitzhenry & Whiteside, 1987.

Berketo, Paula. *Oakes Garden Theatre and Rainbow Gardens Restoration Study*. Niagara Falls, ON: Niagara Parks Commission, 2000.

____. *My Times: Living with History 1947–1995*. Toronto: McClelland & Stewart, 1995.

Berton, Pierre, *Niagara*. Toronto: McClelland & Stewart, 1992.

Campbell, Marjorie Freeman. *A Mountain and a City: The Story of Hamilton*. Toronto: McClelland and Stewart, 1966.

Carver, Humphrey. *Compassionate Landscape: Places and People in a Man's Life*. Toronto: University of Toronto Press, 1975.

Dendy, William. *Lost Toronto*. Toronto: McClelland & Stewart, 1993.

Dunington-Grubb, Howard. *The Garden Today*. N.p., *circa* 1930, property of Sheridan Nurseries Archives, Georgetown, ON.

Filey, Mike. *Toronto Sketches 7*. Toronto: Dundurn, 2003.

Hicks, Kathleen A. *Clarkson and Its Many Corners*. Mississauga, ON: Mississauga Library System, 2003.

____. *Erindale: Early Times to Evolution*. Mississauga, ON: Mississauga Library System, 2009.

Johnson, Lorraine, ed., *Garden Plants & Flowers: Canadian Edition*. Toronto: Dorling Kindersley, 2006.

Jones, Donald. *Fifty Tales of Toronto*. Toronto: University of Toronto Press, 1992.

Kilbourn, William. *Toronto Remembered*. Toronto: Stoddart Publishing, 1984.

Macdonald, Colin S., ed. *A Dictionary of Canadian Artists*, 5th edition. Ottawa: Canadian Paperbacks Publishing, 1997.

Martyn, Lucy Booth. *The Face of Early Toronto*. Sutton West, ON: Paget Press, 1982.

Mawson, Thomas. *The Life and Work of an English Landscape Architect*. London: The Richards Press, 1927.

McBurney, Margaret. *The Great Adventure: 100 Years at the Arts & Letters Club*. Toronto: Arts & Letters Club of Toronto, 2007.

McCart, Neil. *Atlantic Liners of the Cunard Line*. Wellingborough, UK: Patrick Stephens Ltd., 1990.

Oxland, Evan. Unpublished Dissertation on Howard and Lorrie Dunington-Grubb, 2010.

Paine, Cecelia, ed. *Fifty Years of Landscape Architecture*. Guelph, ON: The Canadian Society of Landscape Architects, University of Guelph, 1998.

Sherk, Lawrence C. and Arthur R. Buckley. *Ornamental Shrubs for Canada*. Ottawa: Canada Department of Agriculture, 1968.

Skinner, Helen. *The Growing Years: The Garden Club of Toronto 1946–2007*. Toronto: Garden Club of Toronto, 2008.

Way, Ronald L. *Ontario's Niagara Parks*. Niagara Falls, ON: Niagara Parks Commissions, 1960.

Wilson, Lois. *Chatelaine's Gardening Book*. Toronto: Doubleday, 1970.

NEWSPAPERS

Port Credit *News*
Toronto Star
Toronto *Globe* (*Globe & Mail*)

PERIODICALS

American Nurseryman (United States)
The Canadian Florist
The Canadian Home Journal
Canadian Homes and Gardens
Canadian Landscape Architecture
Canadian Municipal Journal
Century Home
The Boxwood Bulletin
The Gardeners' Chronicle (UK)
Horticultural Review
Landscape Architectural Review
Sheridan Nursery News
The Sheridan Year Book
Women's Century

INDEX

Numbers in italics refer to pictures and their captions.